I. ROBERT SINAI, a foreign affairs specialist, has traveled all over the world and studied at first-hand the political and social forces about which he writes. Born in Lithuania, he is a citizen of Israel and has lived in South Africa, Great Britain, France, Burma, and India. He has been with the Information Department of Israel's Foreign Ministry and was a member of the secretariat of the Asian Socialist Conference in Rangoon. In the United States, he has been a lecturer at the New School for Social Research in New York City and a consultant for the Foreign Policy Research Institute at the University of Pennsylvania. His articles have appeared in many international political journals.

To Anne and Joshua

The Challenge of Modernisation

THE WEST'S IMPACT ON THE NON-WESTERN WORLD

By

I. R. SINAI

W · W · NORTON & COMPANY · INC · *New York*

SBN 393 00323 X

PRINTED IN THE UNITED STATES OF AMERICA

3 4 5 6 7 8 9

CONTENTS

ACKNOWLEDGMENTS

I am most indebted to my wife, Anne Sinai, for her help, inspiration and encouragement.

Chapter 1

THE WEST AND ASIA

i

THIS is not the first age to find itself plunged in a process of revolution, and it will not, undoubtedly, be the last. But no previous age, in the long history of the Western world, has had to meet the force and comprehend the meaning of the all-embracing, many-faceted revolution which is now moving across all the continents of our distraught world. This is a revolution which has forced its way into all spheres of life. It has left no nation, no interest, no class and no mode of human experience or activity untouched or undisturbed. All the fundamentals of our world have been affected. And hanging over all is the fear and the dread that the penalty for yet another breakdown in the relations between nations could lead to the very destruction of all the major centres of civilisation themselves.

No wonder, then, that Western man is tense, confused and disenchanted. The inconclusive wars which he has fought, the revolutions which he has seen mounted against his very way of life, the reversion to barbarism which he witnessed in as advanced a member of Western society as Germany, the challenge for world leadership which has been thrown out to him, the failures of men and measures which he has experienced—all these have entered into his soul, and instilled a disastrous loss of self-confidence. Fear and insecurity—surely among the meanest of human motives—have again become driving forces in the Western world. Western man has come to suffer from a failure of nerve. He is not only failing to understand the world in which he lives, but he is also tending to forget much of the valuable knowledge that he once possessed. He has come to look upon our epoch as a time of mere troubles. He feels that the life of the world has become treacherously provisional and that the balance of the continents is shifting. There is even a growing feeling that perhaps 'the salt of the earth is moving eastwards', that the world's centre of gravity might shift from the Atlantic Ocean to the Russian steppes, or to the Chinese communes, or to the plains of India or even to the bush and deserts of Africa. The wounds which Western society has inflicted upon itself and which it has received from its enemies have left their mark upon a whole civilisation.

The following pages are being written in the belief that though the West is on the defensive and will remain in that posture for a long time to come, it need not go into decline, that it need not become some provincial backwater contemptuously left behind by the swift march of events, and that the world revolution in which we are all immersed is a challenge which can be met by the application of intelligence and courageous action and by the revitalisation of its democratic heritage. Western society has not already fulfilled all its potentialities and need not be overtaken by any other nation or group of nations. The lamentable failures of the West during the last fifty years, its relative diminution of power, are not due to any shrinking of its inherent vitality, to the exhaustion of its energies or to the depravity of its peoples, but spring primarily from defects which can be removed, from failures of understanding and weaknesses of leadership. There is no lack of means for the solution of all these problems—there is only a lack of minds, of will-power, of suitable men.

The refusal to face unpleasant facts, the desire to believe in comforting panaceas, the pathetic search for simple and cheap short-cuts, the tendency towards complacent relaxation after every great effort, the pursuit of private gain and comfort at the expense of the public welfare, the continued devotion to smooth-sounding and sentimental, liberal, socialist and conservative platitudes in a time of permanent crisis and change, the lack of intellectual vigour and the conservative frame of mind of most of its leaders, the failure of the West to forge the closest bonds of unity, transcending the ebb and flow of national interests, and the decline of its will to serve as an example of high civilisation to the backward countries—all these have played their significant part in the defeats and setbacks which the Western world has suffered.

Yet, in spite of all these distressing facts and though practically shorn of all the imperial power and splendour that the countries of the Atlantic Alliance once possessed, they still retain sufficient economic and military resources for survival and growth. To live through this age of transition and transformation, however, it is not only necessary to possess the sinews of material power. Sufficient power in all fields, constantly augmented, must be wedded to appropriate ideas. And the men who wield this power, the political leaderships elected to manage its affairs, must be guided by a long-term historical perspective, by a tough-minded public philosophy endowed with the insight to understand the world's turmoil and to see beyond the turbulence of the present to the possibilities of the future. Only when statesmen moved by a sense of passion and devotion and fortified by resolution and courage will succeed in combining power, ideas and a supple ability to respond to the swift flux of events, will the Western world be in a position to meet the perils of our age and to use for the defence of its civilisation the grand opportunities which are still available to those who seek them. Notwithstanding the ever-growing feeling that we live in a world which has become too big, too complex and too uncontrollable, it is still possible for man, aroused to vigour and insight, to intervene in the historical process, and to use the freedom which is both his birthright and burden to bend the forces of his environment to his own human ends. Events have not yet taken charge, and responsibility still rests in human hands.

The world revolution of our modern times has found its expression in many disparate but interdependent fields. The collapse of empires, the awakening of submerged classes and nations, the emergence of new, lean and hungry states, the coming to power of new rulers, the rise of new and dynamic great power competitors filled with messianic pretensions and driven along by grandiose totalitarian ambitions, a menacing population explosion, radical shifts in the balance of power, the invention of new weapons—all these are the outward signs of a vast upheaval in international life. Neither the cold war nor capitalism or communism, neither imperialism nor anti-imperialism are, by themselves, the deep-rooted causes of the crises which face our world. All these pressing realities are merely the symbols and manifestations of the revolutionary epoch in the midst of which we live, and in the contours of which we must find our way. All these movements and all our contemporary discontents are, in reality, the consequences of that global change-of-life produced by the emergence of our highly original and highly inflammatory modern Western society and of its expansion throughout the world. At the heart of this movement of rapid and profound change, we confront the confused and protracted dissolution of an old order and the irritating but inescapable need to adjust to this stark reality. This general development might be deflected here or there from its course for some time—or even stopped in its tracks in some places for a few years. But the massive flow of the new forces and energies released by modern society cannot permanently be blocked and will continue to move on its way, affecting all men at all levels of society and in all countries, until the world will have found some temporary equilibrium (which is all that can really be expected) on a new basis.

The world is disturbed and tense and full of explosive forces and situations because many things are simultaneously coming to an end in so many different places. At no other time has the earth's political and social crust been as thin and brittle as it is today. In Asia and Africa, and Latin America, too, for that matter, the peoples are agitated, everything is uncertain and fluid, because an ancient mode of existence is slowly but surely coming to an end. In China there is now going on a vast and dangerous revolution because something there has come to an end with drastic suddenness. In the former metropolitan centres there is a turmoil of readjustment because something of great significance to them has come to an end. In Western Europe every nation is in ferment because many things have come to an end. In America and Russia there are doubts and anxieties, there are gropings for new ways, because many things have come and are coming to an end in their societies and in their surroundings. All over the world, in fact, decaying elements of the past are being destroyed or will have to be destroyed, and all over the world millions of human beings have to prepare themselves for new beginnings, for new thrusts in sociological functioning, for a radical remodelling of their ways of social life.

Arising out of this vast, agitated and agitating world-wide movement then, new ways and methods of life and thought will have to be devised, new great enterprises launched, new institutions organised, new political and social forms contrived, to meet the blind and brute material forces—in politics, economics and technology—which are infiltrating all societies from the most primitive to the most sophisticated.

In the following pages it is my intention to deal with a few of the aspects involved in this wide-ranging international upheaval and crisis. I will try to analyse some of the intricate problems connected with the encounter between the Western and the non-Western civilisations; with some of the problems of modernisation which now face the newly independent countries of Asia and Africa; and with some of the steps that the West should take in order to counter all the hostile forces which are at present so dangerously rampant in the world. In different degrees and on different levels, all the societies of our world confront the acute challenge of modernisation. But before attempting to analyse some of these issues, it is necessary to pass in review some of the dynamic forces which have fashioned our Western civilisation and some of the simple, but powerful, factors which have created the long-enduring civilisations of the non-Western world.

ii

Although it is impossible to draw a sharp and consistent line of division between one period and another, especially in the history of so immense, complex and jagged a process as the rise of a civilisation, it is yet possible to see the period between the eleventh and twelfth centuries as a decisive turning point in European history—the emergence of an autonomous Western culture. For during this time a movement of progress in the arts of life, in thought and human behaviour begins which has continued, through trial and error, down to our own times.

Slowly but surely a new tide in human affairs began to flow and the whole tone of life began to change. Men's outlook upon the world, their attitude to God, nature and to their fellow men was slowly being transformed. As against the city of God, the city of Man began to stand out in ever-sharpening relief. People began to turn from heaven to earth, to feel that even 'fallen man' could, by his own efforts and audacities, improve his lot on this earth. In place of the ancient contempt for the world, of the ideal of renunciation as the foundation of all personal and social virtue, a tendency towards greater confidence in man's capacities becomes manifest. Trade and industry began to make more steady progress. The intellect of Europe began its long and revolutionary march towards new and untried frontiers and all those forces which, in the end, made for greater freedom, in politics, education, philosophy and the arts, began to exercise their influence. New forces were mobilised, which helped to bring about the birth of the rich, diversified European society on which our modern civilisation has been built.

The most significant development in this movement of progress, engendered within the framework of feudal society and ultimately in decisive opposition to it, was the growth of the prosperous commercial city states of Italy. This development, so fruitful in its consequences, represented the revival and the expansion of the most distinctive institution—the city—of the Greek or Roman world and, by extension, the most characteristic invention of the Western spirit. It is in these nervous centres of movement and wakefulness that man has most fully realised his humanity by growth and change. For, according to Ortega y Gasset, the city constitutes the '. . . invention of a new kind of space, much more new than the space of Einstein'. By creating a city, man frees himself from the community of the plant and the animal, '. . . separates himself from the fields, from Nature, from the geo-botanic cosmos . . .' and produces '. . . an enclosure apart, which is purely human, a civil space . . .' It is only in the West that man has made a conscious and persistent effort to separate himself from nature and has opposed, to the idea of nature as imprisoning, the concept of his own individual freedom (precarious though it may be) within it, shaped by his own adventurous intelligence and vital energy.

In Europe, then, cities have always been, from classical times onwards, the centres of social, economic and intellectual life; they have been the architects and builders of civilisation. This is a purely Western phenomenon. No other civilisation has known anything like it. Athens and Rome, Florence, Amsterdam, Paris and London, are not majestically isolated, snow-capped peaks of achievement; they have, rather, always been the intricate channels through which they have poured their culture and civilisation upon the rest of their own societies and rural hinterlands. And from these dissonant urban centres, life-giving and innovating influences have radiated to the rest of the world.

Our modern world starts on its course with the decline of the Middle Ages and with the growth, by an inward ripening, of those forces whose destiny it was to overthrow the medieval conditions of life and thought. Notwithstanding the present-day fashion to emphasise the gradual evolution of institutions and beliefs, it is nevertheless true, as Lord Acton has written in his *Lectures on Modern History*, that '. . . the method of modern progress was revolution . . .' and that '. . . by a series of violent shocks, the nations in succession have struggled to shake off the Past, to reverse the action of Time and the verdict of success and to rescue the world from the reign of the Dead . . .' The new forms of society emerged in turmoil and through a sharp conflict of values.

Bursts of liberated creative energies lifted society out of its medieval ruts and set it in motion. The great voyages of exploration, the Renaissance, the Reformation, the movements of mass emigration, all the industrial, scientific and political revolutions, set the peoples of Europe on the move. A new fluidity swept Western society and great numbers of men in all classes were stirred by a sense of expansion, felt their lives quickened and their horizons enormously enlarged. All these movements of change, each in its own way, and what is even more significant, all in inseparable combination, undermined the medieval and prepared the modern world outlook.

With the Renaissance, some of the outstanding characteristics of modern man began to assert themselves. By rediscovering the greatness of antiquity, the Renaissance released a new movement in the world of thought, art and feeling. A new type of man appeared—a free personality—believing in a new elite of talent and intellect. By finding again a world of great aims, a higher energy was infused into all their restless strivings. They were stirred by the idea of the infinite potentialities of the human spirit; they worshipped the beauty of energy; they initiated all those rational disciplines which finally led to the modern triumphs of science and the enhanced understanding of nature. Looking into himself after a long period of living under a veil of faith and illusion, man was no longer afraid of singularity, of selecting his own ideals and moulding his mind to them. The ban laid upon the growth of the human personality by medieval conformism was dissolved and men began to discover the inward resources of their own natures. They dared to be themselves in all their vigour and variety. The Renaissance helped to shape the autonomous individual who in fact ushers in modern civilisation.

The release of all these pent-up energies gave rise to a powerful moneyed class, filled with a spirit of initiative. They encouraged a new enthusiasm for architecture, for building and rebuilding and generated considerable forces of industrial expansion in the Europe of that time. Man was, furthermore, moved by his own personal efforts to achieve fame, glory and success and to attain something great and memorable, regardless of all the means and consequences. Driven along by these Faustian passions and forces, the men of the Renaissance not only created tyrannies and despotisms, unlimited democracy and pseudo-democracy, they not only engaged in fierce party struggles and violently disturbed the whole course of life, but they also encouraged an astonishing display of genius in art and literature, which have never lost their appeal. These attainments of the free Western spirit will always continue to haunt and inspire the world.

While the Renaissance was essentially the achievement of a comparatively small minority of gifted and creative men—of an intellectual elite that by its very nature worked in a world from which the broad ranks of society were excluded—the Reformation affected much more deeply the life of the people as a whole. It radically challenged the main pillar of authority in the medieval structure—the Church. It sought to renew a whole society by penetrating every sphere of life, public as well as private. By appealing to popular passions, by calling into question the universal and traditional religious beliefs of the people, it broke the chain of authority at the strongest link.

On one level, the Reformation was a revolt against the universal authority of the anachronistic Catholic church, whose religious authoritarianism was unable to contain the new vanities of a growing commercial civilisation, or to come to terms with the ambitions of the emerging and, at first, absolutist national states. Both commercial capitalism and the national state had to break loose from this central authority of the medieval world, and to break down the feudal nexus in economics and politics before they could begin their epoch-making careers in the fashioning of our world.

But the Reformation, in all its aspects, had an even more shattering impact on the life of Europe, on its inmost nature. By refashioning the very image of God, by setting one church against another, by challenging the supreme and sacred values of medieval Europe, it set in motion every force in heaven and on earth. (Even Catholicism had to evolve its own kind of Protestantism.) It asked men to disbelieve and disobey. It broke away from an ancestral faith and defied spiritual and secular authority. It destroyed the altars of the old religion. In place of slavish deference to authority it called into being rebellion. In England it cut off the head of a king. Wherever its spirit of rebellion spread, the human mind attained an unprecedented height of self-assertiveness.

In the course of this prolonged moral and intellectual conflict, the Reformation, especially in its Calvinist and Puritan form, not only fashioned new philosophies of society, new conceptions of economic thought, not only brought about a revolution in the traditional scale of ethical values, but also created a new type of Christian character—a daring, independent and iron-nerved being—determined to remake the world in his image. Calvinism became an international movement which, in its early stages, in the service of its religion, brought not peace, but a sword. The path which it traversed was heaped with revolutions. Monastic properties were confiscated and a widespread transfer of lands to new proprietors took place. The traditional methods of work were transformed and new methods of production were organised. The village community, the main unit of feudal society, was disrupted. Old classes were depressed and new classes exalted. In the heat and fury of peasant wars, of religious wars between states and of civil wars, rural medieval society collapsed and its customary relationships were dissolved.

Above all, Puritanism was one of the most powerful factors which helped to fashion the Western middle class, the most revolutionary and productive class that the world has ever known. No other civilisation has been able to produce anything to compare with it. Puritanism taught the bourgeoisie that it was a chosen people, it infused it with pride in itself and its calling, and strengthened its already vigorous temper. While its theology denied the freedom of the will as a metaphysical principle, the middle class made amends by applying freedom with all the more energy as the practical rule of its life. Although in theory he could do little unless God had chosen him for salvation, the individual was, in fact, left and forced to save himself.

By believing that work is a holy thing, a spiritual effort—the only genuine faith is the faith which produces works—by teaching that religion must be active and not merely contemplative, that the Christian life must be systematic and dedicated, it inculcated those virtues—enterprise, diligence, sobriety and thrift—which were the very qualities most necessary for economic success during the early experiments in industrialisation. Industrial development requires at all times a sustained effort, a willingness to mobilise savings and to take risks, a propensity for innovation, a long vision, and a readiness to postpone immediate profits for even greater gains in the future. The Puritans' zealous devotion to work and thrift, their belief that labour and industry is their duty towards God, gave to the early industrialists of Europe that energy, that sense of self-discipline and confidence needed for the gradual creation of wealth, for the fashioning of an industrial civilisation. In fact, there is no other period in history in which free men have given their energy so completely for the purpose of work as capitalism did. And this drive for work was not generated by external pressure but by an internal compulsion. This absorption in work, this uncompromising commitment to work was one of the fundamental productive forces of capitalist society, perhaps even more important for the creation of our industrial system than steam or electricity.

The Renaissance and the Reformation helped to plough up the soil for the growth of our modern, urban, industrial and democratic society. By emphasising the worth and dignity of the individual, even though at first restricted to 'chosen elites', by spreading the cult of labour and thrift, by turning the attention of man to nature and arousing in him the curiosity to discover its laws, by stressing the spiritual independence of the individual and his duty to stand alone against all the powers of the world, they laid the foundations of our industrial and democratic civilisation.

Another factor which helped to shape our new style of life, our modern outlook, was that confident and radical movement of thought—the Enlightenment. Beginning with the 'methodic doubt' of Descartes, finding vigorous and successful expression in the England shaped by the revolution of 1688, achieving additional dramatic successes in the American and French revolutions, a new movement of thought and action was inaugurated for the regeneration of society, for the amelioration of man's estate.

Individualism and reason were the two forces that were now let loose in European society. Man was encouraged to think for himself. He was challenged to apply the critical powers of reason, without theological predilections and restraints, to all his thoughts, beliefs and institutions. On the strength of his reason man was thought able to lift himself up to the position from which he could understand the world and his own situation in the scheme of things. There thus grew up a body of philosophic and humanitarian literature, which criticised and attacked all that was obnoxious, all that was outworn and unjust in the constitution of European society and in the fabric of its religious and social beliefs. Western science, philosophy and literature have, as a consequence, made the most sustained and comprehensive effort ever attempted by man, to understand himself and his social and physical environment. Western man was stripped bare, and probed, examined and dissected from every possible angle. His biological origins, his mind, his society, his cultural heritage, his religious beliefs, everything about him and around him, was placed under investigation.

The Enlightenment created a climate of optimism and hope.

It made man independent, his own law-giver. It proclaimed the Rights of Man. There arose the belief that all men are born equal and that circumstances were responsible for their subsequent inequality. It demanded that all governments should be based on the consent of the governed. It stood for religious toleration, for freedom of speech and thought, for the rights of the opposition. By putting an end to theological strife, it diverted human energies to the more profitably exciting enterprises of commerce and science. In the exaltation of their own pulsating energies, they discovered new forms of energy and force in the physical world which all men before them had not even sensed. Men came to believe for the first time that it would be possible to rearrange society on rational principles.

A system of government by discussion, that plant of singular delicacy, as Walter Bagehot called it, was gradually established. By means of discussion, social and class relations, the state, all the instruments of rule, were stripped of their mystery and many of the realities of social life were exposed in the light of 'profane deliberation'. Government by discussion stimulated and enlivened thought all through society and made more men more capable of assuming the responsibilities and risks of civilisation and of enjoying its benefits. Men began to believe in progress as an almost unchallengeable principle and in the perfectibility of man and society. Western man was filled with an immense new self-confidence and the highest hopes appeared to be supported by the most austerely rational judgements.

This faith in reason, this emphasis on natural vitality as a principle of being, this acceptance of an ethic of striving, dissatisfaction and renewal, this commitment to a pluralistic and open society, permitted Europe to make unprecedented progress in all the arts of civilisation. Our modern Europe, not as a geographical but as a spiritual entity, was born as a result of these labours, as a consequence of all these daring and disturbing aspirations. These qualities of the European mind have been well described by Paul Hazard in his treatise on 'La Crise de la Conscience Européenne, 1680–1715', who has given there the following definition of Europe:

What is Europe? A thought which is never satisfied. Without self-pity, she never ceases her pursuit of two quests, one towards happiness, the other, which is even more indispensable to her and more dear, towards truth. She has scarcely found an estate which corresponds to this double requirement when she becomes aware, when she knows, that as yet she only holds with an insecure grip something temporary and relative; and she returns to the desperate search which is her glory and her torment.[1]

All these social, economic, political and cultural revolutions helped to break the 'cake of custom' of traditional society, and to create our modern world of incessant change and innovation and of enduring achievements. The change was, of course, not as complete or as stringent as I have so sketchily described it. It was highly irregular, swifter and more thorough in one place than in another and never so drastic or complete as not to leave behind it shreds and patches of the past, both the good and the bad, which still remain deeply embedded in our Western society. Modes of life and thought rooted in Medievalism still exercise their sway over many minds and many countries. Many old superstitions (not to speak of modern ones) still retain a strong hold, and many old abuses (not to mention the new ones created by modern society) are still entrenched. The tensions between the elements of change and continuity still continue to colour and determine the development of Western society. But an epoch-making change was effected, an extraordinarily bold effort was made by Western man to make over his inherited world. This enterprise has been the greatest revolutionary transformation that the world has ever known since man's first attempts at civilisation. As Karl Jaspers has said: 'Our age of science and technology is a kind of second beginning, comparable to the first invention of tools and firemaking.' [2]

With the opening of the nineteenth century, modern capitalism, based on science and technology, began to unfold all its hitherto unimagined capacities and possibilities, and really began to enter upon the inheritance which it had so systematically and grimly been accumulating for itself in the preceding two centuries. A society based on status on more or less rigid

[1] Quoted by Hans Kohn in *The Twentieth Century*. Victor Gollancz, London, 1950, p. 45.

[2] Karl Jaspers, *Way to Wisdom*. Yale University Press, p. 103.

patterns was transformed into a society based on contract, on individual and social mobility. Large-scale industry and the factory system, expansion of the urban population and of population in general, scientific and technical discoveries, expansion overseas, increases in production and labour productivity—all these were the expressions of its conquests. No less a critic of capitalism than Karl Marx himself penned this paean of praise in 1848 to the achievements of capitalism.

> The bourgeoisie has disclosed how it came to pass that the brutal display of vigour in the Middle Ages, which reactionaries so much admire, found its fitting complement in the most slothful indolence. It has been the first to show what man's activity can bring about. It has accomplished wonders far surpassing Egyptian pyramids, Roman aqueducts, and Gothic cathedrals; it has conducted expeditions that put in the shade all former exoduses of nations and crusades.[1]

In its subsequent evolution, capitalism has continued to revolutionise the economic structure of society from within, has been as constantly destroying old forms and as constantly creating new ones. In economics, as in social and political relations, the history of capitalism is a history of uninterrupted disturbance and agitation. Its technology has disturbed the immemorial rhythm of human societies. It has levelled national frontiers and undermined national self-sufficiencies. It has brought the whole world into its orbit. The velocity of life has been drastically speeded up and space has been reduced. Man has been ushered into a new cycle of civilisation.

However, the bourgeoisie was not only responsible for a fantastic increase in wealth and production, for an all-round rise in the historical level. The European peoples who passed through the trials and tribulations of the industrial revolution had to pay a stiff price for the new opportunities that capitalism was making available to the nations of the West, and for the material advantages it was providing. The living body of society was ruthlessly operated upon. Industrialisation and modernisation worked themselves out through millions of human lives, through millions of labouring and struggling human beings.

[1] Communist Manifesto.

Enclosure acts drove peasants off the land. Craftsmen lost their tools and livelihoods. The new class of wage earners thus created streamed into the 'black satanic mills'. Women and children crawled on their hands and knees, pulling trucks in mines. Working hours stretched for as long as sixteen hours a day. In the slums of the new manufacturing cities, overcrowded and insanitary tenements provided a niggardly shelter to this new race of working hands. They were condemned to a grovelling mode of existence. They had to suffer poverty, inequality and the denial of democratic rights.

Perhaps even more painful than the bodily suffering which it caused, capitalism turned the psychological and spiritual world of its workers upside down and inside out. By thrusting them into industrial society, by hauling them through the drama of proletarianisation, it tore up their traditional life by its roots. The scars left by this upheaval in the lives of the working classes are still to be found today, on their bodies and in their souls. But having passed through this furnace of change, the working class emerged tempered with new inner resources of spirit, endowed with new skills and strong and virile enough to oppose its interests to the interests of the capitalist class. It could become a power in the land.

The economic ambitions which Puritanism helped to release and which enabled capitalism to make over the world have, in their turn, created a host of intricate problems which the re-forming and humanitarian efforts of more than a century have not yet solved. Economic expansion and the accumulation of wealth, instead of being the servants of an ampler and more generous ideal of human welfare, became more often than not the masters of society. Instead of riches serving man, man has tended to become enslaved to the glitter of wealth, considered as an end in itself. The freedom of the individual, as it came to be practised by the fast-rising capitalist class, soon became a rampant selfishness, ignorant of social obligations. It has tended to stress immediate individual satisfactions as opposed to the long-range public needs of the community as a whole.

The technological civilisation which capitalism has created has not only freed man from feudal restraints; it has also produced giant corporations and bureaucracies to stifle the

individual in the routine webs of organisation and in the pressures
for a new kind of conformism. Science has not only released new
human possibilities of abundance and liberation; it has also
tended to mechanise and impoverish human life. Universal
education has not produced a society either more wise or even
more knowledgeable. A vast and insidious mass culture—in
radio, films, television and popular journalism—has developed,
which attempts to stamp out all individual differences and to
reduce everything to the lowest common denominator. The
entry of the masses into the historical arena has produced our
modern mass society, with its overcrowded cities, its huge and
lonely crowds and its day-to-day men, without a sense of worth-
while purpose and not having anything great or inspiring to
which to give themselves. Our modern commercial civilisation
does not provide modern man with great enough aims.

The elements of civilisation have, it is true, reached more
people than at any other time in history. But the general intellectual and spiritual level of modern society has unfortunately
been lowered. The belief in equality, as it has been implemented
in our commercial democracy, has tended to encourage uni-
formity and to lower the standards of excellence. It has been
disposed to put quantity before quality, superficial satisfaction
before arduous struggle, opulence before culture and mediocrity
before greatness. While the specialised functions of the community are performed better than ever before, the generalised
direction lacks vision. Authority has moreover been eroded, the
sense of public responsibility has been diluted and popularity
with the neighbours or with one's 'peer group' has become a
supreme criterion. In place of a coherent and bold public
philosophy we have public relations and the catchwords of the
advertising agency. And sometimes one has the feeling that the
image of modern man lies in T. S. Eliot's line in 'Burnt Norton':
'Men and bits of paper, whirled by the cold wind.' Sentimentality and farcicality are at present deluging most of the
lands of the West and man himself lets himself float on the
lightest current.

The age of the Enlightenment did more than any other century in Western history to attack the powers of traditional
ignorance and of senseless tyranny. By its healthy, manly

and upstanding rationalism, by its encouragement of free, imaginative speculation, through the new scientific mentality which it fashioned, it energised the minds of men, helped to fashion the mental climate of our modern world and produced some of its most permanent achievements. But we can now see that quite a few of its characteristic assumptions were one-sided and deficient in depth of vision.

Their conception of Man as an animal guided by reason ignored the deeper, irrational forces which shape, drive and bend the individual to their peremptory demands. They were unaware of the 'seething cauldron' of the Freudian Id, of the blind and destructive energy of man's instinctual impulses. They failed to understand that civilisation is an ambivalent, precarious compound, just as man is an ambivalent, precarious organisation, and that the tragic 'dialectic of civilisation' is the result in part of this interaction between the opposing powers of reason and unreason.

Their faith in the perfectibility of man and society, their belief in progress, were, furthermore, rather naive and shallow. Man is not born free and good and he is not everywhere in chains, only because of his environmental situation, or because of any particular system of property relations. He is on the contrary a divided and fallible creature, divided in the deepest layers of his unconscious, as he is on the highest levels of consciousness, tainted with corruption and glorified by reason, capable of freedom and ruled by blind necessity. Man is both creative and destructive, swayed both by love and hate. He is as much moved by his passion for creation, for justice, for truth, for the fulfilment of an ideal as he is by his greed for power, domination and gain. Man is both imperfect and unperfectible, an eternal battleground between conflicting urges and impulses, host alike to seeds of nobility and ignominy.

They, moreover, did not foresee the contradictions of a free society, the new possibilities of tension and conflict that it would create. They were unaware of the nature of the struggle for power and domination in society. They did not take into account the fact that man tends to become intoxicated by power and that men's ambitions and lusts enter into every relationship and every institution, distorting and corrupting his most generous aspirations. They did not foresee the increasing sharpness of the conflicts between nations, races and classes. They overlooked the powerful strength of the forces of habit, custom, tradition and inertia which are both a drag and a necessary safeguard in every form of human society. The world inhabited by man is not as tractable as the philosophers of the Enlightenment, of liberalism and of socialism in all its forms imagined it or imagine it to be. Although man is capable of exerting himself in a variety of modes and directions, a variety which is almost inexhaustible, there are still limits to the possibilities of realising human aspirations, as there are frontiers, both natural and man-made, against which man's ambitions can only collide in frustration. Imperfect man can only create an imperfect society, a parody of his soaring expectations, always at war with itself, always reaching out for ideals which ineluctable reality snatches from its grasp. Every form of society is thus a painful and antagonistic process, never a harmonious or finished conclusion.

Above all, the philosophers of the Enlightenment lacked the tragic view of life. Only a humanistic philosophy which accepts the tragic nature of human destiny can understand human history in all its incongruities, paradoxes and overpowering grandeur. Viewed in this light, history is then a permanent, an eternal, conflict between man, driven by sublime discontents and aspirations, and the inherent limitations of his own nature and of his environment, unable to transcend 'the antagonism at the heart of the world'. All man's bravest efforts, all his quests, all his discoveries, can never really eliminate or overcome the primordial pain and contradiction at the very heart of things.

The strength and dignity of Western civilisation at its highest levels lies precisely in its awareness of the 'giant agony of the world' and in its faltering but uninterrupted efforts, from age to age, from generation to generation, never to accept it as final, never to lamely surrender itself to it. Sisyphus will never succeed in pushing the boulder to the summit, but the ever-renewed effort to do so is the secret of his human dignity and nobility.

In spite of all its terrible shortcomings and flaws, in spite of its fratricidal struggles and at times uninhibited violence,

Western civilisation still presents the richest, the most versatile and the most dramatic pageant that history has ever seen. It has sustained a higher level of creative activity in freedom—in ideas, literature, music and all the arts and refinements of civilisation—over a longer period of time than any other society. In general, it has imposed greater demands upon itself, burdened itself with more strenuous duties and it has had to confront greater difficulties and tensions than any other civilisation. Western society is the freest that history has ever known, but it is also the most enslaved—enslaved in service to unequalled standards of ambition and discipline and in making exigent demands upon itself. For Western civilisation is synonymous with a life of effort, of striving, ever set on excelling itself. If it should ever lose or squander these moral imperatives, it would lose its very soul, its *raison d'être*.

It has, on another level, furthermore, had the vitality to produce from within itself those movements which have arisen to correct its abuses, to reform its defects and to humanise its social relations. It is only in the West that democracy, liberalism and socialism have emerged, rooted in its own organic growth and the resultant of its own inner, spontaneous dialectic.

Before discussing some of the new tasks that face Western society, it is necessary to stress and re-emphasise the crucial fact that without the immense contribution that capitalism has made to Western civilisation, the life of Western man would still be hemmed in by all the limitations and degradations of traditional society. Capitalism and the modern technology which it has pressed into its service has made it possible for the West to contemplate a future which could be more dignified, more humane, more free, and perhaps even more maturely civilised, than anything that mankind has ever known in the past. For it should now be clear that the fashioning of a modern class of entrepreneurs, the creation of an industrial civilisation, the establishment of a democratic form of government for our mass society, are in fact the most difficult, the most challenging tasks that mankind has ever confronted. No other civilisation has ever solved the problems that now confront us or has ever had to live with them. We have, in fact, only begun to grapple with some of their far-reaching consequences. And to realise all these complex tasks, even in their preliminary phases, is to achieve the break-through, the dramatic entry into a new universe of existence.

If socialism or radicalism has any mission at all today, it is to battle with all the complex problems created by our modern world; created by the very fact of modernity. Modern man clearly stands before a void out of which immense possibilities both for good and ill may grow. Having broken with the past, having left behind him so much that has become obsolete and inadequate, living in a highly fluid society with rapid change as its hallmark, modern man must now atone by creative ability for his break with tradition. The bow of modern life has to be strung to the highest possible tension. Without building a new space for the cultivation of the human mind, without encouraging freedom and non-conformity and a dedication to excellence and experimentation, the vigorous continuity of our society might well be endangered. If the Western world does not have the courage and capacity to move beyond the complacencies and self-deceptions of official society, at all its levels, then our very survival might well be put to question. The present mediocrity of its governing classes and their attachment to the petty formulae of statesmanship can only prepare further defeats for Western civilisation.

The mission of contemporary radicalism and liberalism, of democratic socialism, is, then, to serve as the representatives of the radical principle within Western society, as the gadfly of civilisation. Its task is to help humanise and civilise the industrial societies which capitalism has created, to bring this powerful machine of movement and disturbance under more conscious control and planned management, without, however, sacrificing its inherent dynamic, and without removing its really productive elements. Both capitalism and socialism, both private property and public property, will have to co-exist in the same society for as long as we can foresee. Its goal should be to guide and divert economic energies to serve those human ends—in education, social welfare, urban renewal and reconstruction and cultural growth—which even our modern reformed capitalism has everywhere neglected. Its responsibility is not only to bring the masses of the nation to share in more equal proportions the material advantages and opportunities which modern industrialism has made available but to make it possible for them to share, in however attenuated a form, the highest cultural achievements (which have always been the property of a minority) of the Western spirit. This attempt to civilise a whole people, to raise it to higher levels of consciousness and self-awareness, is an extremely difficult and unprecedented enterprise and it will be more of an uneven process, of a fluctuating tendency, than a final conclusion. It will demand an incalculable expenditure of reforming and creative energy, determination, mental alertness and time.

The only genuine form of socialism, then, is that which stands on the shoulders of capitalist attainments, which has been moulded and penetrated by its fruitful consequences. It can only be, if at all, a post-capitalist development. Every other form of socialism is either a farce or a fraud, masquerading under a false name, as is communism. The democratic socialist programme can in fact only be implemented in a society which has assimilated into its bloodstream, into its unconscious, those values, those aspirations, those disciplines which have entered into the making of our Western civilisation. Without this rich and varied history, without a society absolutely saturated with the ideas and ambitions and restraints of a democratic form of government, without the memories and the heritage left behind by all these revolutionary movements which I have tried to describe, not only is the society poorer in human resources and less developed in its mind, not only does it lack that sense of human worth which is the precondition for any further progress, but its social, economic, cultural and human foundations can just not be strong enough to support this new adventure in human civilisation. Democratic socialism is only possible in those societies which have undergone this sustained training and development of the human personality, this severe process of acculturation.

iii

The greatest transformation that mankind has ever experienced, both in scale and depth, has been taking place during the past five hundred years or so in those countries which belong to Western civilisation. The West, the youngest member of the human family, from the point of view of culture, developed such wealth and power, revealed such a wide range of individual initiative, was so creative in so many diverse fields, that it became the master of the world. Starting with the fifteenth and sixteenth centuries it burst out of its European confines and spread itself throughout the planet. Spurred on by a spirit of adventure and curiosity, lured on by prospects of wealth, in search of a new trade route to the spice markets of the East, Europe sailed as far and wide as the waters of the oceans would carry it. Navigating the seas it was stimulated and emboldened to further stretch its faculties beyond the customary circles of thought and action. The naval and merchant adventurers who discovered new sea-lanes, who forced open closed kingdoms and disturbed static societies, who shattered the mental crystallisations of centuries, and opened up the world, were the pioneers of a new epoch in human history. Unwittingly, they awakened sleeping dragons, and hurled millions of men towards unsuspected goals. The contacts which they established with the seemingly opulent civilisations of the Orient, with the frightening primitiveness of Africa, have produced fateful consequences, the full import of which we have still not yet grasped, and the full consequences of which we are still to face in the future. This movement of exploration and penetration has furthermore created our interdependent modern world, the Great Society in which we live, perturbed and divided, heaving and vibrating in all its various nationalities, continents and cultures.

The new (though in itself ancient) world they found was strange, and in its essence in sharp contrast with the one they had known at home. It was as if they had passed out of one universe and into another. They came now into contact with the lands of 'perpetual dawn' in the East, whose societies, after an initial outburst of creativity, had remained motionless and frozen for millennia. They discovered the countries of endless landscapes, whose limbs reached up skyward to thin-aired Himalayan peaks and fell below to dazzlingly hot plains and formidable jungles. They went among the multitudes, clad in soft shining Eastern silks and ragged cottons in the spice-laden bazaars of gold and bronze-statued cities and heard of the mysterious hinterlands far off in the continental distance. Populous islands lay, broken off from their mainlands, like green astral bodies embedded in the treacherous seas. There were jungles impenetrable to man, full of an entangling arborescence, the domain of prowling tigers, jaguars and elephant herds, moving like stately and terrible thunder.

From these arid and elevated lands, with their extensive steppes and plains, masses have, since the dawn of time, suddenly poured forth to conquer and devastate whole continents, destroying the existing civilisations that they found and being devastated in turn, without, however, at any time changing the repetitive and oppressive pattern of Asian civilisation. For in these parts of the world, nature was more than man could cope with, as it was not in Europe. Against the overwhelming hostility of physical environment, man was overshadowed and frustrated in all his efforts. In these extreme zones, man did not come to free movement. He could not find or gain freedom within himself, against the majestic and malignant pressure of his natural environment.

The steppes, the jungles and the desert or semi-desert wastelands that mark the continent of Asia have throughout time defied the controlling hand of man. Where the climate is not too severely cold, it is too hot and lassitudinous. Inland Asia is extremely cold in winter and extremely hot in summer. Monsoon Asia and Africa move between the two poles of tumultuous downpour and scorching heat. Some of the soils are poor and apt to erode. The vegetation is either too meagre or too profuse. Locusts, pests, floods and drought can destroy in a day the work of years. Termites undermine monuments. The jungles can smother man in their sensuous embrace. The humidity spreads a carpet of green rot over everything and blights it all. The smiling, colourful and attractively mysterious surface of life only covers up a scene of insidious poison and slow decay. There is no gentle rhythm of the seasons, no modest variations of heat and cold, to provide the most favourable physiological stimulus to activity and enterprise. In all these countries, nature does not appear in a benevolent light, but rather reveals itself as the relentless enemy of man and has, in the majority of cases, destroyed both his self-confidence and his pride in life. Man is both dejected and heavy-laden, oscillating between fatalism and frenzy, tossed between despotism and anarchy.

Against this background a kind of civilisation grew up which has had no parallel in the history of Western Europe. Karl Marx, utilising mainly the views of such classical economists as Richard Jones and John Stuart Mill (who had themselves taken over ideas held by Adam Smith and James Mill), formulated the highly illuminating concept of a specific 'Asiatic mode of production', which was the foundation, in his view, of a specific form of Asian society—Oriental Despotism. Professor Karl Wittfogel, in his book *Oriental Despotism*,[1] basing himself on these thinkers, has also made a stimulating though exaggerated and one-sided attempt to provide a theoretical picture of the autocratic framework of Oriental society. Distinguishing between a farming economy that involves small-scale irrigation (hydroagriculture), practised mainly in ancient Greece and in Western Europe, and one that involves large-scale and government-managed works of irrigation and flood control (hydraulic agriculture), he designated the civilisations of the Near East, India and China and the higher agrarian civilisations of pre-Spanish America, as well as certain hydraulic parallels in East Africa and the Pacific areas, as 'hydraulic society' or 'hydraulic civilisation'. In his analysis all these societies are located in the zones of 'agrarian despotism'. Without entering into a discussion regarding all the details of these theoretical constructions, I shall here attempt to describe in brief some of the main forces which, in their intricate interactions and interdependence, have shaped the character of Oriental civilisation. Though using this concept of an Oriental civilisation, it should, however, be clearly understood that within this broad, general framework there are vast diversities and differences between the different national units. Yet these differences, as will be seen, have not precluded the presence of an impressive array of common characteristics.

Confronted by the vast extent of their territory, the almost

[1] Yale University Press, New Haven, 1957.

continental nature of some of its leading societies (China and India) and by the threatening and overpowering nature of their physical environments, most of the Asian governments were compelled, almost from the very beginning of their attempts at civilisation, to assume tasks of a magnitude far beyond anything undertaken or contemplated by any European government before the modern age. Karl Marx has explained this need in the following terms:

There have been in Asia, generally, from immemorial times, but three departments of Government: that of Finance, or the plunder of the interior; that of War, or the plunder of the exterior; and, finally, the department of Public Works. Climate and territorial conditions, especially the vast tracts of desert, extending from the Sahara, through Arabia, Persia, India and Tartary, to the most elevated Asiatic highlands, constituted artificial irrigation by canals and waterworks, the basis of Oriental agriculture. . . . This prime necessity of an economical and common use of water, which, in the Occident, drove private enterprise to voluntary association, as in Flanders and Italy, necessitated, in the Orient where civilisation was too low and the territorial extent too vast to call into life voluntary association, the interference of the centralizing power of Government. . . . This artificial fertilisation of the soil, dependent on a Central Government and immediately decaying with the neglect of irrigation and drainage, explains the otherwise strange fact that we now find whole territories barren and desert that were once brilliantly cultivated, as Palmyra, Petra, the ruins in Yemen and large provinces of Egypt, Persia and Hindustan; it also explains how a single war of devastation has been able to depopulate a country for centuries, and to strip it of all its civilisation.[1]

To execute all these vital and gigantic works of irrigation and flood control, the ruling classes of these societies had to have the power to mobilise the labour power of their peasant masses. As a consequence, all these societies were based on one form or another of forced (*corvée*) labour, recruited on a temporary though recurring basis. This forced labour was then used not only for fundamental hydraulic purposes, but also for the construction of gigantic defence fortifications and roads, and

[1] Karl Marx, *On Colonialism*. Foreign Languages Publishing House, Moscow, p. 33.

for the building of cities, extravagant palaces and temples, wondrous gardens and tombs. The masters of all these hydraulic societies were great builders and they built on a monumental scale. The Great Wall of China, the Pyramids of Egypt, the temple cities of India, Burma and Cambodia, are all splendidly impressive monuments to their builders and organisers.

By means of taxation and land revenue, moreover, a major portion of the societies' wealth—from agriculture, from handicrafts and trade—found its way to the central government and its bureaucracy. All this surplus wealth was used to support the extravagance, the policies and wars of the various courts and dynasties. Their lavish expenditure on display and building created the general impression of wealth and magnificence which so impressed the casual traveller who only visited the great cities. But in fact all these countries were poor; their peasantries in particular lived close to the minimum subsistence level. And the vast state organisations which they so laboriously fashioned could not prevent the frequent floods, droughts, famines and pestilences which devastated whole provinces and cruelly smote the life of their peoples.

Within this framework there arose the political despotisms which ruled in all these societies without exception. Political and administrative power was concentrated in the hands of the central, royal authority. The central government, ruling through nation-wide bureaucracies of one kind or another, amassed so much power that no other group could or was permitted to challenge its leadership. The imperial bureaucracy of scholar-gentry, developed by China, was the most remarkable example of this form of administration.

Facing the central government there was, then, only the politically unorganised people. The monarch's excessive power was derived from the pathetic servitude of the masses. The very word for an Indian peasant—*rayiat*—means 'one of a herd', and there is no herd without a controlling master. Determined to monopolise every source of profit, to squeeze as much taxation out of the people as the traffic would bear, suspicious of uncontrolled private initiative, the central government managed to stifle the growth of a class of private entrepreneurs. Afraid of independent groups of power, it organised and controlled a monopoly of military force. It prevented the rise of an independent church. These despotic states effectively inhibited the non-governmental forces of society from developing into organisations strong enough to counter-balance or to oppose the central political authority. Power, in the Orient, was never divided and was never a subject for political discussion. No great political controversy ever engaged the passions of the people. Power was almost a fact of nature—an elemental force to be taken for granted like the giant landscape itself.

In all these agrarian despotisms, the state became stronger than society, the central authority was raised in barbaric splendour above the mass of its people, whose principal role was to serve it, to bow down to it.

If the city is the centre of gravity of Western civilisation, the village is the basic unit of Asian society. Gandhi's saying, that '. . . the heart of India is in its villages . . .' was equally true of the whole of Asia in the past and is still true of most of it (with the exception of Japan) today. Notwithstanding all its diversities and divisions, Asian civilisation has been and is still today a civilisation based on agriculture and rooted in its myriad villages, which are its characteristic expressions. This contrast between Western towns and Eastern villages is another highly important factor differentiating Europe from Asia.

While the cities of the West have been the builders of our dynamic industrial civilisation and of our free democratic society, the villages of the East have helped to create and support a society of an entirely different kind—patriarchal, conservative, immobile and despotic. This has been a society enslaved to ancient and unquestioning rules of life, governed by tradition and custom, bereft of the spirit of growth and innovation and moulded by an outlook which was based on an absolute identification of nature and society. In these villages man became so adapted to the environment that he was almost completely absorbed by it. The great civilisations of Asia and Africa have always been essentially huge, anthropomorphic vegetations.

Though at the mercy of the despotic state, yet the Eastern village was essentially a 'free' village. Although there was the scourge of untouchability in India, there was no serfdom anywhere and slavery did not play an important role. These villages were almost self-contained and self-sufficient communities, combining agricultural pursuits with domestic industry. The bulk of the village population consisted of peasants working their own small plots. The system of intensive agriculture, the pressure of over-population, the lack of capital and mechanical ingenuity, the primitiveness of their implements, the laws of inheritance whereby the property is divided between all the sons, the government's fear of 'strong property', all precluded the cultivation of large areas by individual families or by big landowners. No big landowning class developed in Asia, no stable aristocracy or hereditary noble order was permitted to grow, to limit the range of the royal despotic power.

The Eastern village also represented an association which was largely self-governing; but this did not make it democratic nor its life idyllic. They had to pay extremely heavy taxes in cash or in kind to the government or to its local representative, and they always had to meet official demands for military and labour service. But apart from these onerous exactions, the central government's control did not generally extend very far down into this basic unit of traditional Oriental society. The village elders, sometimes elected, sometimes nominated, sometimes attaining their positions by a subtle combination of age, inheritance and personal influence, performed most of the tasks of local administration. They were the guardians and the carriers of the traditional order of society and the representatives of orthodoxy. Through them the bonds of dependence were maintained and tightened. But this level of organisation, nevertheless, executed many important functions: local irrigation works and self-defence, the upkeep of temples and other religious establishments, mutual aid, mediation in personal disputes. They dealt with petty crime, they re-allotted holdings, controlled the relations between the village craftsmen or servants and other villagers, and often even levied the taxes among the households. The most important feature of these communities, however, was their conservatism, their lack of inner freedom, their absolute devotion to the totems and taboos of their patriarchal society.

Enveloping all these communities there is a sense of life

robbed of all significance. Man is both degraded and mocked. The peasantries are all haunted by the fear that the earth will lose its fertility, or that spring will fail to return. They are obsessed by an almost panic concern to maintain the size of their populations. Surrounded by malignant demons and spirits, threatened by the unruly forces of nature and society, they were led to seek the intervention of occult powers whom they must try to propitiate or coerce by means of offerings, spells, worship, to protect their precarious though unchanging position in the natural and social order. Precarious though it was, it ensured and continued for millennia. Dynasties disappeared, kingdoms broke up, war, famine and disease desolated them, conquerors swept over them, tax collectors and moneylenders robbed them, but these villages remained unchanged and unaffected, always ready to resume the old burdens and to submit tamely to the same degrading routine.

Writing about the possible dissolution of these 'semi-civilised, semi-barbarian' communities of India, as the result of British interference with their economic bases, Karl Marx has left this memorable description of their character:

Now, sickening as it must be to human feeling to witness those myriads of industrious patriarchal and inoffensive social organisations disorganised and dissolved into their units, thrown into a sea of woes, and their individual members losing at the same time their ancient form of civilisation and their hereditary means of subsistence, we must not forget that these idyllic village communities—inoffensive though they may appear—had always been the solid foundation of Oriental despotism, that they restrained the human mind within the smallest possible compass, making it the unresisting tool of superstition, enslaving it beneath traditional rules, depriving it of all grandeur and historical energies. . . . We must not forget that this undignified, stagnatory and vegetative life, that this passive sort of existence evoked on the other part, in contradistinction, wild, aimless, unbounded forces of destruction, and rendered murder itself a religious rite in Hindustan. We must not forget that these little communities were contaminated by distinctions of caste and by slavery, that they subjugated man to external circumstances instead of elevating man to be the sovereign of circumstances, that they transformed a self-developing social state into never changing natural destiny, and thus brought about a brutalising worship of nature, exhibiting its degradation in the fact that man, the sovereign of nature, fell down on his knees in adoration of Hanuman, the monkey, and Sabbala, the cow.[1]

What Marx said about these Indian village communities is more or less true of the whole peasant world of Asia.

With the partial exception of China, today's great cities of the East are new. Until the last century, the cities of the Orient were no more than administrative centres, outposts of the territorial state, closely tied to the ruling dynasty and subordinated to the royal autocracy. In contrast to the West, the cities of the Orient lacked political autonomy.

The Oriental city was no *polis* in the sense of antiquity and it knew nothing of the 'city law' of the Middle Ages, for it was not a 'commune' with political privileges of its own. Nor was there a citizenry in the sense of a self-equipped military estate such as existed in occidental antiquity.[2]

The prosperity of these cities did not depend primarily upon the enterprising spirit of its inhabitants but rather upon the activities of the imperial administration and on its power. The Asian city created as an imperial fortress had even fewer formal guarantees of self-government than the village.

The excessive power of the central government, its overwhelming organisational and military strength, always prevented the civil and military officials, the merchants and artisans living in these cities from acquiring a position of autonomy and from becoming foci of successful resistance to the despotic central authority. The merchants, moreover, at all times ranked too low in the social scale and neither developed the ambitions nor possessed the means to aspire to independent rule. The lower classes were mainly underlings and beggars, hewers of wood and drawers of water for the court and the bureaucracy. No association of citizens arose, for there were no citizens. An assertive middle class could not and did not develop.

The bureaucratic state, furthermore, did not assure any

[1] Karl Marx, *On Colonialism*, p. 36.
[2] Max Weber, *The Religion of China*. The Free Press, Glencoe, Illinois, 1951, p. 13.

'fundamental freedoms of the individual' nor did it enact decisive legal institutions, fixed and guaranteed by the state. The situation of the merchant or the artisan was always uncertain, his temporary security depending on the goodwill of the official class which could always exact arbitrary contributions from him. The lack of all these rights and legal safeguards helped to inhibit the growth of an independent form of capitalism such as developed in the occidental Middle Ages.

A revolutionary form of entrepreneurial capitalism did not develop in all these societies, not only because of the bureaucratic despotism which prevailed, but also because all these societies lacked the particular kind of mentality necessary for its growth. The mental attitudes rooted in the ethos of the different Asian states was a highly important factor frustrating the development of this form of society.

In China, Confucianism was the ideological and ethical system which helped to shape its political and social institutions. Basically, Confucianism was a this-worldly outlook which inculcated the idea of adjustment to the world, to its orders and conventions, among its adherents. In its view, both the orders of the world and of society were considered fixed and inviolate. The balanced tranquillity of the empire and the harmony of the soul could only be maintained if man fitted himself into the internally harmonious cosmos. And the individual could best attain salvation by adjusting to the eternal and supra-divine orders of the world and hence to the requirements of social life. His main objective should not be full self-realisation, but harmonious social relations. Duties, not rights; filial piety, not individuality; decorum and etiquette, not spontaneous display and feeling, were stressed. Pious conformism to the fixed order of secular power reigned supreme. All these obligations were further strengthened by the cult of ancestor worship which united the living with the dead and with the generations to come.

In contrast with most other traditional societies, a high degree of national unification and of material progress was reached in China, which made it a great empire and a civilised country. It was a civilisation which was practical and energetic, knew very real refinements and was rich in both charm and sensitivity. But, by stressing as a cardinal virtue ceremonial and ritualist propriety in all the circumstances of life, it enabled the Chinese to escape from that 'uneasiness of the mind' and prevented them from knowing anything of that 'divine discontent' which is the precondition of intellectual and social progress. For them, nature and life was eternal rhythm rather than unending struggle. It suppressed not only the aggressive impulses but the healthy, vigorous and creative ones as well. Confucianism was in intent a rational ethic which reduced tension with the world to an absolute minimum. And animistic magic, as the only other form of popular religion, supported this traditionalist fear of innovation by warning against the danger of stirring up evil spirits and producing evil charms, which would result from any disturbing activities.

All these ideas and assumptions helped to produce a certain type of Chinese character. Max Weber has called attention to some of these traits:

The striking lack of 'nerves' in the specifically modern European meaning of the word; the unlimited patience and controlled politeness; the strong attachment to the habitual; the absolute insensitivity to monotony; the capacity for uninterrupted work and the slowness in reacting to unusual stimuli, especially in the intellectual sphere. All this seems to constitute a coherent and plausible unit but other seemingly sharp contrasts appear. There is an extraordinary and unusual horror of all unknown and not immediately apparent things which finds expression in ineradicable distrust. There is the rejection or lack of intellectual curiosity about things not close at hand and immediately useful. These traits stand in contrast to an unlimited and good-natured credulity in any magical swindle, no matter how fantastic it may be. In the same way the strong lack of genuine sympathy and warmth, often even among people who are personally close, stands in apparent contrast to the great and close-knit cohesion of social organisations. The absolute docility and ceremonial piety of the adult towards his parents hardly seems compatible with the alleged lack of love and respect for authority in small children.[1]

Completely absent in the Confucian ethic, then, was any tension between nature and deity, between ethical demands and

[1] *The Religion of China*, p. 231.

human defects, consciousness of sin and need for salvation. The Chinese soul had never been revolutionised by a prophet or by a prophetic religion.[1] Hence those psychic inner forces, freed of tradition and convention, for influencing conduct and shaping character were never generated. Without these inner forces, the individual lacked an autonomous inner core as a counter-balance in facing the world. Few dared to deny tradition and stand alone. Confucianism helped to tame the masses as well as the scholar-gentry, but by so doing it also took away from them all those inward aspirations which have fashioned the Western autonomous personality. Having stripped man of the stead-fastness of personal freedom, which was the instrument of Western progress, they created a static, frozen kind of society, sunk in the degrading life of mere custom.

Although they discovered paper, printing, the magnetic compass and gunpowder, they failed to develop a modern science and technology. And although they sanctioned revolt, a success-ful revolt brought in its train only a new ruler, not a new order. Chinese society was incapable of movement and evolution and was caught in a process of virtually circular development. Lacking freedom, the Chinese people came to see themselves as 'born only to drag the car of imperial power' and the burden which pressed them to the ground 'they came to regard as their destiny'.[2]

In contrast with the prosaic Chinese society, fixed among a firm and definite reality, India is a region of fantasy and dream, of a boundless imagination. It is a society deeply penetrated by religion. Hinduism, the predominant religion of India is, how-ever, not an organised church nor has it a strict set of religious dogmas. It is, rather, a mysterious and amorphous entity, made up of a body of ideas, beliefs, values and customs. It has been the basis of the country's thought, art, law and social structure. Religion has permeated all its activities, domestic and social, political and economic. Religion has, in fact, obsessed the Indian mind to the detriment of more worldly pursuits.

The three main ends of life recognised by the Hindu religion

---

[1] The Chinese soul 'wandered' in its world, it never attempted to establish the supremacy of soul over the alien, the environment.

[2] Hegel, *The Philosophy of History*.

are Karma, Dharma and Moksa. Karma is the doctrine of moral consequences. Man is not an isolated, autonomous individual with a sense of sin and revolt, but a link in a potentially endless chain of lives. This is the doctrine of the transmigration of souls. According to it, each life is only one of a series and its content depends upon the will and behaviour of the individual. Every action, good or bad, has its consequences and each soul enjoys or suffers in every life the consequences of its actions in previous existences. By great exertions and suitable exercises, man may ultimately escape from this endless chain of births and rebirths, into a direct union with the Brahma—an immanent God or World Soul.

Dharma is a comprehensive word, covering law, social usage, and duty. It refers to the regulation of life in all its aspects. In India, everybody is born to his own place in the universal scheme of things, and wears the signs of the department of life to which he belongs. The aim of the individual is to become absolutely identified with the tasks and interests of his social role. He should even subordinate to this his public and private character. In terms of India's philosophy of duty, the composite group takes precedence over any of its individual components.

All self-expression, as we know and care for it, is therefore ruled out, the precondition to participation in the group consisting not in cultivating, but in dissolving, personal tendencies and idiosyncrasies. The supreme virtue is to become assimilated wholeheartedly and without residue—to the timeless, immemorial, absolutely impersonal mask of the classic role into which one has been brought by birth (*jati*). The individual is thus compelled to become anonymous. And this is regarded, furthermore, as a process not of self-dissolution but of self-discovery: for the key to the realisation of one's present incarnation lies in the virtues of one's present caste.[1]

India's static, departmentalized and mutually co-operative hierarchy of castes, crafts and professions demands that from the very first moment of life the individual's energies and aspirations should be devoted to the service of the divine. The individual is not free to choose; he belongs automatically to a species—a family, a guild and craft, a group, a caste. This

[1] Heinrich Zimmer, *Philosophies of India*. Meridian Books Inc., New York, p. 152.

principle of a divine order determines to the last detail the regulations for one's public and private conduct. Only by accepting these rigorous rules, only by practising all these prescribed virtues, can the individual lose himself, dissolve the temporal accident of his own personality and be absorbed into the boundlessness of universal being. This is the power of Dharma.

This depersonalising 'principle of specialisations' is pushed even further by the subdivision of the ideal life-course of the individual into four stages. The first stage is that of the pupil. In this stage the pupil identifying himself unquestionably with his Guru (master) must become nothing but the vessel into which his master's knowledge of his vocation is poured. This phase is ruled exclusively by obedience and submission. The second stage is that of householdership. The youth, now a man, must take over the paternal craft, business or profession, is given a wife, begets sons, supports the family and does his utmost to identify himself with all the tasks and rules of the traditional head of the household. In the second half of the individual's life, he must begin to prepare himself to cast aside all these worldly roles, throw off all possessions, break from the desires and anxieties of his married life, and turn his back on the duties of society. He must now enter upon the third stage, that of the 'departure to the forest'. And the fourth, that of the 'wandering, holy beggar', the 'homeless wanderer', indifferent to the world and 'identified with the eternal self'. He is now released from narrow groups, family ties and possessions. Rule and duty cease to be binding. He has now attained release from all the desires, ambitions and fears of secular life, the delusions of social interests. Through yoga, self-discovery, one reaches the phase of absolutely unconditional identification with the super-personality of the divine will, which is beyond his natural life, beyond his individual ego, beyond the moment in time.

Moksa—or salvation—is the attainment of freedom from action, from desire and from the material world. Moksa has impressed itself on every feature, trait and discipline of Indian life and has shaped its entire scale of values. By far the greatest measure of Indian thought has been concerned with the supreme spiritual theme of liberation from 'the passions of the world's general illusion'. For Hinduism, God is more real than the world. There is no higher purpose in life than eventual re-union with the abstractly universal, and all doctrines, disciplines, devotions and ecstasies are but means to that end. This world, however, ultimately has no substance at all. To obtain deliverance, to achieve Union, man must escape from the endless round of births and deaths, from the cruel bonds of passion and desire. He can only escape by realising that the world is illusion, by annihilating his spiritual and physical existence, by purging the passions because they inevitably lead to action and therefore produce only suffering and delusion. In its highest degree, this negation consists of perfect mental immobility, the annihilation of all emotion and all volition. Man in the Indian vision is a plaything and slave of natural forces; and the things of this world are regarded as mere dust. The Hindu feels himself to be utterly at the mercy of the destructive forces of death (disease, plagues, warfare, human tyranny and injustice) and the inevitable victim of the merciless flow of time (which destroys individuals, wipes out towns and the splendour of realms and crumbles even the ruins to dust). For Hinduism, life is not something of great worth, touched by the divine, but is a mere fever. Hinduism is a world renouncing system, and its strongest impulse has been to deny life and to treat it with contempt.

India's religious mentality, its caste system, its other-worldly outlook, have all helped to shape a certain kind of society. This system was by no means barren in material achievements and cultural attainments. It left behind remarkable architectural remains. It produced many schools of philosophy. Its arts and sculpture have been both intricate and grandiose. Yet, when all has been said, this most religious of peoples has produced a society which has supported some of the world's greatest superstitions and barbarities. Its social fabric has been more outwardly impressive than human within. The devotion to Brahma is less obvious than the worship of the cow; the few genuine mystics have been lost in the vast crowd of fakirs, temple prostitutes, fortune-tellers and snake-charmers. Its energy has been spent in worship rather than in thought. In place of compassion men have prostrated themselves before the terrible Shiva, the God of destruction whose ritual demands were often cruel and bloodthirsty. Humbly crouching and abject before victor and lord, the Indian has more often than not been recklessly barbarous to the vanquished and subject. The prosperity and splendour of the court rested most of the time on the wretchedness, the poverty and oppression of the masses. The Hindu pantheon has been as corrupt as the Indian government.

After a brilliant start, Indian civilisation has had a long and infinitely slow running down, always a prey to conquerors. Even Nehru has viewed Indian life as a

sluggish stream, living in the past, moving slowly through the accumulations of dead centuries. The heavy burden of the past crushes it and a kind of coma seizes it. It is not surprising that in this condition of mental stupor and physical weariness, India should have deteriorated and remained rigid and immobile while other parts of the world marched ahead. . . . The urge to life and endeavour becomes less, the creative spirit fades away and gives place to the imitative.[1]

The society which existed in India before the coming of the British has been a society that has stressed stability and security as against progress and movement. The social structure based on the caste system and joint-families demanded strict conformism to social and communal usage and suppressed the growth of the autonomous individual. Instead of stimulating the activity of the individual soul it has condemned it to the most degrading spiritual serfdom. The Indian social order was unfavourable to economic progress and to the development of diversified social classes. Instead of expanding the sympathies of the people, it has contracted them. It afforded few opportunities for the virile growth of the human spirit. Hegel has left us this intuitive passage about India which perhaps expresses some profound truth about the country:

There is a beauty of a peculiar kind in women, in which their countenance presents a transparency of skin, a light and lovely roseate hue, which is unlike the complexion of mere health and vital vigour—a more refined bloom, breathed, as it were, by the soul within—and in which the features, the light of the eye, the position of the mouth, appear soft, yielding, and relaxed. . . . Such

[1] J. Nehru, *India Rediscovered*. Oxford University Press, p. 10.

a beauty we find also in its loveliest form in the Indian world; a beauty of enervation in which all that is rough, rigid, and contradictory is dissolved and we have only the soul in a state of emotion—a soul, however, in which the death of free self-reliant Spirit is perceptible. For should we approach the charm of this Flower-life—a charm rich in imagination and genius—in which its whole environment and all its relations are permeated by the rose-breath of the Soul, and the World is transformed into a Garden of love—should we look at it more closely, and examine it in the light of Human Dignity and Freedom—the more attractive the first sight of it had been, so much the more unworthy shall we ultimately find it in every respect. . . .[1]

Asian civilisation, whether in its Confucian, Hindu or Buddhist forms (Buddhism will be discussed later, when we analyse Burmese society), was predominantly an agrarian one. Its twin bases were the self-contained villages and the despotic state, responsible for vast economic enterprises and ruled by a centralised bureaucracy and army.

The economies of these societies formed an integral part of what Marx called the 'Asiatic mode of production'. These economies had certain resemblances with the economy of the ancient world; slavery, for example, was tolerated; but slaves never occupied an important role in either agriculture or industry. Then again, it had some features in common with medieval Europe—the guild system, and some of its religious values—but it was without the Manor and has never had free cities to stimulate innovation and protect enterprise and to give the businessman an honoured position in the society.

It was, in fact, an economic system in radical opposition to anything that the West had developed. Its special character, its uniqueness, is to be found in its incapacity to transcend itself. It was condemned to a 'life in death'; from century to century its essential identity with itself was scarcely altered. Its capacity for novel ideas, for novel aspects of old ideas, for change and experiment and adventure was frozen. Hence, whatever the superficial resemblances that could have been detected between it and the conditions of Europe in the medieval ages, it was never at any time in its history involved in

[1] *The Philosophy of History*. Dover Publications Inc., New York, p. 140.

THE WEST AND ASIA

a similar process of revolutionary transformation. In spite of the unsurpassed industry and capacity for work among the Chinese, and in spite of the economic achievements of the Indians in handicrafts, no independent system of capitalist production developed, no bourgeoisie grew to prominence. They lacked both an adequate circulation of wealth and of ideas. Both society and man repeated themselves from generation to generation, unable to break through the passivity of perpetually renewed identical circles. Its wide-ranging thought and speculation concentrated on interpreting rather than destroying its inherited traditional beliefs; it failed to develop our modern scientific and philosophic outlook and its revolutionary and explosive consequences. Oriental wisdom and morality have never lost their traditionalist character.

Ruled by a despotism which had managed to suppress all class struggle, without a sense of sin and therefore of rebellion, lacking the feeling of a profound disjunction between the individual and his destiny, without a sense of tragedy, its individual members tied to the divine unconscious or the magic body of the race, Asia never produced its own Renaissance, Reformation and Enlightenment. None of these societies have ever known what spring is: they have never experienced a sense of refreshment and renewal. Asia has known wars and massacres, it has experienced conquests and anarchy, it has participated in intrigues and revolts, but it has never given birth to those political and social revolutions which have inaugurated a new epoch of civilisation, which have changed the lives, the habits and the values of whole peoples. Asian history is the history of an inert being, without sufficient resilience to defy destiny. It experienced no dramatic turning points in its history, no new social forces arose to alter the destinies and outlook of its peoples. Its instinctive conception of government has been that of a ruler who gives orders and is unconditionally obeyed. Throughout the long centuries of its existence there is hardly a sign of any mass aspiration to freedom, any indigenous popular effort at social justice, any concerted will to social progress. Asia preferred stability and 'peace of mind' to tension and struggle, static adjustment to dynamic enterprise. The interests of the empire, of the community, of the caste, of the family, were cultivated in opposition to the aspiring, discontented, free individual in revolt against the injustice, the failures, the inevitable incompleteness of the world. Man was never endowed with outstanding rank in this society. In Asia, man has always been part of a group, at all times subordinated to ends larger than himself, willing to lose himself in something immense, in a horde or in a dynasty, in a pyramid or a Nirvana. Asia never found what Europe discovered—man—individual, self-conscious, expansive; seeking, acquiring and tormented. Asia lacked social spontaneity and fertility. Its religions and philosophies stupefied and paralysed its peoples. Its social structure stripped them of the highest qualities of humanity. One age died only to be born again, decked out in exactly the same garments. Its history was a history of reigning dynasties, but not of peoples.

Chapter 2

IMPERIALISM AND ITS CONSEQUENCES

i

STARTING with the fifteenth century, the West began, systematically, to break in upon the ancient peoples of America, Asia and Africa. At first they went into these countries in search of trade and high and quick profits; later, in order to defend their trading rights and profits, or to forestall their Western rivals, they began to intervene in the national governments. Finally, they established their domination over most of these countries and ruled their territories as alien conquerors. At the time of the first world war, Britain, France, Russia, Germany, Holland, Belgium, etc., were in control of vast empires and together constituted the predominant force in the world.

Western imperialism was, however, not merely a movement inspired by capitalist interests or motivated by narrow commercial considerations. Profits and power, idealism and cupidity, violence and constructive upbuilding, avarice and service, all helped to fashion its character. It was one of the far-reaching consequences of that magnificent outburst of creative energy which recast the traditional European order of society and the surplus energy of which was drained off and turned against the primitive, decaying and stagnant societies of the non-European world. Imperialism was not, in the main, the work of a few trading corporations, governments and states. It was brought into being by hundreds of thousands of colonists, pioneers, missionaries, explorers and adventurers, moved by all these contradictory impulses and responsible for both unprecedented constructive and destructive enterprises. This was, in short, a complex movement embracing economic interests, the nations' will to power, and the desire to spread more civilised notions of life. The pursuit of economic profits, dreams of national glory and prestige, political ambitions, the aspiration to play a leading role in world affairs, the feeling that they were the agents of a higher form of civilisation, the desire of missionaries to convert souls, all these coalesced to impel the West to embark upon the very hazardous but exciting adventure of imperialist expansion.

Western imperialism was so successful, furthermore, not because of any special iniquity on its part and not because of the amount of violence that it employed, but primarily because, beginning with the Age of Discovery, a sudden and dramatic disparity in cultural and political energies, in economic and social productivity, opened up between Europe and the rest of the world. The anarchy and disintegration of states and societies that they encountered, the backwardness, bankruptcy and internal divisions which they found on their arrival, the vacuums that developed as a result of this process of dissolution, the military weakness that they met on the field of battle—all these conditions made it possible for the West to extend its influence and, after centuries of unparalleled daring and resolution, to establish its ascendancy. Very rarely did the Western colonisers meet with political entities and social structures filled with an inherent capacity to resist this new, strange and formidable challenge. Almost nowhere did they find peoples who were endowed with the awareness of a freedom of independence worth sacrificing their lives for. In a world of relentless power-struggles between states, and of unremitting competition between nations and ideologies, imperialism of one kind or another will always be present as a danger or as an actuality as long as these fatal weaknesses, disparities and unbalances prevail between nations and civilisations.

Like so many other human efforts, the imperialist enterprise, too, was inextricably mingled with evil and corruption. It was responsible for the horrors of slavery and the slave trade. It decimated whole groups of primitive peoples in America, Africa and Australia. In its early mercantilist phase, it plundered the countries it penetrated. A destructive form of racial superiority, particularly among the Anglo-Saxon powers, insulted and humiliated the self-respect of the native peoples over whom they ruled. They left behind them a trail of cruelty and megolomania. Their rule did involve economic exploitation and it was not based upon the freely given consent of the governed. They did pursue narrow and restrictionist political, economic and social policies. Western industry did ruin ancient handicrafts and its land policies did disrupt whole populations. The foreign rulers and the foreign companies did tend to discriminate against local interests and to neglect the training of local managerial manpower. More often than not, the colony was only treated as a market rather than as a community of human beings. In general, the imperialist powers found it much more congenial to support and associate with the more backward, reactionary and less enterprising elements within the native societies.

Western domination over their colonies quite naturally had highly significant spiritual, political and economic consequences for the Western world. It led to a great enlargement and enrichment of its view of the world. New concepts, new goods, new uses, new learning and skills, new art forms and ideas, innumerable legends and myths, all flowed to it from its colonies. Its political and psychological effects were apparent: a rise in self-confidence, a sense of power and dominion, increased military resources (including the service of native soldiers), and a general feeling that they were the leaders and masters of the world. In addition, empire provided a field of activity and a source of high earnings for both the ambitious and the laggards and dregs of Western society.

On the economic plane, too, imperialist domination produced important economic consequences for the ruling powers. The doctrine of the super-economic exploitation of the colonies has been a stock-in-trade of all anti-imperialist literature (Lenin and Hobson, for example) for many years. John Strachey, in his *The End of Empire*,[1] has quite lucidly and effectively punctured the extravagant claims of these schools of thought. After examining thoroughly the arguments and data concerning the 'drain of unrequited value extorted from India and the West Indies by Britain' and which was supposed to have greatly helped Britain to industrialise, he comes to the sober and more valid conclusion that this was never as much and was never as effective a factor as had been and as is still supposed. He argues on the contrary, that while in the mid-eighteenth century the British 'take-off' into industrialisation did receive

Victor Gollancz. London, 1959.

some impetus from 'unrequited imports', it was by no means the largest factor in Britain's pioneer accomplishment of primary industrialisation. He claims that the agricultural revolution marked by enclosures, and the break-through in technique associated with the steam engine, which was occurring at the same time and place, were the major immediate influences responsible for Britain's industrial revolution. These two factors, plus the surplus wealth extracted from the exploitation of the working classes, and the 'terrible initial fall in the peasants' standard of life' provided the resources which were many times as important as the unrequited imports of all the imperial spoils. What was true of British rule in India was probably true of the rule of most of the other advanced European countries. Though some colonies produced a greater surplus, many more produced a smaller one and some were probably dead losses. The present wealth of the West has not been produced by imperialist exploitation, but is the painfully won product of the hard work, the arduous efforts, the suffering, the enterprising skill and the intellectual and cultural audacity of the Western peoples and of their ruling elites. Emerson has said that 'India fell to British character'. It is even more profoundly true to say that Western wealth and the achievements of Western society are the products of the fervent and resilient Western character.

As against all these negative aspects of Western rule, one must, to set the historical record straight, take into account all those particular respects in which Western rule was both positive and productive. Imperialism was far from being only political domination, racial arrogance and economic exploitation. It was a vivid example of culture-contact on a vast scale, of that encounter and collision between cultures which constitutes and generates the history of civilisation itself. The intrusion of Western colonialism into all these territories was the most revolutionary event in the centuries-long history of the non-Western peoples. For the first time in their prolonged and unchanging histories, a force burst into the societies of Asia and Africa which introduced techniques, ideas and institutions that they had never experienced before. By disturbing the existence of their ancient peasant communities, by partially destroying their native domestic industry, by replacing the ancient system of despotic government with a new form of administration tinged with Western liberal ideas and practices, and by holding up the image of a radically opposed world outlook, they launched a process of change and development such as these societies had never experienced before in all the thousands of years of their history.

Imperialist conquest established the rule of law and order in all the territories under their control. For many decades it preserved them from foreign attack. With only a handful of soldiers and administrators, they succeeded in throwing a net of internal and external security over vast territories which had previously been prey to lawlessness and anarchy. They stimulated a new sense of political and economic unity. They protected the rights of individuals and communities more fully and impartially than any previous regime. Even if government was not based on the popular will it yet permitted the growth of an organised political opposition which no previous Oriental state had ever tolerated.

Having established conditions of law and order, all the forces of Western rule—administrators, businessmen, educators, missionaries, etc.—were able to begin to exert their influence over the native societies.

Western economic enterprise brought the economic life of all these territories out of its ancient isolation into the network of the modern world economy. Large-scale capital investments imparted advanced technical skills and scientific knowledge. New crops were developed, new industries were started up, new commercial institutions were founded. Railways, roads, canals and irrigation works, the whole 'infra-structure' of modern industrial development, were built. The seeds of a modern working class and of a modern middle class were planted and began to sprout. Despite all the exploitation that took place, a considerable increase in the wealth of these societies was, in fact, realised.

As a result of contact with the West, new cities grew up. Bombay, Calcutta and Madras, Shanghai, Tientsin, Canton, Rangoon, Djakarta, Colombo and Saigon became centres of economic enterprise and political ferment. The growth of these commercial and industrial cities, the spread of municipal self-government, represented a radically new principle in the organisation of oriental society. The fashioning of these cities with all their new skills, interests, ambitions and stimuli, probably represents the West's chief achievement in the east.

Stirred by its own liberalism and humanitarianism, and faced with the need for a large body of indigenous administrators, the Western rulers launched a programme of education, social welfare and even political training. Schools were opened, hospitals built, medical science introduced, and gradually even organs of local and national government, on some form of democratic basis, were established. The French were, in a way, the most daring of all the Western powers in theory, in this regard, though they fell far short of their intentions in practice. They alone attempted to assimilate colonial peoples to the French people and believed that it was the mission of the French nation to spread the benefits of French civilisation and culture among them. Their aim was to treat the subject peoples as possible participants in the 'fraternity of a common French civilisation'. This was partly carried out through education, and when coloured representatives even took their seats in the French parliament. And in India, Macaulay was boldly optimistic enough to believe that the teaching of the English language could civilise the country and liberate it from 3,000 years of despotism, superstition and debasement, and create 'a class of persons, Indian in blood and colour, but English in taste, in opinion, in morals and in intellect'.

The Western powers as a whole, by their educational and welfare activities, by the research of their scholars and archaeologists, had a considerable effect on the general stock of ideas by which the elites of these societies came to guide their lives. Over the years, Asian youths began to find their way to European seats of learning. London, Paris, Berlin and Leyden became magnets, attracting an ever-growing number of students. Some even began to study such subjects as engineering, physics, medicine, geology and chemistry, which their societies had never cultivated before. European scholars provided the material for the writing of Indian history. A few Dutch scholars reconstructed from inscriptions the history of the empires of Java and Sumatra. Even the new orientalism, which has now become so fashionable in the East, is not a pure replica of the traditional original, but has been shaped by what European research has discovered about the East.

The new art forms, especially in prose and painting, which have been developed, have little or nothing in common with the earlier traditions. Asian literature and art, meagre though they still are, have borrowed freely from the work that is being done in the West. Foreign scholars even played an important role in fashioning the new languages of Asia and thus have helped to shift a whole world of thought and expression. And although the missionary attempt to evangelise the peoples of Asia met with failure, this Christian attack on the spiritual foundations of Asian countries also had a limited effect on the religious thought of the peoples.

The contact between Asia and the West, furthermore, introduced the elites of Asia to the vast treasure house of Western thought and experience. The mental ferment this has brought about is inscribed in highly irregular lines over the whole Asian landscape. Western rule introduced into the Orient its post-medieval world view and thus challenged its whole ancient cosmology. The French Revolution, British liberalism, Marxism, democratic socialism, the Russian Revolution, all have won adherents and inspired the various movements of reform which sprang up in all these territories. Perhaps the best justification of Western intervention in the East is the fact that it brought these countries into contact with all the invigorating principles of Western social life (and with many of its heresies). Western history and Western education gave direction and shape to Asian aspirations for national independence.

Panikkar has given this broad summary of the Western impact on the mind of Asia:

The period between 1870–1914 thus witnessed the first large-scale meeting of Asian and Western minds. The mental ferment that this contact caused in Asia cannot be dealt with simply as a challenge to the established traditions of the past; it also sowed the seed of the new thought which in time replaced the learning of the ancients and placed the Asian countries on the road to intellectual progress. The Asian countries again became scientifically minded. Their social thought took them beyond Confucius and Manu; their history began to take in the lessons of other countries. Besides all this, the essential point for our purpose is that in every one of the countries of Asia, the leadership in the movement which ultimately displaced European supremacy belonged to those who had been trained by the West under the aegis of imperialism. Not only Mahatma Gandhi and Jawaharlal Nehru, but the founders of the Indian National Congress and the successive generations of Congress leaders were trained in the West. In Japan, it was the group of explorers sent to the West by the Shogunate that led the movement for the reorganisation of the State. In China, though the deposition of the Manchus was not the work of Western-educated people, the building up of the revolutionary movement that followed was led by men of Western training. In Indonesia, Indo-China, Burma and Ceylon it is the men and women educated in the West—the 'Wogs' (Westernized Oriental gentlemen) as the European contemptuously called them—that provided the leadership.[1]

Western rule in Asia was, then, not mere exploitation as has been alleged by nationalists and communists alike, but had many constructive and revolutionary consequences. If one serious charge can be levelled against Western imperialism it is that it was not revolutionary enough in its multifarious activities within the territories under its control and that it did not, in the essential work of civilisation that it was performing, sufficiently disturb or transform the archaic societies with which it came into contact. It innovated too little and too slowly. It did not effectively destroy the inbred stagnation of Asian society, nor did it adequately industrialise these countries. Even more important: it did not prepare sufficient modern men, Western men, indispensably necessary for the management of a viable and independent nation in the merciless twentieth century. It did not adequately prepare either the human or the material conditions essential for the further rapid development of these countries.

The Western impact on these societies was fundamentally a superficial one. Western rule operated on the surface of Asian life and did not affect its ponderous subterranean foundations. It did introduce some of the techniques and instrumentalities of the industrial revolution, it did build a number of imposing island cities, it did construct a new political system based on a

[1] *Asia and Western Dominance*, Allen and Unwin, London, 1959, p. 490.

radically new conception of law and government, it did introduce many Western ideas, notions and concepts and it did spread a knowledge of its languages among the educated classes. But this foreign system in all its aspects did not radically transform all these masses of mankind. A partial Westernisation penetrated only the upper layers of society. The life and thought of its peasantries, the overwhelming majority of its populations, was largely untouched. It did not transmit a new coherent or vigorous philosophy of society to their elites, nor did it inspire them to work out a suitable ideology and programme for the solution of their immense problems. The Western ideals which they acquired did not in fact interest the deeper energies of their personalities, nor did they stimulate the primitive impulses which constitute the heart of man. It failed to propagate its civilisation or to extend its spiritual citizenship to its subject nations. It clearly did not change the instincts or the character of all these peoples, nor even of their elites. While a small minority did acquire some of the technical skills necessary for a modern technological society, they understood little of the values or the ferment on which Western society as a whole reposes. They were never really culturally contaminated by the West. They only acquired a veneer of Western life; its health and vigour escaped them. Except in a few outstanding cases, there was no genuine cultural conversion of souls. Although the West ruled Asia, it never in any way converted it. And this distressing consequence, far from being a source of regret, is in fact considered as a badge of pride by many educated Asians. Confronted with the multitudes of their empires, with the rigidities of their customs, the Western rulers soon enough began to feel that they were not strong enough to interfere with the lives of their subjects. Their original ambition to modernise their colonies was quickly exhausted. The mere handful of Europeans who administered these territories could not and were not willing to radically alter the channels in which their daily life continued to flow.

Even in the heyday of empire, in the second half of the nineteenth century, the majority of officials were of the opinion that the Asian societies under Western rule and influence should be developed along Asian lines. Impressed by some of the ideas developed by the Orientalists, they held that Asia should be reconstructed 'upon a purely native model'. These men, most of them out of sympathy with their own industrial societies, incapable of coping with its dangers and opportunities, sought to escape the pressures of the modern world by dreaming of building 'Arcadias in Asia' (and then later, in Africa), based on the idea of service to unspoiled and childlike peasants and craftsmen. Most of these officials were far happier moving about in regal isolation in the villages of Asia than they would have been as ordinary functionaries in the West's industrial centres. Although they understood that some of the gross abuses like slavery, suttee, child marriage and some of the more outrageous superstitions would have to be eliminated, they were yet convinced that the introduction of industrialisation and modernisation would bring even greater evils. Out of tune with the modern world from which they came, they found a cheap kind of refuge in romanticising the Asian peasant, praising the simplicities of village life and the virtues of the un-sullied, natural man. Surrounded by all these alien multitudes they found a vacuous satisfaction in assuming the role of Gods to the distant and worshipful mass below.

In the period of disillusionment that followed the shocks which the liberal democracies suffered in the first world war, the institutions of primitive peoples were rediscovered as cultures worthy of preservation. Under the influence of the late Professor Malinowski, the functional school of anthropology in particular laid great stress on the need to preserve the delicately balanced functions of these primitive cultures. In his view a society's environment imposes a pattern, each particular custom, institution, function, having evolved in response to some impulse—some need of survival or security, of climate and geography—and all the parts are closely interdependent. This school of thought believed that a break at any one point would dangerously disorganise the functional unity of the whole. They (and the colonial offices which were influenced by these considerations) were therefore highly apprehensive of any initiative which would produce disrupting culture contacts. Tribal institutions and indigenous customs (the policy of 'indirect rule') were maintained and encouraged, particularly in British Africa. By the end of the second world war, the Western powers everywhere were supporting and administering obsolete forms of society and had lost the inner confidence required for a programme of innovation and modernisation.

Another fatal mistake that has been made has been the ever-increasing emphasis that both the colonial rulers and their nationalist opponents have been placing on purely political (and today purely economic) solutions to the complex and many-sided colonial situation. The colonial question came to be looked upon and is in fact still now regarded in almost exclusively political terms. A naive faith was propagated and spread in the curative potentialities of national independence. This exaggerated stress on mere political solutions prevented the nationalist leaders and the world at large from facing the realities of the colonial situation and from analysing the true ground of their backwardness, which in fact had fundamentally nothing to do with imperialist rule. A society is backward, not only because its economy is backward, but because its people are backward. It is backward people who create a backward society. The colonial question is basically a question of cultures and of peoples at different stages of development. Political ambitions, therefore, did not march together and were not inspired by a sense of mission for the task of recasting the foundations of their own society. Political advancement came to be thought of as an end in itself, without inducing any serious thinking about how such advancement was to be used. To achieve national independence is relatively a very simple matter, to build a new society is something involving qualities of a different order of magnitude. In fact, their enhanced political status has halted any critical consideration of the true reasons for their retarded development; has deflected thought from considering the true causes of their former dependence and present inferiority; and has thus given birth to a superficial optimism about their future prospects. The only heritage of this kind of approach is the production of a consummate mixture of complacency and presumption.

It is, furthermore, not true, as some have said and as so many believe today, that as a result of Western rule the lives of these societies have been turned upside down and inside out, that their social fabrics have been pulverised and convulsed and that all these 'petrified fossils' (Toynbee) have been corroded. Despite the disturbance which Western rule has effected, the non-Western world has continued to cling to its own traditions, values and habits. No fundamental breach of cultural continuity has occurred anywhere. In none of these countries was the traditional society abolished or anything new developed to its logical conclusion. The peoples were more inclined to spasmodic efforts at rebellion than capable of building up a movement for creative freedom. The more superficial elements of the intellect and the conscious mind were influenced by new Western ideas, particularly the idea of nationalism, but the subconscious, containing the powerful instinctual forces which shape character and give strength to the passions and the will, has as yet only slightly been stirred. These 'unadapted' societies will only begin to come to terms with the problems created by the irreversible encounter between the Western and the non-Western worlds when the psychic energy present in the subconscious will have been excited and canalised into a determined effort to realise some of those radical changes in basic character structures and values made necessary as a consequence of this fateful encounter. The awakening of the subconscious can only come about through a powerful shock, or through a series of shocks, which will arouse the imagination of its leading strata and force them to rethink their past and to redefine their basic values and aspirations. This shock they have as yet not experienced. For the process of Westernisation is not only one of passive adaptation but of radical transformation and involves a genuine mutation, a revolutionary process of rebirth. A new civilisation can never arise without the disintegration of the old one. And this process of rebirth, this intervening period of deep crisis, the precondition for the creation of a new society capable of coping with the immense problems of the twentieth century, is a prolonged and stormy process which by its very nature will have to stretch over many generations, and even then suffer all the distortions and corruptions to which every human effort is heir.

The nationalist movements which arose in opposition to Western rule have, during the past fifteen years, scored unparalleled successes. The anti-colonial uproar which is now so audible in the underdeveloped and backward parts of the world has been the second of the two great emotional and political issues—the first one being communism—which has dominated the political and intellectual life of the post-war period. The political emergence of the Afro-Asian peoples has shaken the former world structure of power and has produced a fierce competition between the two main power blocs for influence over them. Before discussing the implications of all these outwardly dramatic events it is necessary to attempt to analyse the character of some of these nationalist movements and their offspring, which have now come to power in all these countries and whose leaders are now being courted by all the leading powers of the West.

Undoubtedly the most significant, the most responsible, the most impressive of all these movements in the non-communist part of the world has been the Indian National Congress. Not only was it the largest of these movements, but it also succeeded in mobilising the most capable group of political leaders to represent it. The Indian national movement, however, was at first entirely a product of the cultural contact between India and Great Britain. The injection of English ideas into Indian life awakened the Indian desire for nationhood and led to its demands for national independence and freedom. In the course of its development, Indian nationalism, at first almost entirely a product of British inspiration, began to oppose not only Britain's political domination but to object to its cultural influence as well. Indian nationalism soon came to feel that its moral mission was to protect national customs and the destiny of the country from the pernicious influence of British culture. It represented an awakening of national forces, reasserting the validity of a native tradition against the wholesale influx of foreign influences. Panikkar has well described, in more general terms, the essentially conservative nature of all these movements.

Nowhere was it a movement starting from the bottom, an up-surge of social protest caused either by the sufferings or the awakened conscience of the masses. Its strength lay essentially in the desire of each nation to conserve what was its own, and its leadership, as we shall show, was drawn from classes which, by intellectual tradition, tended to be conservative. It was not the desire for progress or for betterment that was originally at the root of the Asian revival. It was the determination to resist the foreigner who was pressing his attack in all directions, political, social, economic and religious. It was the desire for national strength and not for revolutionary changes that was the main motivation of the changes in Asian communities. It was the case of ancient societies calling forth and mobilising their dormant forces to meet an aggression.[1]

The Indian nationalist movement against foreign rule and the amorphous revolt against age-long social injustice and economic exploitation was, therefore, right from the start married to the defence of the archaic ideals of India's ancient social structure. The weak and irresolute liberal Westernisers and reformers who did arise in India were thus opposed by the new mass nationalism led at first by Tilak and then later by Gandhi. Culturally, these two leaders and their many followers belonged to India's hoary past and consciously shared all its prejudices and petrified outlook.

Tilak, for example, who has been called the 'Father of Indian Unrest', was mistakenly convinced that the Hindu middle class had become 'denationalised' under the influence of English education, manners and ideas. He believed that India was losing its soul and acquiring a slave mentality because of its indiscriminate borrowing from the West. He therefore supported, as part of his nationalist agitation, the Anti-Cow-Killing Society, opposed the Age of Consent bill, was hostile to the government and mission schools, favoured the use of the vernacular languages in place of English, spread the cult of home-made cloth and tried to revive ancient festivals and exalt ancient heroes. Tilak, who was a militant nationalist and quite ready to use violence to attain his aims, firmly believed that only by a revival of Hinduism, that only if India asserted its 'Asianism', could the country be saved and win back its dignity and independence.

[1] *Asia and Western Dominance*, p. 315.

After the first world war, Gandhi in particular came to symbolise this revivalist and conservative aspiration, although in comparison with the general run of Hindu traditionalists he also embodied, on a much lower intellectual level, the best of its moral inspiration. For all these groups, the very fact that the Indian people had remained backward was not a cause for lament but a virtue of great merit. Gandhi not only denounced British political domination, but rejected Western civilisation in all its forms. 'One effort is required,' he said, 'and that is to drive out western civilisation. All else will follow.' In his eyes, the West's industrial and democratic civilisation was merely materialistic and destructive of harmony and community. For him, India's salvation was to consist of a revival of its traditional handicrafts and of its ancient village form of life. By practising poverty, India would recover her soul and go back to a 'peasant golden age'. Gandhi was convinced that it was his mission to teach wisdom to the West and preach revolution to his own countrymen.

Nirad Chaudhuri, in his remarkable book *Autobiography of an Unknown Indian*,[1] has described Gandhiism as follows:

Only the noble slave could have propounded this doctrine, a slave who was too weak, too modest and too meek, and too passive to break his chains, but was capable of making them immaterial in an ecstatic contemplation of his hypostatis of goodness and right. Those other men—strong, courageous and creative, who never flag because they are sustained by the urge of life, and an intuitive pre-vision of the future they are bringing to birth, who are symbolised for me by the young horsemen of the Parthenon, would not only have rejected this servile morality as unacceptable, but also deprecated it out of a feeling that it was alien and opposed to the law of life.

Weak and paralysed at home, with a feeling of wounded national pride, knowing in their heart of hearts that they suffered from a kind of inward senility, the fatigue of untold and unchanging centuries, they yet created for themselves a vision of India's peculiar and unique place in the world. They began to extol India's spiritual and metaphysical profundity over and against Western materialism and its intellectual shallowness.

[1] The Macmillan Co., New York, and Macmillan, London, 1951, p. 430.

Indian religiosity and pacifism was going to save the world from the effects of Europe's inherent aggressiveness and its propensity to permanent strife and chaos. This goal was openly proclaimed: 'You shall help to create, to spiritualise an epoch, to Aryanise the world. And that nation is your own, that epoch belongs to you and your children and that world is no mere tract of land but the whole earth with its teeming millions.'[1]

These champions of India's spiritual uniqueness and special religious message to the world were the Indian equivalents of Russia's nineteenth-century Slavophiles (though without their essential physical vitality and spiritual restlessness), who also believed in Russia's unique future, who were also convinced that Russia was 'a God-bearing nation' destined to become the world's 'Third Rome'. For them primitive but spiritual Russia was superior to advanced and cultured Europe. These Slavophiles eulogised rural handicrafts as specifically Russian, and exalted the village communes as the incarnation of the Russian virtue of collective living. For them, collectivism based on the self-abnegation of the individual was far superior to the Western ideal of the free individual, pursuing his own independent goals and ambitions. The existence of these communes, they were convinced, showed quite clearly that Russia could follow her own path of social development and need not adopt the dehumanising European model of industrialisation. Uncertain whether they were Eastern or Western, hankering after Europe and at the same time repelled by many of its features, the elite and intelligentsia of Russia was haunted by the question whether their country should follow the beaten track laid down by the West or whether it should find its own way. The drama and agony of Russia's modern history can only be understood in the light of the issues raised by this fateful controversy. Armies, doctrines, hopes and delusions marched and counter-marched across this political and intellectual battlefield.

Russia's prolonged, intense struggle between the forces of Westernisation and Russianism or Slavophilism, which still continues today, though in a completely new context, is now being repeated, on a much lower level, in all the newly inde-

[1] Quoted by Hans Kohn, *The Twentieth Century*, p. 23.

pendent countries of Asia and Africa and even in the more 'Westernised' countries of Latin America.

Gandhi and his disciples and followers were only the most extreme representatives of this archaic trend within Indian society. But some of his ideas and sentiments, in one form or another, have influenced the thinking and outlook of its intelligentsia, of the overwhelming majority of India's ruling group and even of its more 'radical', non-communist socialist opposition. Gandhiism as the modern embodiment of India's antiquated heritage has left an indelible mark on India's contemporary society.

Apart from intellectuals of Parsee origin, or that small group of Westernised intellectuals influenced by the late M. N. Roy and now centred around the *Radical Humanist* magazine, Professor Edward Shils, who has written an interesting study on the 'Culture of the Indian Intellectual',[1] discovered that most of the Indian intellectuals he had met, interviewed or encountered through their writings, seemed to be 'Quite firmly rooted in India, in its past and present.' He found that most of the intellectuals are bound to Indian society and culture and accept its essential religious sentiments, ritual observances and family obligations. They are still influenced by astrology and astrological predictions. Even those with a scientific training or outwardly committed to radical views somehow seek to justify this strange attachment of theirs. (An interesting sidelight on the contradictory cultural influences which shape the mind of the Indian intellectual was provided in the course of an interview with a young Indian student who was doing post-graduate research in higher mathematics at the Hebrew University. He explained that the results of his research might possibly be useful within about twenty years. Yet, when asked about his attitude towards the 'problem of the cow in India' he replied with vigour that he believed in the 'holiness of the cow' as the symbol of 'mother India' and claimed that India is possessed of a great and ancient spiritual force which is both ineffably superior to anything that the materialistic-minded West has produced and which could serve as an

[1] Jan.–March 1960 and April–June 1960 issues of *Quest* magazine, Bombay.

example to Western civilisation.) Besides, Indian intellectuals, like everyone else in India, are caste conscious. Caste affiliations influence their behaviour, limit the range of their interests and sympathies and stunt the growth of their individual personalities. The Indian intellectual, moreover, despite his contact with the secular West, still possesses quite an elaborate religious consciousness. This involves not only the performance of religious exercises and devotions but also includes his fascination with the Hindu ideals of renunciation and withdrawal. The third and fourth stages in the Hindu theory of the four stages of life—the stages of release from all the desires, ambitions and fears of secular life, of 'departure to the forest' and of the 'homeless wanderer'—continue to have a tremendous spiritual power over most of them.

While being Indian in his inmost self, the Indian intellectual is none the less a troubled and divided human being. Victor Anant, a young Indian writer, has poignantly described the mass of contradictions inherent in their way of life:

It means that people like me are heirs to two sets of customs, are shaped in our daily lives, by dual codes of behaviour. For example: my generation on the one hand declared its agnosticism and on the other tamely succumbed to the old rituals; we yearned for romantic love but were reconciled to marriage by the well-established method of matching horoscopes to a girl selected for us by our parents; outside our homes we smoked, consumed alcohol, and ate meat, when available, but at home we were rigidly puritan and vegetarian; we glibly talked about individual salvation although we belonged to a very closely knit joint-family system.

Until India became independent there was, in the minds of most of my generation, no dismay at the contradictions inherent in our way of life. This was due to moral inertia and flabbiness. If we had then tried to come to terms with our two influences, we may have been able to see them as mutually antagonistic and we would then have been compelled to make a choice. The majority of Indians were engaged in a struggle for political independence, but the method of warfare corresponded to our mental slovenliness and to our physical lack of energy; 'freedom' was a national enterprise and all our moral anguish could be contained in one word—slavery.[1]

[1] 'The Hypnotized People', *Partisan Review*, Spring 1960, p. 311.

The Indian intellectual is beset with all these contradictory influences on many different levels. Despite the fact that he is 'quite firmly rooted in India' he yet has a nagging feeling that he is insufficiently Indian. He is concerned about not being Indian enough. He feels himself alienated from India and from the life of its common people. While they themselves are attached to India's ancient social pattern, they are yet ashamed that their country is not a modern country, that its institutions do not correspond to the needs of the modern world. On the one hand they are frustrated by their recognition of their country's inferiority and on the other they hug the vain idea that it has a unique message of harmony and peace for the rest of the world. While buoyed up by all the talk of 'Asian revival', by the reality of India's new influence in the world, which is more a product of Western weakness than of Indian strength, they are yet deeply worried about the melancholy fact that India is not an 'intellectually independent country', that it is nourished neither by its own intellectual resources nor supported by its own contemporary intellectual efforts or achievements.

Attracted by England as the home of 'modern thought', accepting the idea that science could liberate India from its poverty and slavery to the past, influenced by a primitive and garbled version of Marxism, playing around with the ideas of existentialism and its emphasis on human beings living a life of freedom and authentic choice, yet in all fundamentals submitting to the pressure of traditional Indian assumptions and institutions and in captivity to an antediluvian culture, the Indian intellectual is, then, if not a 'battlefield of severe internal conflict', at least a highly disturbed and unhappy wanderer between fundamentally clashing worlds of cultural values. They are divided between their attachment to a decaying past and their gropings towards an incoherent future.

The most interesting and tragic example of this duality of the modern educated Indian is, however, the present prime minister of India, Jawaharlal Nehru himself. He represents in his own personality a fragile synthesis between East and West, while at the same time he embodies the relentless clash, in his whole outlook, between the values of Asia and Europe. All the contradictory impulses which are present within the more advanced ranks of Indian society also find an even more extreme expression in him.

Yet, despite all these Hamlet-like flaws, Nehru is incomparably the most creative and positive force in all of non-communist Asia. In comparison with all the other non-communist leaders of Africa and Asia, he is a man of modern education and culture who would like, on his own terms, to change and rebuild India and to lead it into the twentieth century. To translate this wish into reality, he has tried, although not with much success, to spur, urge, prod and scold India into some form of activity. Since independence he has allowed himself very little rest and he has been the most dynamic factor in Indian society. Unfortunately, to be fruitful tirelessness must be allied to understanding and guided by strong will-power. This, as shall be seen, Nehru has regrettably lacked. Nevertheless, it must be admitted that Nehru is the only Indian leader who has thought out and worked out for himself and for the country some sort of political, economic and social programme for the reconstruction of Indian society.

His broad aim is to create a modern, secular and socialist society, to be achieved by democratic consent and not by coercion; by planning, through persuasion and not by violence. To realise these long-term socialist aims, his government has launched a series of five-year plans. Explaining the purpose of the first plan in 1951, Nehru said:

Our economy and social structure have outlived their day, and it has become a matter of urgent necessity for us to refashion them so that they may promote the happiness of all our people in things material and spiritual. We have to aim deliberately at a social philosophy which seeks a fundamental transformation of this structure, at a society which is not dominated by the urge for private profit and by individual greed and in which there is a fair distribution of political and economic power. We must aim at a classless society, based on co-operative effort, with opportunities for all. To realise this we have to pursue peaceful methods in a democratic way.

Democratic planning means the utilisation of all our available resources and, in particular, the maximum quantity of labour willingly given and rightly directed so as to promote the good of the community and the individual.

Nehru's programme of reconstruction has three main objectives; the transformation of an ancient society by changing its age-long institutions, abolishing untouchability and rearranging its family life by purely legislative means; a planned development of its economy by utilising the latest technical achievements of the day, by concentrating on heavy industry and by encouraging the growth of a new scientific outlook; and by the implementation of agrarian reforms including the gradual redivision of land holdings and the reorganisation of rural life through community development projects.

These three main objectives, limited and superficial though they are, without in any way going down to the roots of India's problems, yet constitute the most serious attempt made by any of the newly independent non-communist Afro-Asian countries to bring their peoples into the modern world.

What then is lacking in the Indian effort? For it has been admitted, by almost everybody who has studied the Indian effort with sympathy and intelligence, that some vital ingredients are missing, that within the exotic Indian puzzle a number of indispensable pieces have disconcertingly been mislaid or lost. I do not believe that these missing elements have very much to do with the magnitude of the plans so far drawn up. Nor do they spring from a lack of sufficiently educated people, as is the case in all of the other new countries. Nor even are they the result of a lack of sufficient resources. Of course, the Indian effort in all these fields could vastly be expanded. But basically, India lacks the vital ingredients necessary to transform the dream of modernisation into reality, because its ruling groups, including Pandit Nehru himself, have never come to grips with the essential problems and deficiencies of Indian society. None of them have really accepted the crucial fact that Indian society is a mouldy anachronism that has stifled and perverted the development of the human character and the human personality, and that only by a 'series of violent shocks' (Acton) can India shake off the palsied hand of the past, which seems to cling so tenaciously to this country, its institutions and its people, rescue the nation from the reign of the dead and provide it with that inner core of tough virility, that 'creative tension', in its national life, which are the prerequisites of progress. Nehru has often said that he is a socialist, a philosophical Marxist, that he even accepts the ultimate ideals of communism, whatever they might be, but he has never come to terms with the harsh but valid comments that Marx made about India and he has not accepted their full implications for his programme of transformation.

One need only compare India's enterprise of modernisation with some of the other successful or even partially successful modernising movements to discover how puerile the Indian effort really is. I shall not at this stage compare their endeavours with the arduous exertions of the Western peoples, or with the inhuman but highly effective methods used by both communist Russia and China. But let us, for example, compare India with Japan: Japanese society, during its period of modernisation, not only produced enough discontents and ambitions within the Japanese elite, of such a nature as to permit substantial innovating elements with sufficient energy and capacity to take the nation down new paths. It also managed to fashion enough men of courage and strength, who were ready to confront some of the ugly realities of Japanese society itself and to act as leaders of that political revolution which swept away Japan's feudal order. And these Meiji leaders were revolutionary enough, at the beginning of their efforts, to look with single-minded hope to the future and to turn their backs with contempt and shame upon their past. Dr Erwin Baelz, a German doctor called to the new Imperial Medical Academy in Tokyo, describing in 1876 the outlook of the Meiji leaders, had this to say about them:

'The Japanese have their eyes fixed exclusively on the future, and are impatient when a word is said of their past. The cultured among them are actually ashamed of it. "That was in the days of barbarism," said one of them. . . .' Another Japanese friend, questioned about Japanese history by Baelz, replied: 'We have no history. Our history begins today.'[1]

This outlook, unfortunately, did not persist for too long and that is why Japan is the schizophrenic society that it is. But

[1] Quoted by William W. Lockwood, 'Japan's Response to the West', *World Politics*. Centre of International Studies, Princeton University, Oct. 1956.

without this original approach, Japan would never even have succeeded in creating the semi-modern society that it has.

An even more apt comparison can be made with Turkey. It took Turkey a century and a half of half-hearted and self-defeating efforts at Westernisation before a bold and revolutionary national leader, Kemal Ataturk, arose with the courage to accept all the consequences of the encounter with Western civilisation. Before his arrival on the scene, the prevalent ideal of the Ottoman ruling class was to introduce only isolated elements of Western culture, especially in the field of military techniques, into their society. They thought it was possible to adopt only those techniques required for immediate self-preservation and thus to escape the necessity of turning their society upside down. For many generations they tried to cultivate the illusion that it is possible to 'hasten slowly' along the treacherous road of modernisation and to avoid the surgical operations which the situation of their country urgently demanded. In spite of repeated demonstrations of this fallacy, they continued to believe that a new culture was not an organic way of life which must be taken or left as a whole, but that one could, nonchalantly, with the most responsible sense of caution, play about with it as if it were a harmless curiosity shop from which one could pick and choose glittering ornaments and exotic curios, which could somehow be fitted into the old crumbling structures, and which would not call into question the fundamentals of their society. It took the Ottoman ruling class five generations to learn that the bare minimum of modernisation was nothing less than the attempt at the ultimate maximum.

The Ottoman policy of 'staggering' the process of Westernisation corroded the national society, made a mockery of all their policies and efforts and finally led to their humiliating defeat in war and to the total collapse of their empire. It was only at this critical juncture of Ottoman fortunes that Kemal Ataturk found his opportunity for audacious action and directed all the strength of his demonic will-power to the waging of a 'total war' of social and cultural transformation. In a number of Napoleonic-like measures, the revolutionary dictator set out to destroy the whole creaking structure of the Ottoman state, its social organisation, its political system, its bureaucracy. He flouted Islamic custom by tearing the veils off Muslim women's faces and degrading the fez as symbols of traditional demeanour; simplified the national language by changing its alphabet; and disestablished religion. By means of this political, intellectual, religious and emotional revolution, he aroused the energies of the Turkish nation and lifted it to that pitch of psychic and social malleability which enabled the country to begin to recast its traditional order and to launch itself on the road of economic development. Within the framework of these behavioural and institutional innovations, he began to develop the country's economic resources, to build its modern, political structure, to undermine its rural isolation and to compel the Turkish people to come into the modern world.

He forced the villagers themselves to build new village schools; he built new urban centres to be the nerve centres of his great adventure in social change, and shook the people's 'oriental mentality' by promoting mass literacy. He used the power of the state to change the folkways of the people and to transform its fundamental daily needs and desires, first of the new elite, then of the ancient mass. Taking unashamedly the modern West as his model, transferring Turkey's intellectual affiliation from the Islamic to the Western cultural tradition, he set out to create 'New Turks'. He aimed to transform Turkish behaviour and to revolutionise the Turkish psyche.

In spite of all the efforts which have been made in Turkey during the last forty years, with all their ups and downs, with all their advances and backslidings, Turkey is still not a modern society. But it is not a traditional society either. Recent events have only too conclusively shown that even a country like Turkey, the heir of a once powerful empire, which was at one time the terror and scourge of Europe, has still a long, long way to go before it will attain a modern level of civilisation. This by itself is not at all surprising. What is surprising and disheartening is the widespread current belief that the modernisation of the traditional societies of Afro-Asia, most of them on a much lower level of civilisation than Turkey ever was (and some with no tradition of civilisation at all), without its traditions of independent rule and its endowment of national vigour, can be affected by all kinds of 'tricking short-cuts', by all sorts of 'fallacious facilities'.

Returning to the problem of India, then, it becomes highly doubtful whether these titanic historical tasks can be accomplished by men who are deeply divided within themselves and who are floundering pathetically in a welter of conflicting intentions. And it most certainly cannot be carried forward by a national leader who once described himself in the following terms:

Indeed, I often wonder if I represent any one at all, and I am inclined to think that I do not, though many have kindly and friendly feelings towards me. I have become a queer mixture of the East and West, out of place everywhere, at home nowhere. Perhaps my thoughts and approach to life are more akin to what is called Western than Eastern, but India clings to me, as she does to all her children, in innumerable ways; and behind me lie, somewhere in the subconscious, racial memories of a hundred, or whatever the number may be, generations of Brahmans. I cannot get rid of either that past inheritance or my recent acquisitions. They are both part of me, and though they help me in both the East and the West, they also create in me a feeling of spiritual loneliness not only in public activities but in life itself. I am a stranger and alien in the West. I cannot be of it. But in my own country also, sometimes, I have an exile's feeling.[1]

This shrewd and wistful self-portrait was, it is true, penned many years ago, but basically it retains its validity today. For Nehru is still a 'queer mixture of the East and the West, out of place everywhere, at home nowhere'. A former president of Congress who is now in opposition, described him a few years ago as a man 'who is neither an Indian nor a European. He is a Eurasian.' In pre-independence days, he was torn between his vague beliefs in socialism and modernisation and his troubled faith in Gandhiism and his leadership of the nationalist movement. Although ideologically he found Gandhi 'sometimes amazingly backward' he yet believed that he was in action 'the greatest revolutionary of recent times in India'. He came to see in him 'a unique personality' and felt that it was

[1] Jawaharlal Nehru, *An Autobiography*. John Lane, The Bodley Head, London, 1936, p. 597.

'impossible to judge him by the usual standards or even to apply the ordinary canons of logic to him'. Nehru could not judge Gandhi by the usual logical standards because he could not reconcile his capitulation to Gandhian traditionalism with his essentially superficial modernism. This irrational attachment to Gandhi has in fact eroded whatever strength of character and conviction he ever had and he has spent his life in a futile effort of rationalising the latter's obscurantist ideas. On almost every other issue there was and is the same ambiguity and ambivalence.

Nehru admires the achievements of the Soviet Union, is in sympathy with the ultimate aims of communism (the vaguer and more high-sounding these are, the better), yet dislikes the means which they have applied—ruthless suppression of all contrary opinion, wholesale regimentation and the unnecessary violence. He has described himself as a nineteenth-century liberal and is a genuine supporter of India's connection with the British Commonwealth, yet at the same time he has been more critical of British and Western misdeeds than he has of Russian crimes. And while wanting to make India a modern society, he has also discovered, in the process of letting 'India grow upon him', the virtues, the vitality, the flexible character of India's traditional stagnant society, 'its majesty of soul'. The truth is of course that he detests the sluggish society which he sees all around him and yet feels himself its powerless prisoner. Although he believes that Gandhi's methods were and are both morally right and effective, he has yet acted in opposition to them in many fields since his death. Nehru has become the 'guiding star' of a centralised state; he has created a sizeable professional army; he has used the police frequently against his own people; he has acted as a power politician (as in Kashmir and Goa, for example), and not as a 'saint'. And for those, almost the whole old leadership of Congress in all its levels, who are the simple-minded followers of Gandhi, who, in fact, form an integral and unconscious part of the Gandhian tradition, he has shown nothing but contempt. While they believe in prohibition, abstinence, simple-Hindi, hand-spinning and self-sufficient villages, his government has been cool towards prohibition, has provided some funds for family planning, has done little for Hindi and not much for hand-spinning and has emphasised the importance of heavy industry and of bringing the villages into the money economy. He has even outraged his party and 'educated' public opinion by proposing (although nothing much will be done about it in practice) the establishment of agricultural co-operatives, if necessary on the Chinese pattern. Although Nehru uses the Congress, relies upon it and is its chief vote-gatherer, he yet gives his trust mainly to non-Congressmen. Congress in any case has become over the years a huge, unwieldy organisation, without a soul or a real doctrine of action. It has become largely a gathering of corrupt and self-seeking politicians practising self-indulgence despite their Gandhism, who have been forced by the pressure of their problems to mouth fashionable socialistic slogans but who care little for either socialism or modernisation. His party has revealed itself in fact as a great sham. It remains what it has always been—an organisation rooted in orthodox Hinduism—practising caste discrimination, worshipping the cow, indulging in superstitions and connected with those unenterprising economic interests, landlords and businessmen, largely consisting of orthodox Hindus.

To counteract his disillusionment with the party which he leads, he has therefore surrounded himself with two opposed sets of new people. One consists of advisers or even ministers (Professor Mahalanobis and Krishna Menon, etc.), influenced by communist ideas but without being communists or even non-communist radicals, and the other of former pillars of British rule who, though they are the most competent and trained people in India, are not in any way the determined innovators who are demanded. He has had three non-Congress finance ministers, three non-Congress governors of states, and appointed many non-Congress ambassadors. His minister for Community Projects and Co-operation, which he considers the most revolutionary instrument of his socialist programme, was once the head of the branch of a foreign firm in India. And while proclaiming on every occasion his undying belief that India's superior way is the way of non-violence, he has yet openly expressed his regret that the Indian national movement did not go through the harsh and violent school of struggle which the Chinese communists had to endure and traverse before they attained power, and which would have steeled India's weak and flabby national character and toughened its leadership for the responsibilities which now face them.

Nehru has always been a man who has worked by compromise and reconciliation, vacillating between sharp alternatives, always divided and hesitant, always subject to the pulls of mutually opposed forces. Although he has been prepared to innovate in detail, his whole philosophy belongs to a tradition which events are now overtaking and he has never been able to bridge the gap between his fumbling efforts and the new conditions and needs of his own country. His political style has thus been shaped by a powerful need of his personality for compromise, for mediation, for smooth-sounding emotional formulae which do not bind one to a definite course of action. The middle ground where Nehru stands provides him with neither enough force nor enough faith. He is the prisoner of an outmoded way of life and an out-of-date philosophy. He has therefore always yielded to the influence of stronger personalities than his own. In all the great disputes of nationalist politics, he pursued a middle-of-the-road position (as he has in India's foreign relations since independence), trying at all times to reach reasonable and pragmatic solutions which more often than not meant no more than brushing the problems under the carpet in the hope that they would, somehow, be forgotten and disappear of their own volition. Nehru has always tried to jump the abyss in two jumps.

All these attributes, good enough perhaps or not too harmful for the leader of a well-established and strong society living in times of 'normalcy', were also helpful to the leader of a struggle against the basically humane form of British imperialism. (They would have been of little use against conquerors of the Nazi or Japanese type.) But it is becoming more and more clear that these are not the qualities required for the modernisation of India, are not really appropriate for effecting an economic revolution, and for meeting the threats posed by the imperialist ambitions of the two vast and neighbouring totalitarian empires, China and the Soviet Union. The task of liberating India from British rule was simplicity itself compared with the task of changing the life and character of the Indian people and of safeguarding its national independence. Torn by all these opposing loyalties, dimly aware of his own flaws and weaknesses, frequently disgusted by the spectacle of corruption and back- wardness presented by his own party, without however doing anything about it, Nehru has, during the last few years, shown all the signs of declining vitality. He has been losing his grip. He has tried more than once to resign. He has admitted that he has felt 'flat and stale'. He has found himself out of tune with his countrymen and repelled by the 'morals' of his party followers. In May 1958, Nehru told a news conference that 'An atmos- phere is growing in India that I found not only disturbing but suffocating.' His own work had come to be the work of

some kind of robot or automaton. . . . I was physically fit but getting querulous. I sense coarseness and vulgarity growing in our public life. In the Congress Party and the whole country idealism is fading out. We in India suffer from a split personality. One part is of the highest moral standard. The other part completely forgets about it. We are losing our sense of mission. What to do? I don't know. It is not easy to stop. You can't draw a sword and cut off the head of this enemy.

Then, looking to the future, Nehru said: 'We may win certain elections but we are losing our soul.'[1]

But Nehru was again undecisive even about resigning. The panic which followed his announcement among Congressmen, their pathetic appeals to him not to leave them as 'orphans', led him once more to capitulate and he agreed, sick in mind and heart, to continue to represent the unborn future in India.

Even so sympathetic and conventional a biographer as Michael Brecher was forced to come to the conclusion that

social and economic change since 1947 have been less than that pledged . . . and less than required if India is even to approach the goals set by Nehru in the past. . . . The inadequacy of land reform suggests one of Nehru's weaknesses as a political leader: the gap between words and deeds is often wide. . . . Over the years he had denounced many unsavoury features of Indian public life, but the matter frequently rested there. He has criticised

[1] *Time Magazine*, 12 May 1958.

nepotism and corruption in the administration but has never acted against them. He has deplored the cesspools of disease and degradation that are the slums of Delhi and other major cities, but they remain. He has castigated black-marketeering and other nefarious aspects of Indian business life: in the earlier days he even threatened to shoot or whip the guilty. But these practices continue. . . . By this constant verbal attacks on things which offend his sensitivity, often without following through with harsh deeds, he has tended to 'cheapen the coinage'. . . . The gap between words and deeds suggests something else. In some instances it is not the lack of time to follow through or the inability to change institutions overnight; rather it is a tendency to shrink from radical deeds. . . . Nehru is a social reformer; he is not a social revolutionary. . . . He vacillates in the face of alternative courses of action, all of which seem to have some merit. He is completely lacking in ruthlessness. But there are times in the affairs of a nation when ruthlessness is desirable, and with it a strong will to follow through the logical imperatives of a policy decision. It may well be that Nehru is an excessively pure democrat . . . he seems to have a compulsion for universal consent. Partly this is due to his stress on mass participation; but in part it is due to an instinctive playing to the gallery, a desire to please the crowd, the ultimate basis of his political power.[1]

The failure of Nehru to rise to the heights of leadership which the situation of his country requires is only one symptom—the most interesting perhaps—of India's malaise, of its split mind, of its disease of spirit. But in fact, all those groups and classes which have come into contact with Western ideas and ambitions are infected with the same malady. They are all not only the victims of the present but of a long, long past which they refuse either to understand or to cast off. Some want to build a modern society while still clinging to the ancient ways which have lost their binding force. Some want to take refuge in the past, to go back to the ancient order without however being able to make their way to it. They seem to be as incapable of acquiring new values as they are of developing their old ones. Almost all of them are frustrated by their position in their own society, tormented by aspirations which exceed their capacities in either direction.

[1] *Nehru. A Political Biography.* Oxford University Press, 1959, pp. 624, 627.

While their traditional institutions deteriorate, the creation of more satisfying modern ways dangerously lags. There is both a desire for progress and a resigned preservation of every traditional situation and structure. But among all the active ranks of society there is the same fatal lack of a coherent image of a desirable national future.

Mr C. Rajagopalachari, one of India's 'grand old men', a close friend and disciple of Gandhi's, India's last Congress Governor General, has, with the help of an extraordinary assortment of collaborators, founded in 1959 a Conservative opposition party called the 'Swanatra' or Freedom Party. This party, frightened even by the blundering and half-hearted attempts made by Congress to edge towards the twentieth century, has proclaimed its belief that only by going back to the values and practices of India's 'golden past', that only by returning to Gandhi's pristine teachings, can the country be saved and rejuvenated. In a programmatic declaration, Mr Rajagopalachari described himself as 'belonging to the centuries before Christ' and declared that 'he would not give up the old and take to the new'. In place of innovations, the party pleads for Dharma, the traditional Hindu system of law, social usage and duty, bound up as it is with the whole caste system. He has said that he wants 'Dharma restored in India, and I want young men to fight for Dharma. The material enemy was an insiduous and dangerous enemy. We want to raise Dharma in life and lower material values.' He wants the people to return to religion, to the old culture patterns which are 'the very marrow of the nation'. He believes that his party should make every effort to foster and maintain spiritual values and avoid the dominance of the purely materialist philosophy of life which thinks only in terms 'of the standards of life'. But with the same breath the party announces that its programme for increasing the national wealth is to give full play to the profit motive and to increase the incentives for private enterprise, both in industry and agriculture. They furthermore claim that it is premature to think of economic equality now and that instead the wealthy classes should be made aware of their duty to the community, not by compulsion (that is, by legislation), but by being converted to the Gandhian principle of trusteeship.

In terms of this principle, those who possess wealth should hold it in trust for society and share out voluntarily what they feel they can spare of their material possessions. And this in a society where what charity exists is more often used for the protection of cows than for the treatment of infirm and destitute human beings. They are, therefore, against taxes on private industries and against ceilings on the property of the bigger landowners. Trusteeship in fact denies the freedom and dignity of the individual and aims at making eternal wards of the majority of mankind, under the perpetual tutelage of greedy and conscienceless trustees covered with a mist of spirituality. It is only necessary to add that this party is the most pro-Western of all the Indian political parties and has even been enthusiastically received by certain organs of private enterprise in America.

Contrary to the illusions spread by sentimental liberal and socialist thinkers and journalists and by just plain ignorant ones, and contrary to the illusions hugged by all the Western governments, whether socialist, liberal or conservative, India under Nehru is not on the threshold of breaking through the barriers of stagnation and backwardness, and is not at the point, at present, and may never even reach the point, of 'take-off' into self-sustained industrialisation and modernisation. And India has nowhere reached that position, not only because it is politically inefficient and corrupt (most societies seem to be able to stand a tremendous amount of political inefficiency and corruption), and also not only because of the slow rate of economic progress,[1] but positively because of the deep-rooted prevalence of reactionary social ideals, emotions and habits among wide groups of the people, from the most primitive villager to the most eloquent graduate of the London School of Economics and Political Science, and negatively in the absence of a revolutionary urge to recast its society and to revolutionise its lifeways and thoughtways. India is today the frustrated, the deeply neurotic society that it is, without a spirit of bold initiative, ardent enthusiasm or creative energy because, as M. N. Roy has pointed out (without however making

[1] India's plan, in fact, is in relation to the size of the population, even rather smaller than Pakistan's.

much impression on his countrymen), it has not attempted that complete reconstruction of the established order, of every department of human existence, including the human mind itself, which is so insistently demanded. In his view,

India needed not only national independence but a social revolution, a radical and complete social change not only of the political regime, not only of economic relations, not only the abolition of capitalism and landlordism but a change in the entire outlook of the people, in their whole mental make up. As a matter of fact, this latter change of our mental make up, our view of life, in other words, a philosophical revolution, was a precondition for the social revolution which is the need of the time.[1]

Surely it should be recognised that a society which still practises untouchability, which still operates within the framework of hereditary castes, thus virtually eliminating prospects of promotion through hard work, which considers manual labour as degrading and believes that it is more respectable to do nothing at all than to supervise, let alone toil, which accepts and sometimes actively encourages primitive and animistic beliefs about the sacredness of special varieties of trees and plants and animals, where cities and rivers and locations are regarded as sacrosanct, that such a society resting on such beliefs is a pathetic anachronism and irrevocably condemned as being out of place in the modern world.

The social structure under which India lives is in almost every respect in sharp conflict with its professed aspirations. It is therefore much easier, with all its fatal consequences, to transplant in isolation the fruits of economic and political development than to assimilate and take over the seeds out of which they have grown. Treated in such a way, these fruits of economic and political development have a way of distorting and even inhibiting the society's progress. Western rule, for example, imported medical improvements in isolation without lowering the birth-rate, and it therefore merely increased the population, laid the basis for Asia's present population explosion and thus not only lowered *per capita* standards but also produced the dark clouds of population pressure which hang over the world. Import the outward forms of democratic

[1] *Radical Humanist*, 2 December 1956.

government to an authoritarian society, marked by mass illiteracy, cultural backwardness, intellectual stagnation, blind faith and obedience, conformism, unrestrained leader worship and immeasurable inertia and one will find that the so-called 'popular vote' (obtained in any case by all kinds of illegal manipulations and pressures) only tends to reinforce all these maladies and vices of the national society. A society of this kind is really incapable of receiving the idea of democracy without drastically diluting it and bringing it down to its own authoritarian level. In general, it can be said that when the language of Western politics is transported to societies, divorced from the complex and strenuous tradition in which it has value and dignity, it becomes a debased, grandiloquent jargon, by which tyranny and corruption is made to seem constitutional, and inflated pretension to look like the genuine thing. All the well-known Western concepts—liberty, democracy, reform and progress—take on a nightmarish meaning in these countries. In India, democracy has given encouragement to all the centrifugal forces in its society (linguistic divisions, communalism, etc.); far from destroying caste it has only strengthened it; and far from undermining the great power of authority it has only served to increase it. It has enabled the people to submit uncritically to the whims and caprices of one man and has created almost a one-party regime, however factious and divided it is. A deeply rooted national tradition which teaches people that they must be satisfied with their social slavery because it is their Karma, which proclaims that the highest virtue is to be reconciled to fate, which really believes that its culture is the model pattern of all cultures and cannot be improved upon, can never generate the disturbing and explosive will to freedom or progress, or development. India can in fact never advance towards its proclaimed goals unless and until it has the courage, the strength of character, to free itself from its bondage to this tradition.

Nehru's India is in a way committing the same errors as the former foreign British administration, though with much less excuse. Like its predecessor, it too functions merely at the top of society, without being able either to make contact with the masses of the people or to stir them out of their immemorial passivity. The changes which it is introducing are mere ripples on the surface of India's vast human ocean. Even the most enlightened Indians believe that they can bring about an economic revolution as a kind of academic exercise, without soiling their own hands or changing their own characters. But an economic revolution, not to mention a social revolution, is not something you accomplish by writing a scientific report, it is not something that you merely administer even with the most 'brilliant' group of civil servants, however necessary they are. It is on the contrary a laborious enterprise, made by a 'creative minority' of men and women who have in the first place changed themselves, made themselves fit for these tasks, and who in conflict with the accepted institutions, values and habits of their environment are then ready to transform and regenerate their own society. The present-day leaders of India are not at all aware of these compelling necessities and seem, moreover, to believe in their hollow conceit, that 'what has been planned virtually exists and that what exists need not function in order to be admirable'.[1]

Without a clear and comprehensive programme of radical reconstruction, thwarted by a fatal split between its office-bound bureaucracy and its inert masses, India lacks that zeal for self-improvement which the country requires if it is to move, in Nehru's words, 'Out of the dead past into the living present', and to be able, if not to compete successfully, at least to stand up to the efforts and drive of China. But this is precisely what is not happening. In 1959 a United Nations mission came to India to examine its community development plans, which were originally designed to set on foot a 'total modernisation of the villages'. The mission, however, found a most disturbing state of affairs, a whole series of grave defects which were placing in jeopardy all of the country's development plans. Cyril Dunn, of *The Observer*, has summarised some of its conclusions:

The mission discovered officials, apparently out of touch with the real needs of the people, going in for 'coverage achievements'. They gave the villagers new council offices, brick schools, steel play-chutes for the children and paved streets useful only during the

[1] Cyril Dunn, 'Changing India', *The Observer*, London, 10 April 1960.

THE CHALLENGE OF MODERNISATION

three or four months of monsoon. None of these embellishments had done anything to reduce the underlying poverty and hunger.

The report shows that the villagers had not been persuaded voluntarily to abandon unproductive habits dictated to them by custom, religion and their own indolence. Irrigation channels and field drains were not being dug with the result that water coming down from the great new concrete dams in the mountains was saturating, not rescuing the arid land, and now threatened 'a national calamity'.

Where the peasants could expand from one to two crop farming they were not generally doing so, with the result that irrigation provided at enormous national expense was being wasted. All the voluntary labour needed for the dull and heavy jobs had declined from two days per adult per year at the start of the plan to one day now.[1]

Despite all its rather widely-trumpeted though misguided efforts, then, the Indian peasant has not in any way been aroused to activity or motion. As a result, India is now tending to rely too much on external aid and not enough on its own internal efforts. The government has failed to mobilise or exploit the vast manpower of its villages. It has given priority to luxury over production. Lacking a genuine agrarian reform, it has not been able to arouse the interest of the peasant in the hard work that is needed. Usury is still a great evil. There is little family planning. Indian production is failing to keep up with the growth in population. A professor from the sacred Hindu city of Nasik has suggested that the villagers have withdrawn into a world not so much of true religion but of fantasy. 'Their poverty is terrible,' he says, 'and their contentment inexplicable.' He seems to feel that they need the advice not of economists but of psychiatrists.

The popular picture of Nehru's India is that of a reasonable country, guided by the methods of compromise and accommodation, tolerant and moderate, open to every wind of doctrine and influence, always ready to remove the sharp edges of principles, to round off all corners, and to reconcile all conflicts both at home and abroad. In fact, it is the home of a confusing, unintelligible and paralysing jumble of contradictions. It has

[1] *The Observer*, 10 April 1960.

chosen a political and social approach which arouses vague expectations without being able to satisfy them, which proclaims its belief in modernisation without understanding what is involved in its fulfilment. Its attempts at transformation take place in a framework of stagnation. Its educated classes are torn between their fascination with Western ideals and their attachment to archaic, traditional practices. It wants to acquire the outward forms of modern civilisation while reluctant to pay the high price in change and disturbance which it demands. It wants to change society without changing the character structure of its people on which every society rests. Its elite wants to revolutionise society but without revolutionising their own primary beliefs, habits and values. It would like to awaken village India but without understanding that this can only be done by an army of ardent village workers firmly committed to this goal and dedicated both in heart and mind to modernisation. It wants to build a new structure of national life on the flimsy, disintegrating foundations of the old. In the perspective of history it may yet be seen that India was handed over to 'straw men' in Churchill's rather wounding phrase. It seems that the Indian character as at present constituted is too soft and flabby to stand the wear and tear of the great changes that the country has to undertake. A society of this kind, split not only in its social life but in its psyche, lacking that intrepid hardiness of mind and body which is required, can only make the gestures of progress, but cannot respond creatively to its own predicaments and build, with faith, energy and hope, its own future.

Perhaps one can better understand the problems of India and its prospects by following the brilliantly provocative analysis which Nirad Chaudhuri has made of the course of India's history in his book *The Autobiography of an Unknown Indian*, from which we have already quoted. He argues that the main cycles of Indian history are really the periods of India's successive affiliations with one form or another of foreign rule—the Aryan, the Islamic and the European. He thinks that there has never been any civilisation in India which has not had foreign inspiration behind it and has not been substantially created by vigorous incoming foreign ethnic elements. Whatever political order or civilisation has existed in India, has been due to the powerful external force which was dominant there at any particular point of time. He asserts, furthermore, that this foreign aristocracy was never defeated by a truly creative indigenous opposition and was never transcended by a genuine national resurgence. The active opponent of foreign rule in India has always been the country and its climate.

There are many geographical regions in the world which are utterly incapable of developing a high civilisation, but there is perhaps not one other which so irresistibly draws civilisation to it and strangles it as irresistibly as does the Indo-Gangetic plain. It is the vampire of geography, which sucks out all creative energy and leaves its victims as listless shadows. The high mean temperature together with its immense daily range of rise and fall, hardly allows the human body to attend to anything more fruitful than the daily adaptation to the weather. The unbroken flatness of the plain finds its counterpart in dullness of the mind, in monotony of experience and narrowness of interests.

This terrible milieu has told on all the foreign immigrants into India. His energy has been drained, his vitality sapped and his will and idealism enfeebled.[1]

As long as the foreign rulers were reinforced by a continuous stream of fresh recruits from the home country, as long as the metropolitan people have remained vigorous and creative, they have managed to maintain their dominant position in the country. As soon as this source, however, has begun to dry up, or has become exhausted, both they and India have fallen into decay. Then he maintains there occur phases in Indian history '. . . which have the appearance of being periods of national freedom and resurgence', but which are in reality only periods in which the fossilised and atavistic indigenous opposition finds an opportunity to rise to the surface, engages in a futile pursuit of the social concepts transmitted to them by the preceding foreign rulers and in an inefficient manipulation of the political machinery left by them, without being strong or creative enough to build a new, viable civilisation of its own. In his view, the degeneracy of the indigenous opposition (the 'internal proletariat' as he calls it) has at every given point of time

[1] *Op. cit.*, pp. 492–3.

been greater than the degeneracy of the foreign ruler. And when one group of foreigners is exhausted by the geographical environment, and has lost its will to rule, there has always been another to take its place. Viewing India's present efforts, weaknesses and difficulties, one can only, in trepidation, wonder if these sombre conclusions are going to repeat themselves again.

iii

We have spent some time trying to analyse the nature of the Indian response to its fundamental problems, because we believe that it is the most serious attempt that is being made anywhere in the non-communist section of the underdeveloped parts of our world. There seems to be very little doubt, however, that in the long run this attempt at modernisation will be found to have been a minimal and distracted effort in no way commensurate with what is so urgently required. Inadequate as India's total effort is, it yet stands out in its sense of responsibility and earnestness, as compared with the pathetic and farcical meanderings of the governments of the other Afro-Asian states. To get a fuller picture of what is happening, we must then examine briefly some of the broad trends in some of these other territories.

Wherever we look, we find that the ruling elites, faced with the massive problems of modernisation for which they have no coherently suitable answer, are tending to find refuge in the myths, legends and ghosts of the past, while continuing at the same time to pay lip-service to the modern ideas and slogans which they have picked up in the course of their contact with Western rule. Nowhere in these countries have the present governing groups seriously decided upon the image of civilised life that they would like to project to their own peoples. Faced with the need to choose between the relentlessly demanding modern world and their simple, primitive and lethargic native traditional world, they flounder in hesitation and indecision. They are agitated by various and hostile intentions. Because they have not made this fundamental choice they continue to speak about the ideals and techniques of the modern world while in fact continuing to live and breathe within the crumbling walls of their effete, traditional societies. At the deepest layers of their minds they are, in fact, guided not by the ideas of the modern world but by their own traditional shadows. Unable to resist the appeal of the modern world, yet unwilling to break with the traditional habits, customs and social relations which have condemned their societies to servitude and stagnation, they continue to straddle the two systems of civilisation. What the Lebanese Christian, Albert Hourani, once wrote about his own countrymen, applies with even greater force to the leaderships of all the Afro-Asian states.

To be a Levantine is to live in two worlds or more at once, without belonging to either; to be able to go through the external forms which indicate the possession of a certain nationality, religion or culture without actually possessing it. It is no longer to have standard values of one's own, not to be able to create but only able to imitate. It is to belong to no community and to possess nothing of one's own. It reveals itself in lostness, pretentiousness, cynicism and despair.

The post-independence history of Indonesia offers a frightening illustration of how irresponsible this kind of 'Levantine' leadership can be. Since 1949, when Indonesia became formally independent, it has been caught in a slow but seemingly irresistible (though at an Asian tempo) process of disintegration which it appears no political force in Indonesia can arrest. Independent rule has been a reign of corruption and demoralisation. Indonesia has never known internal stability. It has experienced one wave after another of internal rebellion, ranging from those organised by the Darul Islam fanatics who want to set up a theocratic Moslem state, to the Sumatra Rebels, who consisted of some of the country's outstanding military and intellectual personalities, and who were goaded to take this extreme path by the bottomless corruption and inefficient, light-headed tyranny of the central Java government. Its attempt at parliamentary government dedicated to merge its dozen ethnic groups and 114 different languages into a 'new unity in diversity' has collapsed in national division and anarchy, provincial revolts against the centre, and has been replaced by a 'misguided democracy'. While Indonesia has moved away from a pseudo-democratic form of government it has not produced any responsible and appropriate political substitute.

Independent Indonesia has failed to achieve economic growth and the standard of living of its masses is lower today than it was in 1938–40. It has managed to get rid of the skills and experience of its former Dutch residents, while not developing any new, indigenous group to take their place. Its agriculture is scandalously unproductive. In spite of favourable natural conditions, Indonesian yields per acre are barely one-third of the yield achieved in good modern cultivation. It has been estimated that the Paris of 1789 had more skilled industrial labour and experienced management than that supplied by the 90,000,000 people of Indonesia today. Oscar Gass, a highly competent economic expert on 'development problems', has stated that 'the physical resource base of Indonesia, both for agriculture and industry is superior to that of Japan', and that 'nowhere between the Persian Gulf and California is there an equal resource base for a great petro-chemical industry'. Yet the country's economic situation has, during all this time, been going from bad to worse. After almost twelve years of independence the present Indonesian elite has not even so much as begun to develop any effective method of fostering economic growth.

Indonesia's present ruling group has, however, not only managed to disorganise the country's economy and reduce its government to a state of chaos, it has also succeeded in systematically removing and driving away nearly all of its most 'Westernised' and competent intellectuals and leaders from positions of power and influence. Alienated from the mainstream of indigenous cultural life, too rational and balanced to sink to the low level of flamboyant demagogy practised by a Soekarno, lacking those qualities of character necessary for a life of political action in a backward society, these 'Westernised' intellectuals have permitted themselves to be reduced to impotence and 'internal exile' by those who are the champions of a more primitive and reckless variety of nationalism. Criticised for the failures of his policies, Soekarno once responded by saying that his critics did not understand the uniqueness of Indonesian circumstances and values and did not appreciate the special 'Indonesian way' of doing things. What, then, is this Indonesian way of doing and saying things?

According to its exponents, the 'Indonesian way' is supposed to rest on the well-known Indonesian traditions of consensus, compromise and avoidance of opposition. It is based on such local customs as *runkun* or the 'spirit of conciliation', which means that in cases of conflict the guiding principle must be to find a 'reasonable solution' that will eliminate all traces of resentment. Another custom is that of *gotong royong*, a term denoting mutual assistance and common work effort in many parts of the traditional village society and which is besides based on the practice of all the elders discussing a proposition until they are in unanimous agreement. In this kind of discussion there is no vote, because votes produce majorities and minorities and such a division only leads to unhappiness and opposition. Indonesians are taught to respect their elders, always to 'give joy first', that 'circumlocution is the best policy' and to practise *halus*—the ability to adjust passively to circumstances.

Superficial observers of Indonesian society have claimed that all these customs and formal patterns of behaviour have made Indonesia into 'a highly civilised nation', a 'land without tensions', characterised by 'democratic relations between the big and the small' and guided by almost limitless tolerance and a refined politeness. But all these aspects of the 'Indonesian way' also reflect the utter absence of individuality, the utter suppression of dissent, the utter lack of a coherent sense of purpose, where the inner core of moral self-assertion and independent judgement is almost non-existent, where the need to conform is all-powerful and where there is universal fear of injury from those who wield power and authority. There is, however, another face to the coin of Indonesian adaptability and passivity. This finds expression in *kasar*—the blind, rough, primitive plunge into brutal action, embodied in the demented agony of the man who runs amok, who for no apparent reason throws off all the customary restraints and tears through his village wielding his razor-sharp parang against everything in his path. The Indonesian hovers between passivity and running amok.

The people of Indonesia thus do not only suffer from economic starvation, but even more crucially from a profound emotional starvation, from a crippling form of psychological frustration which prevents them from developing those personality traits needed to come to grips with the new problems created by their contact with Western rule. The old traditional lifeways and thoughtways have become obsolete, in a community subject to the challenge of a process of novel and disruptive change. The 'Indonesian way' of doing and saying things, in fact, only permits the country's ruling elite to escape and evade its true problems, only helps to build up individual and social tensions without providing for their resolution. Sutan Sjahrir, the first socialist prime minister of Indonesia and one of its leading 'Westernised' intellectuals, once said in a private conversation that 'there is always a lot of noise and the threat of action in Indonesia, but nothing really seems to happen there'. Soedjatmoko, one of Indonesia's most brilliant intellectuals, commented on his country's intellectual situation by saying: 'In Indonesia, people first take up positions and then one suddenly finds that their resolution and firmness have just simply melted away and dissolved. Hinduism, Buddhism and Islam are all soft religions and they produce soft and shadowy people.'

Oscar Gass has indicated the true nature of the 'deep revolution' which Indonesia requires. He has written:

If such observations may be permitted a friend who is not a countryman, the deep revolution which Indonesia needs is perhaps first, one in modes of thought and, second, one in modes of discourse. The mind and hand of man could, no doubt, build a creative society in contemporary Indonesia. The Indonesian hand does not lack sensitivity and adaptability to the acquisition of skills. But the mind must first effortfully, painfully remake the foundations and workings of the mind and then learn to speak what it has thought. Directness and the discipline of the issue are sadly lacking and these can be acquired at no sacrifice of true personal consideration. Such change is what is hardest. Repetitious commonplace and pallid courtesy will not help.[1]

But Indonesia has as yet had no 'deep revolution' and no group of men exists to bring such a revolution about (apart from the communists—but that is a different matter). Even the

[1] *Commentary*, February 1960, p. 160.

development-minded, 'Westernised' political intellectuals lack the will-power, drive and ruthlessness to implement the changes which are necessary. Instead we have the frenzied and pathetic posturings and gyrations of a Soekarno, who is today the 'great charismatic' figure of Indonesian politics and a leading representative of the Afro-Asian camp. Oblivious of the realities of his own country he now wavers on the thin line between charisma and paranoia.

On the one hand, he continues to orate about the 'fire of revolution' and to warn his countrymen that they should see to it that it 'does not die or grow dim, not even for a single moment'. And on the other he persists in his real role as a great playboy, who loves official cars, motor-cycle escorts, uniforms and women. He loves crowds and adoration and is always ready to rouse them to some irrelevant and costly nationalist demonstration. In so far as he has any kind of political philosophy, apart from his primary desire to occupy the highest seat of power and pomp, it is a meaningless jumble of mystical and aggressive Javanese nationalism, of anti-Western imperialism, blended with bits of Marxism, fascism and leader-worship and a large dose of general incoherence. Soekarno has repeatedly expressed his admiration for political and economic collectivism, he has held up communist China (and Nasser's Egypt, of all places) as an example of a 'grand reconstruction' worthy of emulation and announced, after one of his many world tours, that he learnt most from his visit to 'the socialist countries'. Although he has been impressed by 'the socialist countries', he has not been willing to change either his habits or the habits of his people to the extent of making it possible for them to work even half as hard as these countries are doing. He once told a political acquaintance that the key to his political success has been his discovery of the 'horse of anti-imperialism' and that only by riding it hard could he continue to rule. Because of it he has attained a tremendous hold over his dazed and long-suffering countrymen, and he has boasted that if he 'tells them to eat stones, they will do so'. Soekarno has frankly told his people that he is

fascinated by revolution . . . completely absorbed by it. . . . I am crazed, am obsessed by the romanticism . . . Revolution surges,

flashes, thunders in almost every corner of the earth. . . . Come . . .
Brothers and sisters, keep fanning the flames of the leaping fire. . . .
Let us become logs to feed the flames of Revolution. . . .

In fact, Soekarno is crazed and obsessed not by any kind of
'creative revolution', but only by the fumes of his own inconsequential oratory, and he and his supporters are converting the
people into logs to feed the flames of disintegration and collapse.

In Ceylon, too, the forces of Asian Revivalism and chaos are
on the march. The more Westernised groups (including the
Burghers—people of mixed blood and the more advanced elements of the Tamil community) are being purposefully removed from positions of power and influence. The men who
wear trousers (the Westernised) are being replaced by the men
who wear sarongs (the 'Asianised'). The late Mr Bandaranaike
was the first prime minister to represent the growing power of
this destructive and corrupt movement. Raised in an Anglican
household, educated at Oxford, he only rose to eminence by
becoming a convert to a bigoted form of Buddhism. Ceylon,
which has been in contact with the West since the sixteenth
century, whose upper classes were more Westernised than any
other Asian group outside the Philippines, is now yielding to the
facile blandishments of 'Asianism'. It is turning its back on most
of the lessons of Western civilisation which its elite learnt and
reverting to the 'Asian ways' which it seems to find more
congenial.

The system of parliamentary government bequeathed to
Ceylon by the British in 1948 is rapidly running down. Communal conflicts between the six million Sinhalese, most of whom
are Buddhists, and the one million Ceylon Tamils, who are
mainly Hindu, are becoming more fierce. In this Buddhist land,
political assassination was the instrument used by Buddhist
priests and laymen with which to express their resentment of
the hesitant policies of the first Bandaranaike government. A
'Back to Asia' movement embracing a number of Western-
educated Sinhalese intellectuals professing a confused variety of
'socialist' beliefs, and supported by ambitious but backward
Buddhist priests and laymen, has exploited the grievances of the
Sinhalese community to come to power. Unable to bring Ceylon
into the modern world, many have begun to dream about

reviving the glories of the old, despotic Sinhalese kingdom and have demanded the restoration to the Buddhist monks of their ancient political authority. These monks, in their campaign for the re-establishment of Buddhism as the state religion, also preach the superiority of Ayurvedic over Western medicine. In Ceylon, Buddhist compassion and gentleness threatens a medieval type of persecution of the Christian minority. Many of the more extreme representatives and supporters of this movement—sons of small cultivators, minor officials, shop-keepers and the lower middle class generally—believe that only in a backward social order will they find the necessary opportunities for power and plunder.

In the Arab countries of the Middle East, the struggle between tradition and innovation is writ large in the mob violence, the explosive tensions, the erratic policies, the vicious inconstancy of the region. The underlying tensions are everywhere much the same—village versus town, a subsistence economy versus a money economy, orthodoxy versus enlightenment, resignation and indolence versus sober ambition and disciplined activity, Islamic pieties versus the modern, rationalist and positivist spirit, a wild nationalist intoxication versus a genuine movement of modernisation, of national reformation and up-building. Everywhere, even in autocratic, benighted Saudi-Arabia, there is the same agonising and unresolved debate, among the newly forming middle classes, among army officers, white-collar workers and intellectuals between Permanence and Change. This process is working itself out on many different levels. Daniel Lerner has described this process in simple but moving human terms, as it reaches different people in different settings and creates for them 'different dilemmas of personal choice'. He wrote:

In Turkey a grocer exhilarated by the sight of a city must live out his life in a traditional village; in Iran a newly entrepreneurial peasant proudly owns the first store-bought suit in his walled hamlet but rarely dares to wear it among his envious fellows; in Jordan an illiterate Beduin chieftain professes the tribal law of the desert but plans to send his son abroad to school; in Lebanon an educated Muslim girl loves the movies but fears her orthodox parents; in Syria an under-educated over-ambitious clerk dreams of being a

Tito; in Egypt a young engineer has eaten pork in the West and seeks atonement in the Muslim Brotherhood.[1]

The struggle between Permanence and Change in the Arab world is so fierce and so tainted with frustration because, unlike the countries of South East Asia, Islam, which on one level can be considered as a Christian heresy, has been in close and hostile contact with the West ever since it burst out of the deserts of Arabia in the seventh century. The Arabic-speaking Muslim countries have, furthermore, particularly been in intimate and continuous contact with the West during the last seventy years and their repeated but so far unsuccessful attempts at modernisation have scarred the elites of every one of these countries and have been the root cause of all their violent but fruitless revolutions.

Contrary to the inflated claims of its propagandists, the only unity these countries have is the unity of their problems. Solutions they have still not found. But everywhere the traditional order is in decay, everywhere there is the disquieting feeling that the old ways must be replaced because they no longer satisfy the new modern wants which have been aroused. In all these countries these 'Levantine' elites reveal the wry face of ambivalence, inconsistency and incompleteness. They are tragically torn between two cultures—one archaic and constrictive (though with a glorious past), and the other over-developed and beyond their reach. They have been filled with new and impotent desires while continuing to cling to the ancient world from which they have not the strength to escape. Nasser has expressed his own feelings about this fundamental conflict:

Waves of thoughts and ideas came over us while we were not yet developed enough to evaluate them. We were still living mentally in the captivity of the thirteenth century. . . . Our minds tried to catch up with the caravan of human progress, although we were five centuries or more behind. The pace was fearful and the journey was exhausting.[2]

---

[1] Daniel Lerner, *The Passing of Traditional Society*. The Free Press, Glencoe, Illinois, p. 44.

[2] *Egypt's Liberation. The Philosophy of the Revolution*, pp. 67–8.

In no other Arab country are all these conflicts so stark as in Egypt. The Egyptian elite is the most frustrated and desperate because its aspirations are higher and its capacities and resources are inadequate to realise them. Its reach exceeds its grasp in almost every direction. Driven along by the force of nationalism, it would like to enhance the power and prestige of its own country, to increase its rate of economic growth, to industrialise, to raise the living standards of its poverty-stricken and servile masses, to reform its agricultural system and to create a modern nation. Every unbiased observer has reported that the present military junta has changed the pace of life in Egypt (especially in the big towns) as compared with the past. By expelling those who have formerly ruled them, by playing the game of international politics (i.e. by playing off America against Russia) with great skill and daring, by becoming an important centre of Afro-Asian anti-imperialism, Nasserism has succeeded in raising hopes and stirring up ambitions. But as yet it has only dented the real problems of its country and not come to grips with them.

Even the most competent, realistic and radical movement of modernisation would find it extremely difficult to overcome the tremendous obstacles which stand in its way. It would be faced with a vicious circle of poverty, it would have to contend with a rate of population growth which swallows every gain of modern technique and it would have to organise a nation, the overwhelming majority of which has only the most tenuous links with the beliefs and values of the modern world. It would above all have to wrestle with a people suffering from chronic maladies and weaknesses, the product of centuries of adversity and arrested development. The contemporary Arab elites, including the Egyptian military junta, have still not even begun to understand themselves or their societies. They have still not come to terms with the flaws of the Arab as a man, nor with the defects of their whole civilisation.

Overshadowing every other force is the problem of nature as the Arabs have had to face it. The Arab mind and character has been shaped by his struggle against the desert. For centuries they have fought the desert and the desert has always won. The Arab is both its father and its son. Arab society has been indelibly marked by this portentous fact. A merciless history has battered and twisted both his personality and society. The history of the Arabs is the melancholy history 'of spasms, of upheavals'; and of the ferocity of dogmatic, unbending creeds and heresies. Its failure to subdue its own environment has created a social order which, though it has been capable of a whirlwind of conquests in the past, has never been able to conceive, organise or maintain a system of government more advanced than the patriarchal.

The Arab's greatest weakness in political behaviour has been his inability to subordinate his personal interest to the public interest or to comprehend the basic categories of civil society. He has not only not had an appropriate political philosophy, he has shown no great interest in acquiring one. For the Arabs believe that man's destiny is essentially in the hands of God. His tradition of despotic government, furthermore, has crushed free, adventurous thinking and has prevented the growth of an independent school of political speculation. Instead of analysis and speculation, the Arabs have had poetry. Every Arab ruler has always surrounded himself with a court poet whose main business it was and still is, in fact, to 'address and flatter his superiors' and to weave with the magic and richness of the Arab language a web of ornate fantasy and colourful, hashish-like illusion. They have fashioned wondrous pleasure domes of imagery and delight—a Thousand and One Nights World. Caught in these webs of illusion and pretension, the Arab's sense of reality has always been weak. He has besides lacked a belief in the capacity of reason to guide man and in his human potentialities. His ossified totalitarian religion has reduced man to passivity, has stifled his mind, and his whole outlook has been stamped by submission, despair and lack of initiative. Overpowered by the forces of nature and society, living in fear and ignorance, lacking 'science, daring, curiosity and openness', all these societies still do not possess those psychological, intellectual and moral resources necessary for life in our modern world.

Dr Elie Salem, assistant professor of Middle East studies at the School of Advanced International Studies of the Johns Hopkins University has, with great understanding, raised the problem of man as the basic problem of Arab society. He has argued:

There is a lack of belief in the capacity of reason to create, achieve, shape or even destroy man. In relegating all acts of creation to God, man is relieved of responsibility. The need for understanding man, therefore, his purpose and his responsibility in promoting his personality, is most imperative in the Arab world; for without this understanding there is no hope for the modulation of the human problem. If the state is to undertake this function, it first must be governed by men who appreciate these values and who are in turn courageous enough to embark on radically new plans. They must be sincerely convinced of the seriousness of the task and of their accountability to the people and to history. Since we, the Arabs, are not steeped in democratic heritage, it is natural for our leaders not to comprehend fully their role in service; and many of our leaders are not really convinced that they are the servants of the people. It will be some time before this political philosophy is actually believed and followed. For our world has had the misfortune of breeding masses who were always so poor, so ignorant, so reduced, so crushed by nature, religion, and society as to accept their lot without question. For the Arab world, indeed for the whole of Asia and Africa, the problem of the masses constitutes the deepest and most challenging problem of government. . . . The problem of 'man' is the fount from which all the major conflicts in Arab life flow. This theme must be pondered again and again before the other problem, that of nature, is considered. . . .[1]

Having turned their backs on the real and difficult issues which challenge Arab society (as have all the newly independent countries of Africa and Asia), fleeing from the deeply embedded problems that torment their very souls, all the Arab rulers, including the new Egyptian governing group and the Baathists of Syria and Iraq, have sought ephemeral and tawdry substitutes. In Egypt, Nasser has defined his general goal as the establishment of a 'Socialist Co-operative Democratic Commonwealth' and this in a society which has never known anything of socialism, co-operation or democracy. His general ideology, in fact, consists of a hodge-podge, made up of bits of fascism, socialism, a fierce anti-Westernism, vague

[1] *Tensions in the Middle East.* The John Hopkins Press, Baltimore, 1958, pp. 77–8.

schemes of reform and chimerical visions of national greatness. Here, too, we have the stress on 'Arabism' as something that is superior to both Western democracy and communism and as destined to inherit the world after the mutual destruction of the two most powerful world blocs. Attracted by the goal of modernisation, yet accommodating itself to the customs and habits of Islam, displaced between the ancient world of rigidity and sloth and the modern world of mobility and industry, exploiting and appeasing reactionary religious fanaticism, Egyptian nationalism is a highly ambivalent phenomenon. Nasserism, immature and half-educated, restless and dissatisfied, provincial and power-hungry, is thus very far from having a coherent philosophy. It does not even have a consistent doctrine of action. It is merely a muddled and feverish state of mind.

Without the strength to face all their internal problems of human change and growth, the Egyptian elite has become obsessed with the question of Egypt's posture and status in the world, with the idea of national power and greatness. Nasser has, therefore, begun to look far beyond the perennial miseries and weaknesses of Egypt to the glittering but illusory opportunities abroad. It is moved by visions of national grandeur, by an urge for great power status, by a fantastic ambition for empire. One of Nasser's basic theses is that Egypt is uniquely qualified both by geography and history to be the centre of three overlapping circles of activity—the Arab circle, the Islamic circle, and the African circle. Egypt's great destiny and his own heroic duty is to unite these three sources of potential power into one great force, cemented by a single creed, the core of a new Afro-Asian empire, and ultimately of a new form of global imperialism. Suffering from a profound sense of national inferiority, of wounded self-esteem, determined to defeat and humiliate the West, and to destroy Israel, his head stuffed with global fantasies, Nasser has decided that the only way he can get the 'dark and ominous mass' to serve him is by dangling before them the mirage of all these intoxicating national ambitions. But, as in most other respects, all these dazzlingly attractive national goals are to be attained by a country, by a people, by a leadership, inadequately equipped in every way for the fulfilment of any one of these pipe-dreams.

Africa, the newest of the continents to join the ever-growing caravan of national independence, is again confronted with the same problems which I have been analysing, though on a much more primitive level. Pushed into the modern world while not yet ready for it, provided with all the paraphernalia of independent statehood though as yet incapable of sustaining it, the new African elites are involved in the same distracted search for an identity and for answers to their personal and national predicaments. The Negro states of Africa are weighed down with such a burden of backwardness, with such a meagre human past, with so much primitivity and superstition that their reluctance to face the challenge of modernisation is both understandable and explicable. But unfortunately this challenge is going to gnaw at them until they will have found some more or less satisfactory solution.

Africa, south of the Sahara, with the exception of South Africa, has always been deficient in the most essential means of civilisation. Because of its inaccessibility, at least until the nineteenth century, it was also for countless centuries far removed from all the stimulating influences of the higher civilisations. Without convenient natural harbours, her coastline sealed Africa off from the outer world and from all the opportunities and dangers of significant interchanges of life with the more advanced cultures. Immense seas of deserts stood guard against intruders. The mosquito, the tsetse fly and other minute parasites were all able to attack and strike down any invader (and the local populations as well) with such deadly diseases as sleeping-sickness, malaria, dysentery, typhoid, leprosy and the bubonic plague. Africa was thus enabled, undisturbed, to develop and retain its own forms of traditional life and society and was never brought within the provocative range of universal culture. Deprived of the stimulus of connection with the rest of the world, compressed within itself, Africa remained for millennia 'the land of childhood, which lying beyond the day of self-conscious history is enveloped in the dark mantle of Night'.[1]

Taken as a whole, sub-Saharan Africa is also the most tropical of the continents with all that this implies in natural difficulty and intractability. Over immense areas, this African

[1] Hegel, *The Philosophy of History*.

soil has lacked the elements necessary for a stable and continuous form of agricultural cultivation. The soil in many areas is poor, friable and unpredictable. Africa's inferno of heat and humidity decayed whatever was built there and dissolved almost everything back into its voracious earth. Of all the major continents it has the lowest density of population. The overpowering African continent—into which it would not be difficult to pack the land areas of China, India and the United States and still leave room to spare—has, in general, been unfavourable to the rapid growth of the human race. African nature, primeval, relentless and oppressive, has dominated, enslaved and degraded man to an extent unknown anywhere else. Imprisoned by nature, the free human spirit nowhere even had an opportunity of beginning to develop. The African peoples did not succeed in creating a human reality of much depth or elevation. As against the overwhelming reality of nature they appeared as defenceless creatures, as corporeal shadows on the majestic landscape.

The basic defect of African society in the past as at the present time has, then, been its extreme form of historical 'independence'. For the most part of their history, the peoples of Africa have lived in almost total isolation, split up into small tribal units and dependent upon the vagaries of an inhospitable natural environment and upon its brutal control of the balance of births and deaths and the growth of population. Within this framework of isolation the Africans developed a primitive society which exhibited no movement or development of any importance. The African peoples in fact exhausted themselves in the effort to maintain the integrity and secure the survival of all their numberless archaic little groups. African agriculture generally took the form of the shifting cultivation of subsistence crops and was both unproductive and inefficient. Cattle was the most prized form of wealth and was surrounded by religious and magical beliefs and practices. Division of labour hardly existed. Although land was held in common by the tribe or the kinship group, every individual member had the right to use the land allocated to him but without freehold rights to it. Possessions, however, were not held in common; cattle, crops and gear belonged to the households and could not be disposed of even by tribal chief or council. No significant or enduring privileged class—landed aristocracy, priesthood or merchants —developed because this arrested form of society offered no opportunities for social differentiation or advance.

In general, the status of the individual was derived from his membership of the group—family, village and tribe—and was not determined by his individual capacities. It advanced only with age. The African tribesman was thus an integral part of his group and had no thought of ever going beyond it. No effort could be made without the co-operation and the consent of others. Ostracism or banishment from the group was the equivalent of a sentence of death. Tribal life had nothing of the unexpected or the novel about it, the individual was as impotent in any situation which deviated from the customary as he was utterly powerless in the face of his group's disapproval or hostility. Under these conditions individualism or a sense of pioneering and adventure could not develop at all. There was practically no latitude for individual choice or ability. The past ruled tyrannically over the present, custom was elevated over independence. The spirit of innovation simply did not raise its head.

Religion was another vital aspect of African life. African society was immersed in a vast jungle-like variety of religious beliefs. For some it was a simple form of ancestor worship. Others attempted to fashion a more complex hierarchy of gods. Although many tribes had a conception of a Supreme Being, it was not as a rule an object of worship, since it was believed that it took little interest in the everyday life of man. The dynamic of African religion lay rather in animism and in its belief that all objects in nature have souls or spirits which are responsible for practically everything that happens. The African was convinced of the unreality of the material world and the strength of these spiritual forces. Land as the producer and sustainer of life was an object of veneration. The Bushman made gods out of all the animals around him; the Hottentot knelt to an insect, the praying mantis. The Bantu felt linked to the spirits of his ancestors through his cattle, his hut and his ceremonies. The African was convinced that the frequent calamities of his highly uncertain existence—disease, loss of crops or cattle—were all the manifestations of this unseen spirit world and were either caused by a man's enemies or sent as punishment for unconscious sins. In times of distress and illness steps had to be taken to discover which spirit was responsible and to propitiate it by a simple offering. Magic, taboos, curses, omens, talismans, amulets, medicines, divinations, witchcraft and ritual murder were all used and practised to try and appease the spirits which surrounded, protected and menaced him. The African became the helpless victim of this uncontrollable and incomprehensible spirit world which held him in its grip. From all sides and at every moment of his life he was threatened by unknown dangers. Fatalism and lack of initiative, superstition and fear were its inevitable consequences.

Yet African life was not without some achievements. A great deal of its works of art in bronze, ivory, wood, iron, pottery and other materials reveals a high degree of artistry and technical skill. Its music and dancing, its mythology and folk tales were not without variety or intricacy. In West Africa, Benin, Ashanti, Dahomey and the Yoruba kingdoms had managed to fashion a central type of government of some coherence and an organisational system more elaborate than the tribal. It is believed by some that a number of maritime trading cities of African origin grew up and flourished between the thirteenth and the fifteenth centuries on the east coast of the continent. These cities are supposed to have attained a certain level of prosperity through their export of slaves, gold and ivory and to have had trade contacts with countries as far away as China and Siam. The Zulus organised a military power on more than a local basis, which terrorised and uprooted the whole of southern Africa and even threatened the European settlers of South Africa. The Zimbabwe ruins still stand in Southern Rhodesia as the solitary, mysterious vestige of what was perhaps an attempt to build a more enduring form of civilisation.

But all in all, tribal society was probably the most unsuccessful, the most stagnant, form of society that mankind has ever known. African traditional history records migrations, battles and conquests but it never tells of any mental transformations or of changes in social structure. Writing was unknown to it. Nothing of any value was created in that boiling pit of heat and humidity into which they had been cast by fate. It was sunk in darkness and inhumanity, it bred ignorance and incapacity, it practised cruelty and injustice and it failed miserably to grapple with its environment. The slave trade was not only a European invention, it was also actively helped along by African rulers and Arab merchants. Africa's few relatively organised states were despotisms. Famine and disease were the common terrors that haunted it, witchcraft kept the human mind imprisoned in superstition and fear, the individual personality was crushed, originality was suppressed and it lacked not only mechanical efficiency but it was devoid of that spiritual freedom which drives man to discovery and free movement. It had no growing points within it at all. All its energies were harnessed to the stultifying task of maintaining its essentially precarious mode of existence and of upholding the *status quo*. 'They are a rope of sand,' wrote Livingstone; 'there is no cohesion anywhere . . . each village is independent of every other and they distrust each other.' Although some historians have tentatively suggested that on several previous occasions African societies attempted to develop beyond the tribal to the civic and feudal, on each occasion they failed and sank back to their original condition.

And Richard Wright, after having visited Ghana, wrote that he seldom encountered 'what might be called idealism in Africa'. He explained this by saying that

perhaps there was no time for dreaming—and how could one get the notion that the world could be different if one did not dream? Though the African's whole life was a kind of religious dream, the African scorned the word 'dream'. Maybe the plant of African personality was pruned too quickly, was forced to bear fruit before it had a chance to grow to its full height? What would happen to a romantic rebel in an African tribe? The African takes his religion, which is really a waking dream, for reality and all other dreams are barred, are taboo.[1]

In his view, tribal culture also militated 'against cohesiveness of action'. African culture in fact

has not developed the personalities of the people to a degree that their egos are stout, hard, sharply defined; there is too much

[1] *Encounter*, September 1954.

cloudiness in the African's mentality, a kind of sodden vagueness that makes for lack of confidence, an absence of focus that renders that mentality incapable of grasping the work-a-day world. And until confidence is established at the centre of African personality, until there is an inner reorganisation of that personality, there can be no question of marching from the tribal order to the twentieth century. . . .[1]

The Western impact on Africa has been even more restricted and superficial than on Asia. Imperial policy was designed to protect the indigenous peoples against the 'too rapid' introduction of change. Only France made a generous effort to give its culture to an elite, small and inadequate as it is. In the former British territories the half-educated and the semi-emancipated are in power. Behind all the pseudo-revolutionary phraseology, behind all the talk of nationalism, socialism, industrialism and emancipation, there still lurk the ancient, deep-rooted superstitions, fears, anachronisms, phobias and habits of tribal Africa. The tribe not the nation is still the dominant form of social organisation. The paper-thin veneer of Westernisation is even more fragile and limited here than anywhere else. Apart from South Africa, the most advanced industrial economy of the continent, modern economic activities are of extremely recent growth. By and large, modern economic enterprises form only a very small part of the economies of the newly independent territories. And these were established by foreign capital investments and by immigrant skill and enterprise.

African society has, however, been changing, particularly during the last fifteen years. A small middle class, consisting mainly of lawyers, politicians and petty traders now grown rich, has sprung up. New towns have been built and the number of townsmen has increased. The processes of detribalisation and urbanisation have been speeded up. The introduction of a money economy, though still in limited areas, has tended to break down the old subsistence economy and to disrupt the traditional securities that it provided. The rise of migratory labour has shaken thousands of African households as the young men have left their villages and reserves for work in distant

[1] *Resurgent Africa*, August 1955.

mines or towns. New schools, hospitals, housing, roads, ports and power facilities have been built. The 'infra-structure' of modern society though far from adequate has expanded. There has been an acceleration of development in all spheres. Increasing numbers of Africans have been caught in the process of moving from a static society to a more modern, dynamic society. One of the most illuminating paradoxes of Africa, however, is that political emancipation has taken place in those countries where economic development has not even begun to generate the forces capable of passing the 'modernisation barrier', while great economic progress in a modern framework has only taken place in those countries (South Africa, the Rhodesias) where Africans have been denied political rights. Only those African states have obtained independence which are, in fact, incapable of managing, with any degree of efficiency, rationality or honesty, a modern state.

Oppressed by a catastrophic past, tied still by a thousand threads to an obsolete and 'prehistoric society', yet aware of the crucial fact that their archaic tribal society has been disturbed and shaken, the few men who think at all about the problems of Africa have been trying to fill out their nationalism with a more comprehensive kind of content. Everywhere there is grandiose talk about the idea of developing and cultivating the 'African Personality' but without making any serious attempt to understand the terrible weaknesses of this self-same 'African Personality' which made colonialism possible and inevitable. Having failed to come to terms with the true realities of their own society, many are now engaged in a vain effort to re-root themselves in a romanticised past of their own invention. Others, embarrassed by the present poverty and backwardness of their countries, have begun to propagate the myth of 'a great past'. Cheik Anta Diop of Senegal has even attempted in his book *Nations Nègres et Culture* to prove conclusively that Western African Negro culture comes ultimately from Egypt. The former Gold Coast linked itself with Ghana, a shadowy empire in the distant Sudan, which had been overthrown by foreign conquerors in the early Middle Ages. The Islamic peoples of the sub-Sahara regions, having fallen behind the southern coastal peoples in their development, tend to excuse their backwardness by recalling the 'great civilised states' which they had created in the past.

A number of French-speaking African intellectuals have, furthermore, come up with the cult of Negritude as their answer to the problem of the Africans' position in the modern world. One of the basic tenets of this cult is the rejection of Western values and their refusal to grant them universal validity. Although this is more of a cultural than a political concept, it yet reflects their desperate search for a specifically Negro-African form of civilisation. They want to recover for the Negro race a 'normal self-pride' and a 'lost confidence in himself' and to re-create for it a world in which he again 'has a sense of identity' and a 'significant role'.

Aimé Césaire, the Martinique poet who coined the word Negritude, hails the African for the following qualities:

> Hurray for those who never invented anything
> Hurray for those who never explored anything
> Hurray for those who never conquered anything
> But who, in awe, give themselves up to the essence of things
> Ignorant of the shell, but seized by the rhythm of things
> Not intent on conquest, but playing the play of the world.[1]

For Leopold Sedar Senghor, the poet president of the Republic of Senegal, on the other hand, emotion is at the heart of Negritude. 'Emotion is Negro.' He finds a heightened sensibility and intensity of emotion as the African's chief psychic trait. The African's strength lies in his possessing a cultural and communal conscience which is different from Europe where there is an individual conscience. All these qualities, moreover, stem from his 'tropical experience' and the 'agricultural nature of his existence', and from living close to the soil and the rhythms of the seasons. In 1958 Senghor listed as typical Negro virtues '. . . piety, common-sense, loyalty, generosity and courage'. Another writer, Paul Hazoumé, has demanded that certain African traditions should be respected and his good qualities recognised:

If it [the Dahomean people] has no material wealth to offer, it

---

[1] Quoted by Ezekiel Mphahlele in 'The Cult of Negritude', *Encounter*, March 1961.

possesses, despite its seeming barbarity and intellectual barrenness, treasures of soul and mind that its ancestors have accumulated down through the ages: respect for authority and for discipline, keen interest in social welfare, family unity, courage, personal dignity, loyalty in friendship, great honesty, a sense of justice and deep religious feeling.[1]

If these, however, are specific African qualities, then most of us are or have been Africans at one time or another, or none of us are or have been Africans at all.

At the same time, Senghor favours an African form of socialism, 'based on the seminal cultural values of both Africa and Europe', liberal but undoctrinaire, yet prepared to socialise what should be socialised, 'beginning with the rural economy but no more than that'. He has also said that his aim is 'to create a modern nation, an African-Negro civilisation but one that meets the requirements of the present day'. But what is then going to happen to the African's closeness to the soil, to his tropical experience? And how does one reconcile his tropical experience (lived in isolation and stagnation despite all the self-deceiving claims that are being made for it) with the peremptory needs and demands of a modern nation? No answers have been given to these questions because no attempt has as yet been made to find out what are the specific values, habits and emotions that the Africans have to acquire (which are truly universal), and what are the fundamental changes that they have to introduce into their lives and societies before they can even start to think in terms of a modern state, not to speak of a socialist one.

In Ghana a new kind of religion called 'Nkrumahism' has been devised to serve as the ideology of the new elite that has taken over power. This new religion is based on a number of slogans rather than ideas. At its centre there stands Nkrumah himself. Known as the Osagyefo—the Redeemer—he is reputed to be both immortal and infallible, and the most advanced expression of the continent's new African personality. He is being endowed with all the liberating qualities of a new African Christ, as distinct from the old Christ of the

[1] Quoted by Mercer Cook in 'The Aspirations of "Negritude"' in *The New Leader*, 24 October 1960.

white-skinned peoples. Religion and paganism, tribalism and sex, Africanism and socialism, Pan-Africanism and imperial ambitions, neutralism and subversion, authoritarianism and military force, all have been harnessed to provide support for Nkrumah's aspirations for leadership both at home and abroad.

However, the militant and dazzling slogans which the Ghanaian elite uses, the role of African vanguard which they have assumed, have not served to change Ghanaian society itself, or to galvanise it for more than diplomatic action, or to prepare it to face its real problems. Behind this façade there is only bewilderment, incompetence, self-seeking and a paralysing feeling of inferiority. Their African-ness does not represent a new departure but only a 'militant' adaptation to the super-stitions, to the mumbo-jumbo of tribalism, from which they have not liberated themselves. Its only positive aim is anti-colonialism.

For most of the new leaders of Africa, time has not made their ancient gods uncouth but has on the contrary endowed them with a charm and vitality which they in fact never possessed.

Chapter 3

THE BURMESE DILEMMA

i

BURMA is one of the minor countries of South East Asia. It has never played a leading role in the affairs of the region, nor has it contributed much of notable value to its thought or life. The Burman is essentially an Asian provincial. Its disturbed, volatile and fluctuating post-independence history, however, does throw some interesting light on the nature of some of the newly independent countries and on the character of the problems which face them. I shall deal at some length with Burma's situation because of my own personal experience of it. Before discussing the doubtful present we must briefly analyse the simple though enduring past which has shaped and still powerfully influences contemporary Burma.

Burmese society has been profoundly conditioned by its natural environment. Burma is a land of valleys and mountains, lying between the massive ridges that abruptly descend almost in perfect parallels from the Himalayan 'top of the world' roof. All round its inland frontier it is guarded from the rest of Asia by immense mountains, encrusted with dense tropical forest and jungle. Moreover, no main channel of ocean travel touches its coast. In all its history it never had a seafaring boat. In the west, it has been shut off from India by the jungle-covered Arakan and Patkoi mountains. To the east the deep river gorges of the Mekung and upper Yangtze and the towering mountain ranges and vast jungles that lie between them have acted as barriers between it and China. Defended by these formidable natural fortresses, Burma could neither be easily conquered by India or China, nor was it deeply influenced by them.

Burma's overwhelming natural environment not only barred it from steady culture contact with the rest of Asia but it also caged its people and its mind within this containing framework. The Western concept of man's mastery over nature has, therefore, never prevailed in Burma and still does not do so today. In Burma the jungles, the mountains and the wastelands seem like fierce and elemental powers which are passionately insistent upon impressing their presence upon all things. Here all human effort seems to have been made, not to conquer, but to come to terms with this great pressure of nature; to fit man somehow and often only precariously into the depths and fastnesses of jungle growths.

In the hinterland the peasant scratches away, for a few years, at a piece of earth he has hacked out of the green myriad of thickly interwoven trees and jungle arborescence. Then he moves on, allowing the pawing wildness to return. Soon enough the returning jungle belies his work and pours a hot breath of clustering, thick leaves and tangled roots over the patch of seedlings which it had already begun to strangle even at the first clearing. It is certainly true that the savagery of nature has been subdued in several areas. The rich, rice-growing delta is one such example. Mandalay, Rangoon, Pegu and a handful more of small towns have been carved out of the jungle and remain. And yet the whole of Burma, with its towns, its villages and its rice fields, seems to live in the grip of this pervasive force and is spiritually acclimatised to its presence. Nothing is left of the palaces which their old kings built to glorify themselves and their creations. The strong teak walls, the gilt and the lacquer, the ornamental carvings, have fallen, for the most part, into dust; for what the jungle did not reconquer it gave up to the sands to devour. Pagodas remain, because they were built of stone and brick. They stand like some vast, monumental museum in Pagan, amidst the arid sands and neglect of what was once the capital city of the Pagan dynasty. Life clusters round them today in Mandalay and in the other towns. But everywhere else they crown a bare hill or lie hidden in tiny villages woven into the bush and the gigantic creepers; they shelter with the village in the mystery of tall, green, silently pulsating growths. And even the rice fields are linked with the jungle. The monsoon rains come to inundate them and thus provide sustenance. But the unabating and sometimes tumultuous downpour, continuing through interminable weeks, also causes the jungle around the fields to grow more dense, more lavish; seems to make it creep nearer in an effort to reclaim what has been won.

The jungle, portentous and extravagant, holding the secret of unknown things, has also formed the background against which the Burman's life, outlook and personality has developed. The jungle for the Burmese is saturated with fairy presences, with spirits and ogres and Nats. It is a hermitage for the outcast. It provides a place of refuge for the young or the miscreant. Life itself is a jungle in the Burmese philosophy. It is a forest of time, full of giant trees and huge creepers and piercing thorns and snakes and little glades with flowers and aimless, flickering lights in the green darkness where man wanders until his feet are full of the thorns and his back is scarred with the lashes of time. The gate of that jungle is Death, says a Burmese allegory of Buddhism.

The jungle has, above all, closed Burma off for centuries at a time, forming an endless wall of impenetrability against the persistent thrusts of the outside world. Behind all these natural walls Burma was left to develop within its own narrow and isolated society. Until 1824 the Burmese were removed from the main movements of the world and had no interest in trading either goods or ideas with the outside. For all these reasons the Burmese, after they had been torn up by some catastrophe from their native roots in Central Asia on the Sino-Tibetan border and had moved across the frontier into what is now Burma, had only spasmodic contact with their neighbours and in relative isolation, developed their own civilisation.

Within these boundaries, fixed by mountain, jungle and sea, Burma has been able to create a simple agricultural civilisation, and some sort of political and social unity. Its population is composed of a number of distinct ethnic groups with a history of rivalries and conflicts between them and has been formed by waves of immigrants from the central Asian tableland. The earliest to find a permanent home in Burma were the Mon branch of the Mon-Kmer people, who in Indo-China created the magnificent architectural civilisation of Cambodia, and the Karens. These were followed by the Chins. The Tibeto-Burman people first began to make their way across the border into Burma around A.D. 500. And then, between the sixth and thirteenth centuries, came the Thai-Chinese, who have settled in Thailand or Siam and in Burma are known as the Shans. Last of all came the Kachins. Among all the various peoples, the Burmans have long been the most prominent and it is from them that Burma takes its name. Today, the majority of Burma's 19,000,000 people speak Burmese and have come to share, with the Burmans, a common culture.

Burmese society began in the central, dry zone of the country just south of the present site of Mandalay. Pagan was its first capital city. The Pagan dynasty established the kingdom of Burma in the eleventh century A.D., and helped to fashion most of the prominent characteristics and institutions of Burmese society. In the process of conquering and unifying the small states and tribal groups of the valleys and surrounding areas they also succeeded in conquering the Mon kingdom of Thaton, far away in the south, and thus came into contact with those Indian civilising influences which had moulded that kingdom. Mon civilisation was on a far higher level than the Burmese and after the fall of Thaton, Mon cultural influence predominated at Pagan. The Burmese received the institution of kingship either directly from India or from the Mons and also acquired the Buddhist religion as the 'ideology' on which the Pagan dynasty and every subsequent dynasty was based. The royal authority and Buddhism were among the two potent forces operating towards the unification of Burma.

In the thirteenth century Burma was invaded by the Mongol Emperor Kublai Khan and the Pagan dynasty was destroyed. This dynasty was followed by a succession of Shan chieftains, who succeeded in ruling Siam, Burma, parts of Assam and Indo-China during the next 250 years. After the Shans, Burma was temporarily united under the Toungoo dynasty in the middle of the sixteenth century. In the seventeenth and early eighteenth centuries, frequent invasions from China and India undermined this Burmese kingdom. In the middle of the eighteenth century a new Burmese dynasty took power and re-established Burmese control over most of the country. This Burmese state, with its capital at Ava, close to Mandalay, was the last dynasty in Burma and lasted until the British conquered the kingdom in three wars in the nineteenth century. It was governed as a province of India from 1886 until 1937.

The king was the centre of the country's political and religious life. He was not only thought of, and so considered himself, as a divinity in human form, but was the despotic ruler of his people. In secular affairs his will or even his whim was supreme. He was the source of the law, the promoter and defender of the Buddhist faith, the recipient of the revenues and the guardian of the country's security. The highest honour to which a Burmese subject could attain was to qualify as the 'King's First Slave'. Every Burman was the king's slave and could not leave the district, far less the country, without the royal permission granted through the local authorities. He had the divine right to control the lives, the property and the personal services of his subjects. He built pagodas, carried on slave raids, made wars against neighbouring peoples, and collected white elephants, these being holy because the Buddha had once incarnated himself in this form. In Burma the government was traditionally identified with such scourges as fire, flood, famine and evil enemies. The Burmese kings laid claim to these titles:

Ruler of land and sea, lord of the rising sun, sovereign of great empires and countries and king of all umbrella-bearing chiefs, lord of the mines of gold, silver, rubies, amber, chief of the celestial elephant and master of many elephants, the supporter of religion, the sun-descended monarch, sovereign of the power of life and death, great chief of righteousness, king of kings and possessor of boundless dominions and supreme wisdom, the arbiter of existence.

At his installation the king proclaimed himself with the formula: 'I am foremost in the world. I am the most excellent in all the world. I am peerless in all the world.'

Although the king's power was theoretically unlimited, it was in fact circumscribed by custom and the inescapable limitations of a primitive agrarian society. But in his royal palace, within the fortified palace area, his dominion was unquestioned. The palace was the expression of the royal power, the symbolic centre of the universe and the abode of the gods. The ceremonial circling of the palace's walls was one of the king's duties and signified his control over the whole empire. It was sufficient for a rebellion to seize the palace in the temporary absence of the king, to obtain the necessary sanction for its usurpation. Being built of wood and not of stone, however, it was also insubstantial. Within its walls several thousand people, colourfully dressed, draped in silks, jewels and intricate ceremonial etiquette, spent their life in glitter, pageant, idleness and intrigue. At the mercy of the king's moods and caprices, they all lived in an atmosphere of insecurity and fear—fear of spies, fear of the king, fear of tortures, imprisonment and death. At the construction of a new palace or of a new capital it was usual to always bury alive a number of people at their entrances. The idea behind this practice was that their spirits would haunt the palace or the city where they were put to death and attack all persons approaching with malevolent intentions.

Politics consisted of conspiring. The king was always on the look-out for potential rivals and absorbed in the task of crushing them. Because of the uncertainty of succession to the throne, because succession did not necessarily follow the law of primogeniture, Burma's monarchical history was a history of princely rivalries and purges, conspiracies and rebellions. Even when the succession occurred without serious challenge, a period of confusion would follow, as all major government posts in the capital and in the provinces were up for redistribution. A crisis would lead to a period of general anarchy and violence. On the accession of a new king, his relations or other high officials likely to be competitors were often exterminated. But at no time were any of the frequent rebellions aimed at the destruction of the arbitrary royal rule but only at the substitution of one individual or rival family for another in the enjoyment of absolute power.

Nevertheless, Burma's royal despotism was not without some achievements. In Upper Burma they constructed an elaborate system of irrigation works which remained of use for many centuries. And nine hundred years ago, inspired by their newly acquired Buddhist faith, the devout kings of the Pagan dynasty in Upper Burma built an entire city of several thousand pagodas in their capital of Pagan.

Today Pagan still stands as a silent, somnolent mass of gigantic stone structures and quiet shrines, extending over several miles of motionless, hot sand. The tides of history have not changed it catastrophically throughout the centuries. This impressive area of temples, though it was once the capital of a strong Burmese dynasty, was never meant to serve a thriving urban congregation, or to embrace a multitude of humanity, or even to stand among them, in the places where they spent their lives in joy and sorrow, in trade or pleasure. Pagan, with its flow of giant stone monuments, was never like Paris, seething with urban life, where the many churches and the cathedral of Notre-Dame were, but the magnificent religious expressions of the many-sided secular qualities of city life. The kings built palaces within Pagan for their personal use, made of wood, rich with silks, gilded with ornaments and lacquer work, but they were not meant to last beyond the few mere life-spans of mere mortal men. They were destroyed sooner or later by fire, rot or warfare, and only the tracings of their foundations remain in the dust today. The rest of Pagan remains as originally intended, a seemingly endless framework of temples, all of them embodying, architecturally, the original symbolic gesture made (so it is said) by the Buddha to his followers when they asked him how they could show their devotion to his teachings. He placed his square cloak to stand upon the ground, his squat round alms bowl to stand inverted upon the cloak and his staff to stand upright upon that. This pattern of cloak, bowl and staff was endlessly repeated and elaborated upon in Pagan, in stone and brick, and was richly embroidered with the bronze and gold images of the Buddha and his disciples, and with rich carvings and tender-coloured frescoes. Pagan was the gift of Burmese material wealth and power to the life-denying spiritual force they believed in; an affirmation in heavy stone of the ephemeral and illusory nature of life and the world. The high, gothically carved and narrow passages running through all these buildings are full of nooks and arches, carved out of the stone walls to house the cool, remote-expressioned images. They are full of toweringly high, narrow and dim chambers, made incandescent in the dusty gloom by the huge and solid golden images contained in them of the squatting figure of the Buddha. But there is no place for man in any one of them.

The Buddha predominates in Pagan, to man's exclusion, yet the dynasty that built the temples is also in evidence. For the pagodas, notwithstanding the basic similarity of the pattern, speak of a growing Burmese civilisation, with wealth to display, and aware of the cultural riches of its great neighbours which could be adopted and copied. Most of the temples in Pagan bear the indelible stamp of the Indian and Chinese architects who were called in by the Burmese kings to make each new temple greater and more beautiful than the last. The very grandeur and monolithic nature of the pagodas, moreover, tell of the tyrannical power that could be employed by the temporal lords of the land, who could call upon forced labour and use it to construct these heavy, material emanations of the spirit; tell of the conquered peoples who were made temple slaves, to keep the glory polished; and even show, here and there in the frescoes, the forms of the kings and their richly bejewelled courts.

Yet, throughout the centuries, Burma's traditional political structure was more impressively showy at the centre than an effective governing force in the country. One of its difficulties was the fact that there was no noble or educated class to be entrusted with the greater offices of state. Between the king and the peasantry there were no intervening ranks or classes. The king had to pick his ministers and provincial governors from among the ordinary people and consequently the men who were called upon to fill positions of responsibility were as often as not men who had no experience beyond the narrow and confining limits of a village. They were without knowledge of other countries and systems, superstitious and parochial, and without the necessary qualities to manage great affairs of state. The king remained absolutely supreme and his ministers were mere puppets, without roots in any class, who could be honoured or ruined at his whim. There was no powerful nobility or any other class to oppose him, and all the ministers and governors were corrupt and venal. The whole structure was flimsy, unstable and oppressive. The king was more interested to maintain the 'circus-like splendour' of the court than to really govern.

The king's authority was exercised at the centre by a council of ministers, the Hlutdaw, who attended a daily audience to discuss matters of importance. They were also responsible for administering various functional duties of government

which fell within their respective fields of competence—
military ordinance, army administration, river control, royal
granaries, legal matters and taxation. For administrative purposes the country was divided into provinces. Within each province there was a representative of the central authority, the
governor, who governed with the help of numerous subordinates, exercising a wide variety of functions. These governors
were known as the 'Province Eaters'. To be an officer of state,
however, was to hold a post of great hazard. The royal cor-
rection was freely used. Ministers rose rapidly and they tum-
bled down with as much precipitation. The lowest peasant or
the most menial subject could become a high official; and soon
after, the minister or governor might find himself spread out in
the court of the palace with a merciless sun beating down upon
him and huge stones placed upon his chest and stomach. Or
they might be treated even more summarily than this. All
these officials, high or low, whether princes of the royal blood,
ministers of state, maids of honour, royal spittoon-bearers, or
servants of the white elephant, whether at the capital or in the
provinces, drew their remuneration in the form of fees, com-
missions or gratuities, which were either customarily attached
to their office or exacted under pressure.

The administration, as it touched the ordinary villager, was
carried on chiefly by a hierarchy distinct from the royal
government. Over each group of villages, known as a Myo, or
township there was a township headman who held office by
inheritance and was its key political figure. He drew his
authority not from royal appointment but from ancient right,
and was the intermediary between the people and the royal
officers. These headmen constituted some kind of 'local aristocracy' and were the sole lay element of permanence and continuity in social life. They enjoyed wide powers. They were the
police officers, the local judge-arbiters of disputes, they appor-
tioned and collected taxes, assigned service obligations and
recruited local contingents for war.

In these villages the population was divided into two main
groups: the servicemen and the non-servicemen. The servicemen were liable to some form of royal service, usually though
not always military service. The non-servicemen had to pay

various dues and were liable to be called upon for a mass levy in the event of war. Corvees and compulsory duties of all kinds were frequent. The king or some other important official wanted to build a pagoda (to gain merit) and workers had to be supplied. Those who refused to go were flogged. Work levies were also required to dig tanks and repair canals. Similar forced duties involved the protection of the frontier and the pursuit of dacoit bands. The men selected for all these duties could only get off by furnishing a substitute or bribing the official.

As Lord of the People, the king was also, in theory, Lord of all that they possessed. But in fact most people in a village held some land. Burma, being an underpopulated country, never really had a serious land problem. The land did not, however, belong to the cultivator as an individual but to the family of which he was a member. Cultivation was primarily for sub-sistence. The villagers had to pay some form of land tax—sometimes as a share of the crop, sometimes on the area culti-vated, sometimes in silver or copper. Often this revenue was allocated to a member of the royal family or to a high official or to some favourite who became the 'Myosa'—the 'Eater of the Township'.

At the bottom of Burma's structure was a small, depressed and despised class which consisted of executioners and jailors; those who were deformed or incurably diseased; those connected with disposal of the dead; and crown slaves working on the royal lands. Prisoners of war and people guilty of murder, rape and other serious crimes were also used as pagoda slaves or attendants. This class of people were segregated and discri-minated against in pre-colonial Burma and formed a class of outcasts.

Like India, Burma is a society which has been considerably influenced and penetrated by religion. In this case it is Bud-dhism. There are two main schools of Buddhism: the adherents of the Mahayana or 'Greater Vehicle' school are found in Tibet, Nepal, China and Korea and Japan, etc., and the Theravada—'The Way of the Elders' school—is followed by the Buddhists of Ceylon, Thailand, Laos, Cambodia and Burma.

Buddhism, like Hinduism, sees the universe and all forms of life as parts of a process of eternal flux. All forms of life are characterised by impermanence, suffering, and an absence of permanent soul, which separates one form of life from other forms of life. There is no finality or rest within this universe; only a ceaseless becoming and a never-ending change. All creatures are involved in an endless cycle of rebirths, are riveted to Samsara—the 'wheel of rebirth'—and condemned to 'perpetual wandering'.

Buddhism presents its doctrine as a therapy, a treatment or cure of the individual's spiritual and physical ills. It makes four basic statements concerning the condition of man. These are the 'Four Noble Truths' which constitute the heart and core of its doctrine. The first states that all life is suffering. The Buddha said: 'Birth is suffering, decay is suffering, disease is suffering, death is suffering, association with the unpleasing is suffering, separation from the pleasing is suffering . . .' Man is thus subject to pain, illness and disease—physical and mental— is embroiled in disharmony and friction and tormented by dissatisfaction and discontent. 'One thing I teach,' said the Buddha, 'suffering and the ending of suffering.'

The second says that the cause of suffering is ignorant craving. Wrong craving and desire generate the forces which bind men to the endless wheel of rebirth. These include the lusts of the flesh, the will to live, and the craving for the gratification of the passions and the senses. Life is a progress from want to want, not from happiness to happiness. Men who desire life are as men athirst and drinking of the sea. Life is an overwhelming and insatiable thirst; it is not attainment. The tragedies and comedies in which man is involved develop inevitably from the impetus of his cravings for 'things' to which he becomes attached, including life itself, but which are all transitory and perishable. Attachment and the satisfaction of desire only cause disappointment, disillusionment and other forms of suffering. All these cravings are, however, not due to the individual's mistakes or shortcomings, but are rooted in his human way of life, which is 'a pathological blend of unfulfilled cravings, vexing longings, fears, regrets and pains'.

The third and fourth truths show how man can find a way of release from suffering and misery. This can be practised by the ordinary man and is not dependent on divine grace. The third truth states that the elimination of desire will remove the cause of suffering. Suffering will cease by stamping out endless desires. The fourth truth, the noble Eightfold Path, teaches that the individual can stamp out all desire by following the Buddhist path of enlightened self-discipline. By practising the right moral conduct, concentration and insight, release can be attained from the universal law of moral causation (Karma) and the individual can escape from the world of rebirths to Nirvana.

The Eightfold Path consists of Right Understanding, Right Thoughts or Motives, Right Speech, Right Action (that is, according to the accepted moral law), Right Means of Livelihood, Right Endeavour, Right Mindfulness, and Right Contemplation. Stealing, deceiving, adultery, killing and the drinking of intoxicants are the principal crimes. Buddhism cultivates the knowledge of cessation, of the discontinuance of worldly existence, of utter repose by emancipation. To enter the Buddhist vehicle—the boat of the discipline—is to begin to cross the river of life, from the shore of ignorance, craving and death to the far-off bank of transcendental wisdom and liberation from the universal bondage. To reach this bank, after having passed through many lives of increasing self-purification, is to know that one is free and to find oneself on the threshold of Nirvana.

Nirvana is usually described in negative terms, as there is some disagreement about its meaning. For some the secret meaning of Enlightenment is that it is without reality. Others think of it as the dying out of the three fires of Greed, Anger and Illusion, and the stopping of the wheel of rebirth. Some regard it as that condition in which the total loss of personality and absorption in the divine is obtained, and for others it is a blissful, unchanging state of personal existence. It is a condition without fixity, without mobility, without basis; it is the end of will. Man is no more agitated by existence, wretched in itself, still more wretched from the woes which it reveals in others, and he falls into a calm and never-ending cessation of existence. Buddhism yearns to return from the endless whirl and turmoil of existence to the calm of the first beginning.

Buddhism has been and is still so powerful a force in Burma because it has for centuries been served by a numerous order of devotees—the Monkhood. Dressed in their yellow robes, their heads clean-shaven, their faces immobile, with the round black begging bowl in their hands, they have always formed a picturesque and bountiful (much too bountiful) part of the Burmese scene. These *pongyis*, these 'Great Glories' as they are called, performed a number of related functions. They constituted a strong chain of authority between the crown and the people. They were the country's schoolmasters. The monastery functioned as the chief repository of the country's culture and its legal code. There was no village of any consequence without a monastery and without its monks. It was the centre of village life. The monks were at once the village gossips, the source (in so far as they had mastered it) of the knowledge of the Buddhist teaching, the readily approachable consultants on personal and moral problems and, if holy, the pride of the community.

The monastic order was one of the main pillars of the social fabric. It was also highly respected and admired. The monastic order, along with the Buddha and his teachings, was and is recognised as one of the 'Three Gems of the Faith'. To become a monk, to renounce the things of the world, to follow a life of continence, poverty and humility, to seek his own deliverance and salvation, have always been considered as the highest ideals to which a man could aspire. Even the king, though he was the supreme governor of the Buddhist church, venerated the humblest member of the order as his spiritual superior. The people as a whole regarded the monastic order as the highest expression of their spiritual life. Nobody in Burma was in fact without knowledge of the interior of the monastery, and nearly all had accompanied the monks on their begging tours. The most important moment in the history of every Burmese boy was connected with his initiation as a novice in the Buddhist monastic order. The Shinbya (literally, 'becoming a monk') ceremony was one of the most memorable events of his life. Dressed as a prince, because the Buddha had been a prince, he rode in state to the monastery, there to lay aside his crown, cleanse himself, have his head shaved and, after taking the vows of abstinence, don the sacred robe. Both the boy and his sponsors earned great merit for participating in this ceremony.

Although the *pongyis* renounced the world, they did not, like some of the Indian mystics, live in complete retirement from it. The *pongyis* preached, prayed at weddings and funerals and were intimately connected with the life of the people. One of the most common and popular forms of social gatherings was the ceremonial offer of a meal to a group of *pongyis*. At every feast, every rejoicing, the central feature was presents to the monks. The monks set the tone of the society's conduct. For the Burmese Buddhism provided a moral code, an overall ideal of life, though not an insistent one, and constituted an integral element of its whole culture. It provided a full range of activities for the many rather than a difficult philosophy for the few. It was a general frame of reference and a mould which enveloped and gave shape to the whole gamut of experience. It was more pervasive than intense. It inspired the nationalist movement at a later stage and many monks participated in its struggles. Under British rule the monasteries formed centres of Burmese cultural resistance to Western civilisation. It could even be said that, though theoretically the order was barred from politics, it was in fact a permanent though loose political power, keeping Burma secure for Buddhism and preserving the country's stability and continuity.

Though Buddhism was the officially established religion, the older, natural deities of the animistic cults were never superseded and retained a firm hold on the minds of the people. These were the spirits of nature or Nats, like the fairies or trolls of Europe. The term Nat originally meant a 'Lord' and was a spirit which exercised dominion over both people and objects. These deities in fact found a place in the Buddhist hagiology and were amicably tolerated by the monks. According to this belief, all nature is filled with Nats. Millions of these spirits stalk the earth. The highest Nats and the most powerful live in the mountains. But every house, tree and forest, every stone, pool and breath of air has its spirit and they are malevolent beings who must be looked up to with fear and propitiated with offerings. A spirit much feared was one which was twenty-five feet high, whistling and always hungry because its mouth was only as large as the eye of a needle.

Immersed in this ubiquitous, evergreen malevolent world of spirits, the Burmese tended to seek comfort in an abundance of experts who professed to be able to explain signs and omens and to control the evil spirits. Spirit women, astrologers, magic workers, alchemists, wizards and sorcerers, many of them practising their trade within the precincts of the pagoda, were all both popular and consulted. Astrology to the Burmese meant not only the methods of tracing the course of the planets and their influence on human fortunes but also the ritual by which the planets were appeased and made to withdraw their evil influence. Alchemy was a religious cult which aimed not only to transmute base metals into gold, but to fashion an eternally youthful body and thus to halt the natural process of human decay. Even the Buddha himself was not treated as a venerable teacher but as a divinity who must be placated and sacrificed to.

Insulated from both China and India, its capital cities remote from the highways and seaways of the world, Burma then developed in isolation its own form of closed Asian society.

Traditional Burma was a fairly roomy, fertile and under-populated land, based on the customs and institutions of a simple, agricultural civilisation and held together by the bonds of royal despotism and Buddhism. The tempo of government and society were slow and the temperature of life low. Its economic life was primitive, crude and unchanging. In the main life revolved around the cultivation of rice, the rice fields, the pagoda, the happy festivals, the Nats and ghosts of the old animistic culture which had never died out despite centuries of Buddhism. They were a people without either great poverty or great wealth. The distinctions between rich and poor were blurred. By law and custom, women had equal rights with men in property ownership, divorce, inheritance and business. Wants were few. Everyone had enough rice to eat and did not have to work very hard to get his share. Surplus wealth was invested in the purchase of jewellery or in acquiring merit by building a pagoda. The rich man's *longyi* might be made of silk, while the poor man's was of cotton. His house might be of wood, his poorer neighbour's of bamboo. But both lived more or less in the same style, shared the same eating habits, the same cultural life, concepts and ideas, tied to traditional songs and dances, to supernatural stories of fabulous heroes and knaves, to a spiritual climate which stressed the essential insubstantiality and worthlessness of the things of the world. The guiding principle was to increase in merit, so as to be reincarnated at a higher stage of development. Merit was gained not from accumulating but from giving, not through inheritance but from one's own efforts, from doing good deeds. Merit was to be achieved not by pioneering new paths into the future but by moving in discipline and obedience along the customary and traditional byways.

Burmese life, as has been explained, was very strongly influenced by religion—both the official Buddhism and the older nature deities. But as is obvious, Burmese religious life was in no way exclusively directed by the doctrines of Buddhism, neither by some of its profound psychological insights nor by its basic life-denying assumptions. As with most religions, it did spread a number of simple maxims which the people tried to follow as best they could but without essentially changing their behaviour or character. Religion nevertheless contributed to the educational discipline, the standards of moral conduct and the social values by which the people lived. It inculcated a feeling of respect and deference for age and for status. The Buddha, his doctrine, his order, rulers, parents and teachers, all had to be unquestionably obeyed. This doctrine of respect has been described as compounded of fear and love. The Burmese have learnt over the ages much tenderness for the lives of inferior members of the animal kingdom, but at the same time they have shown much disregard of the sacredness of human life. In war they have been both cruel and rapacious and their officers were known as the 'Great Blood Drinkers'. The Burmese have always been extremely proud of their feats of conquest and have gloried in the 'victories' which they gained from Assam in the west to Cambodia in the east. The wars between Burma's different ethnic groups were as merciless and sanguinary as any that were fought anywhere else in the world. Buddhism, adjusted to a primitive agrarian society, did however give an other-worldly tinge to their elementary notions about the world. It has enabled them to accept their simple and uncomplicated life with all its joys and sorrows, with all its inevitable misfortunes and calamities, without demanding much from it or from themselves. No impetus of high ambition moved them to work hard. Few things cut deep. Because gaining merit and meditating on the release of the spirit is a gradual, cumulative process which may take innumerable existences, the Burmese have never been driven by the belief that they have but one life to live in which to realise their authentic human potentialities and that it is necessary to endow this life with worth and dignity. Although they were interested in the past and future in relation to the individual's liberation from the cycle of rebirths, there was little interest in either history or progress. Their sense of separate individuality was extremely weak. There was no feeling that they should exert themselves to dominate their world or to achieve something notable in it. Tradition, conformism, obedience, submission, resignation, 'peace of mind', have been some of its most pervasive beliefs. There was no sense of being in a state of tension with their world or society; there was only superstitious fear of it and a desire to be left alone to enjoy its simple pleasures and consolations. Although the Burmese believed in 'change' in so far as it affected the individual's position in the Buddhist cosmology, the established order and its institutions they regarded as immutable.

Their general pattern of life and behaviour was full of contradictions. There was literacy but also tremendous and astounding ignorance. They set great store on personal dignity and freedom from arbitrary restraint but when in power they were domineering, arrogant and even brutally oppressive. Disciplined behaviour could yield to the most impulsive and unrestrained violence. For the young man, conduct tended to vacillate between a life of monastic withdrawal and participation in the violent daring of the dacoit gang. The Burmese were as capable of displaying much spasmodic energy as of sinking into limitless apathy and idleness. Although Buddhism stressed individual responsibility, it only produced an enveloping spirit of fatalism and passivity. The individual personality was not much developed and the human spirit was never given wing. The Burmans lacked both a fixed purpose and a capacity for perseverance. And quite naturally none of the attitudes and motivations and pressures associated with Western culture were developed.

The Burmese, because they lacked a sharp form of social differentiation, have been called a democratic people and a race of individualists. But the trend has always been authoritarian. Gradations of rank were most minutely and tenaciously maintained. To become the satellite of an official, to place oneself in the position of dependence on an elder or a patron, has always been a natural and congenial ambition. The father in his home ruled over obedient children, poorer relatives and head-bowing servants. The king and his ministers and his officials ruled absolutely and arbitrarily over a peasant population though any man, it is true, could rise to ministerial rank by sheer chance, and the daughter of the humblest peasant might find herself selected either by the stars or the king to become a member of the royal household. Power has always been feared and weakness despised. Political authority was generally abused and once assured of the protection of the government the officials were capable of the utmost meanness, injustice and cruelty. Government was always thought of as a scourge to be avoided at all costs. Burmese life did not lack periods of upheaval and commotion, was not without innumerable massacres and rebellions, but it did lack purpose and novelty and was bereft of the energy of innovation. The society as a whole was without the instinct of growth. Burmese society was both highly fragile and unproductive, unable to confront any serious challenge and without the inner resources to withstand any great crisis. Despite the magnificent and awe-inspiring pagodas that were built, despite its many charming ceremonies and festivals, traditional Burma did not create a civilisation of any universal significance or magnitude.

ii

With the final conquest of Burma by Britain in 1886, the dynamic forces of Western civilisation were let loose upon this isolated, stagnant and backward society. The British impact on Burma provides a striking example of some of the strengths and weaknesses of Western rule in Asia and of the kind of legacy it left to its nationalist successors. Burma was conquered at a time when the British were most self-confident, at a time when the Victorian ideas of *laissez faire* held an undisputed hold over the minds of the civil servants who shaped local policy. The main objective of British rule was economic progress, especially through trade. After the opening of the Suez Canal in 1869, Lower Burma in particular and the country as a whole was systematically handed over to the operations of private economic interests (both foreign and Burmese), and given over to money-making. The result was a tremendous economic spurt forward. Hundreds of thousands of immigrants from Upper Burma brought the wastelands of Lower Burma, formerly swamp and jungle, under rice cultivation. Under British rule a backward subsistence economy was transformed into an important source of rice, timber and minerals and a valuable market. From a sparsely settled region it became the world's greatest rice-exporting area. As an achievement in settlement and economic development, Lower Burma ranks with Canada or the Argentine as an immense Victorian triumph.

In this region alone the rice land grew from about one million acres to over ten million. Before World War II, Burma's annual rice exports exceeded three million tons, out of a world export total of some eight million tons. Burma's teak forests were developed and exploited. Oil exploration began on a large scale at the beginning of the century and by the 1930s produced between two and three per cent of world oil exports. Tin and tungsten, lead, silver and other metals were mined. A modern transport and communication system was built. Some 2,000 miles of railroad lines were laid. Roads were thrust through a formidable interior. Port facilities were established to handle the increasing stream of exports and imports. And an increasing proportion of Burmans streamed into the urban centres which greatly increased in size. Rangoon, which British enterprise built, became one of the most beautiful imperial cities of Asia.

Burma, however, also suffered from many of the worst features of Victorian expansion, supplemented by quite a number of special local ailments. Society was subordinated to purely economic considerations, and the profit motive, unhindered and untrammelled, was given free rein. The laws and relations of the market place ruled supreme. Its economic life, the welfare of the community, came to depend upon the export of a single commodity, which itself was subject to the violent fluctuations of boom and slump. The Burmese cultivators were thrown unprepared into the whirlpool of a money economy, without the necessary training, protection or safeguards. Lacking access to Western banks, without their own credit institutions, they had to borrow money from the Indian moneylenders who infested the country. Much of the land that the Burmese had cleared eventually found its way into their hands. As a result, peasant proprietors were quickly enough converted into tenants burdened with increasing debts and rents and subsequently into a landless rural proletariat, floating from village to village in search of work for wages that were steadily falling.

The Burmese cultivators, unable to face alone the rigours of an undiluted competitive economy, were driven to the wall. Bereft of the support of their customary world, unable to cope with the conditions created by a regime of free competition, they were without protection against impoverishment and social dislocation. While the country became increasingly prosperous, the majority of the people remained relatively poor and quite unable to handle the potent economic forces impinging upon them.

British social policy, moreover, drastically disturbed the old society without, however, preparing or educating the Burmese to live in the new, 'Liberal' social order they were creating. The cumbersome machinery of the old monarchy was abolished. The Buddhist church was virtually disestablished. The old rural headmen were set aside. The old type of village with its bonds of loyalty and obligation slowly expired. Old handicrafts collapsed in face of foreign imports. Burma's traditional subsistence agriculture, in its greatest part, was rapidly displaced by commercial production of a single cash crop for export. Unlike most of the other colonies, Burma's primitive farmers were drawn into a money economy and forced to produce for an uncertain and unstable market. A system of impersonal Western law, designed to encourage free enterprise and freedom of contract and of land alienation, replaced the old framework of social custom. All the outward traditional forms and institutions which in any case were hopelessly outmoded came tumbling down.

It was in the towns in particular that the transformation of the old society was most noticeable. Under Burmese rule the people living in their villages and townships had been cut off from the outside world. Now European, Indian and Chinese immigrants entered the country and quickly began to predominate in all the modern branches of society. Industry and commerce became exclusively foreign with foreign ownership, management and labour. The new industries were carried on completely outside of Burmese life and without any effective attempt to bring the Burmans into the process. Indian workers accustomed to lower wages were imported to make the roads, build the houses and to do all kinds of menial labour. It was much cheaper and less troublesome to do this than to train the Burmans for these tasks. Indians were also employed in the civil service, and were used to perform other administrative duties. The towns became largely 'foreign enclaves', and everything that had the stamp of modernity was foreign. The Burmese, as before, were largely occupied in agricultural pursuits and, apart from being involved in buying and selling operations, they had very few transforming contacts with the modern world. The presence of all these alien groups created a diseased plural society, divided by racial and national hatreds, lacking any profound organic bonds and without a redeeming civic sense.

Yet the British administration was not only a force of disintegration. It also set up new institutions which could have been of great value to a people ready for life in the modern world. Unfortunately this was not the case in Burma. Nevertheless an integrated national administration, run by a professional, salaried civil service, subject to the rule of law was created. The concept of contract, so essential for economic advance, was introduced. Local government was converted from a tribal basis to a territorial one. Modern lay schools were encouraged. The English language was taught. A representative assembly (though not based on universal suffrage) was set up. The net result of all these changes was the establishment, in a country where it was formerly unknown, of the outward trappings of the modern liberal state.

The Western form of parliamentary government, however, was introduced into a country which was not capable of sustaining the standards which it demanded and only became a caricature of its real self. Instead of parliamentary democracy (limited though it was) serving as an instrument of government, it became in fact an education in corruption. The political arena had something of the atmosphere of a jungle. The top political leaders had their own private armies for their own protection and as weapons of vote-getting. The restricted electorate which had the right to vote regarded government as an inexhaustible source of money and favours. Members of the legislature voted for ministers only if they were ready to pay for it. Police officials would find themselves transferred if they intended to bring to justice persons who had the ear of the minister. Some ministers even advised judges what sentence to pass if the accused was a friend of theirs.

Below the top level the whole administrative machine was sunk in a morass of corruption and chicanery. The traditional administrative abuses from the time of the Burmese kings were grafted on to the malpractices of the colonial administration. Petty corruption was universal among the lower ranks of the hierarchy. Some executive officers had to pay a whole year's salary to get or avoid a transfer. An official report estimated that from 50 to 70 per cent of the subordinate magistrates made a business of selling justice. Excise officers amassed quick fortunes. Revenue officers withheld percentages of government loans allocated to needy cultivators. Jail privileges, approval of headman elections, public works contracts, and even altered reports of the outcome of the Buddhist scripture examinations—all of these and much more besides could be procured by bribery.

Although some nationalist leaders tried when in power to tackle some of the country's immediate problems, such as agrarian distress, village administration and regulation of Indian immigration, their efforts produced few results and only increased the nation's dissatisfaction. Divided into many factions, with no party having a clear majority, confused as to aims, enjoying the perquisites of office but without effective power, frustrated by the system of communal electorates and other devices which the colonial government used to safeguard its rule and to preserve the special privileges of foreign economic interests, the system of parliamentary government utterly failed to satisfy the country's aspirations for self-rule.

Burmese political life assumed so many unsavoury forms, however, not only because of British obstructions and short-sightedness. It also arose out of their own deficiencies and general immaturity. U Thant (now the General Secretary of the U.N.) described the Burmese malady in the following terms:

We are a nation of adult infants . . . It often prompts such statements as 'Our Burmese Kings . . . conquered Siam, Assam and Manipur'. . . . Our personal achievements . . . evoke a similar childish emotional response. . . . Proportionately, we have more places of worship than any other country . . . and yet we are the least religious. . . . We have a religion which forbids its priests to meddle in worldly affairs, yet some . . . are more worldly and more debauched than any other religious brotherhood. . . . We do not experience pleasure or fulfilment in the thought that we are grown-up individuals prepared to meet struggle and hardship. We think that the longer we remain impervious to life's warning the luckier we are; that if life would only spare us its blows, we should be happy. Children do not . . . like to think connectedly; they do not like to think at all. . . . Grown-up Burmans have similar . . . dislikes. They leave it to their priests, students, and newspapers to think for them. . . . We refuse to grow up and think for ourselves; we are unable to purge ourselves of the fear of ridicule. . . . Burmese politics have no meaning save to keep Burmese newspapers busy. . . . All our politicians are out to wreck the constitution but at the first available opportunity, the loudest-lunged . . . will not hesitate to swallow his spit. . . . This is a picture of the Burmans as one of them sees them, but we need not despair. Recognition and detection of the causes of the malady are half the cure.[1]

In spite of its many positive features, in spite of some of its

[1] *New Burma*, 8 September 1939: quoted by John F. Cady in *A History of Modern Burma*. Cornell University Press, 1958, pp. 388–9.

good intentions, then, the total effect of British rule was to create a mongrel type of society, discontented enough to demand independence but too immature to be capable of exercising it. The reforms that they introduced did not really strike deep roots. The elements of modern civilisation that they imported into Burma only went skin-deep. The basic habits, instincts and values developed by the old, archaic, despotic society were not transformed. The character of the people was not changed. The fundamentals of the old society survived, despite all the surface changes and disturbances. They cut into the old discipline but without providing a new, coherent sense of national purpose. There was a certain amount of liberation from old traditions, but without a corresponding growth of self-mastery. The educational system gave their students no insights into the realities of the modern world and did not set them high standards to aim at. The uneducated classes were no less a prey to debilitating superstition than before. British rule did not develop an indigenous Burmese middle class of sufficient size or ability to succeed it. And the standards of the tiny, essentially professional, middle class that did spring up were low. Although the new Burmese politicians learnt to manipulate the novel institutions of liberal government, political life was soon enough turned into a vast racket. Principles disappeared; horse-trading took their place. The rewards of office without responsibility produced large-scale corruption and frustration. Crime increased sensationally.

Above all, Burma was transformed into a mere business concern and society became an arena in which men fought for place and profit, regardless of the rules and the means that they employed. As a business concern Burma was relatively successful. But the economic progress that was achieved did not bring the 'people into contact with world civilisation but only with the world market. It failed to solve the problem of equipping Burmans for life in the modern world.' [1]

[1] J. C. Furnival.

It was in the thirties that Burma's political development began to assume those features which came to predominate after it had obtained its independence. Society became more fluid. Groups and individuals were more ready to assert their will for power in conflicts of every kind. The new decade started with a rebellion against British rule. This was followed by large-scale strikes, anti-Indian pogroms and growing political tensions. In 1931 an ex-monk named Saya San started a rebellion against British rule (the first since 1890) among the superstitious peasantry. He promised his followers that by magic powers, tattooing, amulets and charms, he would provide them with immunity against the weapons and the power of the foreigner. Most of his organisers were political *pongyis*. Peasant discontent was here united with a primitive attempt to advance 'religion and the nation' and to save Buddhism 'from the unbeliever'. Saya San was convinced that he was born to be the ruler of a resurrected Burmese kingdom. Over eight hundred troops were finally needed to suppress the rebellion.

Although the Burmese under the constitution of 1935, which separated Burma from India, were given more political responsibility than was enjoyed at that time by any other colonial people in South East Asia, the more radical wing of the nationalist movement was in no way satisfied and still did not feel that they were in control of their own affairs. The 1929 economic crisis which had a disastrous effect on the country's economy, particularly its agriculture, stirred up discontent and diffused it throughout the society. The rising tide of Asian nationalism, the Kuomintang experiment in China, the spread of communist ideas, reinforced by the growing power of the Russian state and the example of the Chinese communists, the influence of the Indian Congress Party, and the increasing power of Japan—all these forces began to affect Burma's political development.

Disillusioned with the quasi-democratic form of government which was in force, many nationalist leaders began to search for some alternative. Some turned to the socialist group within the Indian Congress for political inspiration. Others made contact with the Bengali revolutionary Subhas Chandra Bose. A small group was in touch with the Indian Communist Party. A goodwill mission was sent to Kuomintang China. Some of the younger elements even conceived the idea that communist China might be of possible assistance. One of Dr Ba Maw's lieutenants visited Japan and on his return wrote some articles in which he argued that 'as the West had failed us we must now answer the call of the East'. There was increasing propaganda about the 'New Order in Asia', and that 'Asia is One'. The emergence of totalitarian and authoritarian forms of government in Russia, Germany and Japan suggested that strong government and a more stringent leadership, rather than democracy, were the instruments of national revival and progress. Some began to look to Japan and others to Russia as the 'waves of the future', while not a few were willing to take their chances with both.

Burmese nationalism had at first been closely associated with the Buddhist religion. Its first expression was the formation of a Young Men's Buddhist Association. Monks began to play an important role in politics, and the yellow robe more often than not draped a worldly and turbulent rebel against the ideas and spirit of Western civilisation than a recluse from the temptations of the world. With the spread of Western education, nationalist politics drew into its orbit emerging elements of the middle classes—lawyers, journalists and retired civil servants. This assorted group of well-intentioned but ineffective time-servers, charming in manner but corrupt in practice, outwardly placid and amiable but neck-deep in ruthless personal intrigue, moderate, accommodating but aimless and without power or influence in their own country, could not long survive the new developments that were appearing on the horizon. In the late thirties there was an increasing tendency towards a revolutionary form of nationalism, tinged with socialist, Marxist, communist and even fascist ideas.

Reflecting these new trends, Dr Ba Maw, probably the most educated and capable of all the veteran nationalist politicians, founded a new party, the 'Sinyetha' or 'Poor Man's Party', in 1936. Its programme was a mixture of populism, decorated with some Marxist phraseology. It demanded among other things village reconstruction and tax reductions, regular, periodic elections of village headmen, freer agricultural credit through land-mortgage banks, lower land rents, repurchase of alienated land with government aid and compulsory free education. He described this programme as a form of rudimentary socialism, adapted to Burma's needs. Dr Ba Maw's activities and speeches, during this period, had an important influence upon the thinking of many of the younger nationalists, who were then still at the university but who were later destined to succeed him in the political leadership of the country.

The late thirties also saw the birth of the Thakin movement which grew rapidly in numbers and influence. It soon came to include among its members most of those who were to rule Burma after independence. Starting as a student organisation, it quickly developed into a general, revolutionary nationalist movement. They assumed the style Thakin ('master'), formerly the usual term of address to Europeans, to show that they claimed equality with them and as a mark of their defiance of British rule. By calling themselves Thakins and adopting the peacock as the symbol of their pride they affirmed their belief that the Burmans must be the masters of their own country. The Thakins represented a new element in Burmese politics, bound together by interest, way of life and consciousness of a common task. In them the stubbornly parochial pride of the old Burma only slightly influenced by Western culture came to the fore. The Thakins did not only want to become masters of their country, but through them ancient Burmese forces and habits reasserted their claim to dominance.

The overwhelming majority of them had been educated in the 'nationalist' schools which had been set up in opposition to the 'imperialist' English language school system. Shaped by an educational system which had stressed the preservation of Burmese traditions and of Buddhism as the nation's chief task, stemming from the isolated and hopelessly backward villages and townships of Burma, these young students were the opponents of Western civilisation—as represented by the British authorities in Burma—rather than the potential organisers of the revolutionary transformation of their own country. They did not want to catch up with the West. They wanted to escape from its toils. In their eyes Burma was closely identified with Buddhism. All of them were Buddhists and some of them were even very devout Buddhists. No matter what scraps of modern ideology they picked up, it always had to be coupled with Buddhism to receive their support. And for them Buddhism was not so much a philosophy or religion (most of them did not know very much about it in any case) as it was a symbol and expression of their attachment to the simple village society they had been brought up in and in which they felt at home. Thakin Nu's pre-war novel, '*Man, the Wolf of Man*', placed the blame for the country's troubles quite as much on the apostasy of Burmans who aped the British and rejected the ancient ways as he did on the 'imperialist exploiters'.

Sons of petty tradesmen, small landowners, country lawyers and poor peasants, most of the young people who joined the movement, were naturally more aware of the distress of the masses than were the lawyer politicians who had, until then, occupied the centre of the stage of nationalist politics. Those among them who were more versed in the English language began to read Left Book Club editions and Red Dragon (communist) Books which filtered through to Burma. Sets of Marxist writings were brought back to Rangoon from London by one of the Burmese representatives at the Round Table Conference convened by the British government to discuss Burma's future, and began to circulate among them. There were discussions on the virtues of socialism and Marxism whose significance, however, they barely grasped. Depending on their temperament, education and the strength of their religious beliefs, many of the Thakins were converted to a nationalist form of either socialism or communism.

Yet the Thakins were more practical than theoretical in their approach to nationalist politics. They valued action above thought; and Aung San coined the Thakin slogan: 'We want fools to fight for Burma's freedom'. Marxism attracted them because it provided a plausible explanation of the role and position of foreign capital in Burma and seemed to offer a short-cut to independence. Capitalism and imperialism appeared as indistinguishable in their eyes. The simplistic Marxist explanations that they picked up seemed to harmonise with their instinctive opposition to all those foreign elements (Indian and Chinese as well as British) who, they believed, were exploiting their country and denying them their rightful place within it. Some vague general notions of the future began to take shape. But the young people were far more deeply occupied in actively defying and flouting the British authorities than in trying to understand the nature of the modern world which ruled them. They were far more ready to lay the blame for all Burma's ills on the broad shoulders of the British authorities than to examine their own society, their own hearts and minds as possible causes for their degradation. It was much more important to refuse to bow one's head respectfully to the British dean of the university than to concern oneself with the dazzling array of ideas which impel the modern world; to say with youthful confidence 'Our day will come!' and point defiantly to the stately English houses than to worry overmuch about how to run the country when it did.

Nevertheless, the young students proved to be resourceful organisers and soon spread a network of conspiracy over the country. They roped in other students and dissatisfied youths everywhere, organised trade unions and peasant organisations and set them to hamper British rule wherever they could find a chance. Although they failed to achieve any startling results, their practical activities provided them with valuable organisational experience, instilled them with a capacity for taking risks and helped them to acquire that tactical flexibility, that strength of political purpose which none of the other politicians could match.

Their socialist and Marxist beliefs, however, were not permitted to either cramp their political style or to limit their field of manœuvre. They were as willing to use the strike weapon as to become the champions of Buddhist traditionalism in revolt against the intrusions of Western civilisation in all its forms. They were as ready to use peaceful methods as they were to employ violent means. In order to realise their primary objective of national independence, they were quite willing to accept outside help from any quarter—the Indian National Congress, Kuomintang China, communist China, fascist Japan, or from any other likely source. Only those Thakins who had been attracted by communism were opposed to collaboration with the Japanese after Russia's entry into the second world war.

At the beginning of the second world war, when successful rebellion against the British power seemed possible at last, they began to look for outside aid. Their first impulse was to establish contact with the Chinese communist's Eighth Route Army, whose exploits they had heard of and admired. But they were deflected from this purpose by a chance encounter with an agent of the Japanese secret service, who proved sympathetic. So instead of Yenan, they found themselves in Tokyo and turned to Japanese militarism and authoritarianism, which was then the rising power in Asia, for guidance and for inspiration. Thirty Thakins, the now famous 'Thirty Comrades', were sent clandestinely to Japan for military training and formed the nucleus of the Burma Independence Army, which entered Burma in the wake of the Japanese invaders in 1942.

The Burma Independence Army, which then began to form itself as an instrument of national struggle, consisted of a nondescript medley of adherents. Starting off from Thailand, where Thai and resident Burmese were recruited, the army increased in numbers as it penetrated Burma. Recruits came from all sections of society: politicians, students, village teachers, peasants and workers and just plain criminal elements. All the submerged elements of rural Burmese society, provincial yet pugnacious, streamed into it. Although they fought some engagements in Lower Burma, the B.I.A. did not really make an important military contribution to the Japanese conquest of the country. Their principal tasks were to act as interpreters and guides, as sources of intelligence and as saboteurs behind the British lines. In all these roles they were very effective and of great help to the invaders. Armed with a sense of new power, intoxicated by the military atmosphere, the army also committed many atrocities, was involved in clashes with the Karen minority, and indulged in a great deal of requisitioning, of looting and of other forms of self-enrichment. It grew from a mere handful into a force of about 30,000 men at its peak strength.

Following the collapse of the British administration, the army found itself assuming administrative functions within the country. Working through Thakins, government officers and professional men, they organised local governing committees, and assumed control over abandoned major centres of administration. In the maintenance of law and order all these committees acted with more enthusiasm than justice. Thieves, robbers, murderers and 'spies' alike were tried summarily and sentenced to death. The executions, often carried out by cruel methods, were made publicly. Regardless of its atrocities and acts of oppression, however, the army units served as concentrations of Burmese national power and became the centre of the nation's hopes.

Japan's conquest of South East Asia constituted the most crucial event in the modern history of the region. At one stroke they cancelled the centuries-old Western dominance of eastern Asia. By a series of lightning victories Japan brought about a major shift in the balance of power. The war in all its violent ramifications rent the atmosphere of the times and shattered the normal process of political evolution throughout the colonial countries of the area. It humiliated the Western rulers and exposed their military weakness and lack of native support. By their military conquests and the political concessions that they were willing or forced to grant, by their 'Asia for Asians' propaganda, by their arming of nationalist armies and bands, Japan enormously strengthened and gave a fresh and powerful stimulus to the anti-imperialist movement. It helped to inaugurate a new epoch in Asia's evolution. An old order collapsed with very little resistance and it seemed that things would never be the same again.

The Japanese conquest and occupation of Burma, from 1942 to 1945, served too as a fateful dividing line in the country's political history. It put an end to British rule. The Japanese occupation laid the foundations for a new social order. It contributed in many different ways to Burma's political, economic and cultural advance. It enlarged its knowledge of the modern world. By granting it at least a formal independence it enabled the Burmese to acquire some experience of managing their own affairs. The whole administrative machine, from top to bottom, was now in Burmese hands. They now had their own government, their own supreme court and other courts and tribunals on which their own judges sat. They could now appoint their own foreign representatives. Burma even now had its own Minister of Defence and its own army. For the first time since the final collapse of Burmese power in 1886, Burmans received military training, were provided with arms and were given the chance of acquiring military experience. All these radical changes in their national and private fortunes gave them a new self-confidence and showed them that courage and boldness had their own rewards.

Notwithstanding the havoc and destruction caused by the war, economic conditions were likewise favourable to Burmese progress. The pre-war economic predominance of the British and Indian capitalist communities in Burma was eliminated almost overnight. The evacuation of Indian landlords and moneylenders enabled the Burmese to recover the possession of their lands and thus to solve the hitherto baffling problems of tenancy and land alienation. With no creditors to worry them, the cultivators produced only for their own subsistence and payed neither rents nor taxes. At the same time, the shortage of imported goods and the absence of foreign competition stimulated Burmese industry and commerce. The Japanese set up a central bank and even sponsored an impressive effort to expand cotton cultivation and cloth manufacture. And state scholars were sent to Japan to study such subjects as banking, engineering and industrial management.

The Japanese occupation, moreover, brought the Dr Ba Maw–Thakin 'Freedom Bloc' to power. Under more peaceful circumstances this more militant coalition would probably have attained a position of influence and dominance only after many grinding years of slow political struggle, if at all. The storm and stress of war and occupation enabled them to jump the gun and achieve a virtual political monopoly. Some of their leaders marched from prison, or came out of hiding, to office. Their greater daring and cohesion, their more pronounced political determination, their superior powers of adaptation, their uninhibited ruthlessness and opportunism, made it possible for them to exploit the possibilities of the new situation in which they found themselves and to emerge, after many vicissitudes, as the country's leading political force.

The leading personality in this movement was again Dr Ba Maw. Arrogant, contemptuous of most of his colleagues, well aware of his own intellectual superiority, a lone wolf, basically a Burman yet genuinely appreciative of European civilisation, he stood head and shoulders above all his rivals or collaborators. Dr Ba Maw was the only Burmese politician capable of taking his place among the prominent leaders of the new Asia. Despite his many flaws, despite his weakness for pomp and flattery, he was the most experienced and sophisticated of all the nationalist leaders. He was also an able and energetic administrator and he had the courage to stand up to the Japanese conquerors when required. All these virtues and defects were to remove him from the country's leadership after the end of the war, but while in power he had grouped around him most of the present people whose names are intimately associated with Burma's contemporary history. General Aung San was the head of the Burma Defence Army and the key man in the new constellation of forces that was emerging in Burma. Thakin Mya, the most capable administrator among the Thakins, was the deputy prime minister. U Nu was the unwilling, yet always ready to accept office, foreign minister. His remarkable political road to power was strewn with countless protestations that he was unfit for politics and that his real talents lay in literature and the hereafter. Thakin Tan Tun, who was later to lead the strongest of the communist insurrectionary groups, was the competent minister of agriculture. And men like General Ne Win, U Ba Swe and U Kyaw Nyein were already occupying important positions.

Dr Ba Maw himself became the 'Adipati' or dictator, and all the powers of the state were vested in him. His government was a form of dictatorship, which was no more than could have been expected, and its slogan was: 'One Blood, One Voice, One Leader'. This was rather more high-sounding than terrifying. He declared that action and results must take precedence over 'talk about democratic rules . . . democratic rights . . . democratic bunk'. He added:

We have . . . accepted a revolutionary task. . . . [When] the work is done and the peril averted . . . people may go back to their old political play acting if they should still want to be amused in that way. . . . Man's will and work and sacrifice [must be] the basis of an all-time national plan.[1]

To implement his programme, to stimulate national endeavour, to mobilise Burma's manpower resources and to assist the Japanese, he sponsored his famous 'Four Armies combination'. These were the 'Blood Army' (the fighting forces), the 'National Service Association Army', the 'Leadership (political) Army', and the 'Sweat Army' (Labour Corps). As a reward for all-out effort he proposed that enemy-owned properties, including land, be distributed in recognition of outstanding service and that those in the urban areas who excelled themselves should be given preferential consideration for state employment. He was also ready to build roads and wells for those communities which showed special zeal. A shortage of transportation and poor communications, coupled with widespread corruption and lawlessness, however, made a mockery of most of his plans and efforts.

Dr Ba Maw, the most Westernised of all the nationalist leaders, also made special efforts to accommodate himself to popular Buddhist and animist beliefs, in order to attract popular support. He took the oath of 'Refuge in the Three Jewels' (the Buddha, the Teaching and the Monkhood) and pledged himself to 'defend the Buddhist faith like the royal defenders of old'. He tried to revive Burma's old political traditions by surrounding himself with the trappings of royalty and adopting some of the customs of the Burmese court. Yet this attempt to combine authoritarianism and traditionalism did not produce any substantial or tangible results. There was much more talk than action.

Dr Ba Maw was not the only Burman to reject the democratic philosophy in which he had been educated and to adopt the language and some of the practices of Japanese authoritarianism. The majority of the Thakins were also, after some hesitation, attracted by Japan's claims to be the liberators of Asia, and were fascinated by its military victories and economic achievements. These revolutionary nationalists powerfully responded

[1] John F. Cady, *A History of Modern Burma*. Cornell University Press p. 463.

to such Japanese slogans as 'Burma for the Burmans' and 'Asia for the Asiatics'. General Aung San, the strongest personality among the Thakin leaders, was even more explicit in his acceptance of the authoritarian philosophy. In a draft programme which he drew up for an independent Burma in Tokyo in 1941, he declared his opposition to parliamentary government on the grounds that 'it fostered the spirit of individualism and thus gives a chance to individualistic disrupters and obstructionists to disturb or delay the cause of administration'. He furthermore declared:

What we want is a strong state administration as exemplified in Germany and Italy. There shall be only One nation, One state, One party, One leader. There shall be no parliamentary opposition, no nonsense of individualism. Everyone must submit to the state which is supreme, over the individual. This form of state we call Republic for want of any other name, but it may become when actually in existence and operation, quite a new state-form peculiar only to our country.[1]

Yet his support for a 'strong state' and for a regime based on 'one party rule' did not prevent him at the same time from advocating the creation of an independent Burma, 'a happy, strong and modern Burma' which will strive 'to raise the general standard of living . . . introduce compulsory primary education and make education more practical and technical . . . cancel all domestic debts of the poorer classes . . . ensure land for the landless . . . abolish landlordism . . . modernise agriculture . . .' and determine on 'a definite policy for the industrialisation of the country'. This 'progressive-sounding' policy was going to be realised in full co-operation and with the help of Japan.

Burmese–Japanese collaboration, however, did not last too long. The cruel and insulting behaviour of the Japanese soldiers, the general suffering and privation caused by the war and the occupation, the fact that the Japanese army lived off the land which they plundered, the dawning realisation that Japan's military supremacy was rapidly coming to an end—all these factors incited the Thakins to begin to organise a resistance movement against their Japanese allies. Contacts were estab-

[1] *The Guardian*, Rangoon, March 1957, p. 34.

lished with the allied forces in India and Lord Mountbatten, the supreme commander, recognised and supported the movement. Starting with sporadic actions against the Japanese in the latter half of 1944 the movement rapidly grew in strength and boldness and with the advance of the allies into Burma the resistance movement came out into the open and turned on the Japanese forces. The Burmese gave valuable help in expediting the capture of Rangoon and in sabotage operations behind the lines. Yet the military role which the Burmese resistance played in the defeat of the Japanese forces was a minor one. But the very fact of resistance nevertheless provided an excellent opportunity for the organisation of a new, broad national front to express the people's determination for national independence— the Anti-Fascist-People's Freedom League. The two Thakins mainly responsible for the organisation and leadership of this movement were Aung San and Tan Tun.

The A.F.P.F.L. was a broad national united front, which soon came to include the socialists, led by Aung San, the communists, led in the main by Thakin Tan Tun, the Burmese National Army, the All-Burma Peasant Organisation, the All-Burma Trade Union Congress, the All-Burma Youth League, various organisations of the minorities (Karens, Mons, Moslems, etc.), Dr Ba Maw's Mahabama party and a number of smaller groups and the Maha Sangha organisation of monks. At the end of the war the A.F.P.F.L., backed by all these organisations and supported by a 10,000-strong army with thousands of disgruntled ex-soldiers in the background throughout the country, fully armed, was determined to finally see the Burmese masters in their own house.

With the return of the British army the colonial authorities planned to re-establish British control over the country. They were at first unwilling to meet the Burmese demands for immediate independence and refused to grant the A.F.P.F.L. the dominant position in the proposed Executive Council which it demanded. The A.F.P.F.L. unhesitatingly went into opposition and soon demonstrated that if the governor would not accede to their demands he could not govern in face of their opposition. In this struggle the League enjoyed many advantages. The country was in a state of revolutionary ferment, incapable of going back to the past after all the excitement, privation, challenge and swift changes of the last few years. The A.F.P.F.L., moreover, had under its control a large and growing force of ex-soldiers and resistance guerillas, organised in the People's Volunteer Organisation (P.V.O.) on a semi-military basis, which it threatened to use in armed conflict against the British. Outside Rangoon the country was in a state of turmoil and the governor's authority was increasingly being ignored. In 1946, to support its demands for complete independence, the A.F.P.F.L. called for a general strike of workers and government employees. Beginning with a strike of 3,000 police, the strike fever spread to all government employees and they were later joined by transport and oil workers. For a few days life in the country was paralysed—deprived of railway and postal services and without a police force. This seemingly impressive demonstration of the A.F.P.F.L.'s organisational ability and popular support forced the resignation of the original Executive Council. The time for a decisive change had come.

The A.F.P.F.L. now entered the Executive Council and in January of 1947 Aung San reached an agreement with the Attlee government, which gave the Burmese the right to freely decide their own destiny and to choose whether to remain within or to leave the British Commonwealth. In April elections were held for a Constituent Assembly and the A.F.P.F.L., headed by Aung San, who had now left the army to become the political leader of his people, received an overwhelming majority. While this was still being drafted, Aung San and five other A.F.P.F.L. leaders were assassinated by gunmen instigated by a political rival, U Saw, an act of violence normal enough in Burma, but this time foreboding a period of large-scale violence and disturbance for the country as a whole. Thakin Nu, then Speaker of the Constituent Assembly, was asked to take Aung San's place. A Constitution creating a Federal Union was approved in September and on 4 January 1948 (a date and hour determined on as most propitious by the best available astrologers) the Union of Burma became an independent state, outside the Commonwealth.

Burma was now free. A sovereign government was in power in Rangoon. The Burmese had regained control of their own country and were now free to shape their own destiny. But unfortunately they were soon to discover that independence was not a heaven-sent gift but a cruel testing time, a ruthless challenge and the prelude to a period of danger and trouble. Right from the start the Burmese had to face two serious and threatening problems. The first was the devastation left behind by the war. The country had been twice stormed across by invading and retreating armies and now it had to contend with all their terrible consequences. Its economy was in tatters. Several million acres of rice land had again been devoured by the jungle; the cattle population had declined by one-third; industries and transportation facilities were in large measure destroyed. Cities and towns had been partly destroyed. The people's standard of living had dropped disastrously. A major sustained and heroic effort was needed to repair the damage and to begin to move forward towards higher levels of production and well-being.

But even before they could begin to grapple with all these ruinous after-effects of war, they were suddenly presented with a second, almost fatal, challenge. A few months after the country regained its independence it was plunged into a series of rebellions which only narrowly missed destroying the U Nu government itself. Burma has had a long tradition of lawlessness and violence. Its outward placidity and easy-going amiability has always rested on the most fragile foundations. This propensity for breaking loose had now been greatly aggravated by the dislocations produced by the Japanese occupation and its aftermath. The war had put arms into the hands of tens of thousands of undisciplined individuals and of numerous unruly bands. The semi-anarchy which had prevailed since the Japanese occupation had permitted and encouraged many Burmans to embark upon an orgy of looting and stealing. Burmese society was now passing through a process of acute demoralisation. There was a severe social, political and moral crisis. A century of foreign domination, war, occupation and resistance had released turbulent and persistent personal, poltical, racial and national ambitions and passions and had sharply disturbed whatever equilibrium had existed. And now the Burman's age-old tendency towards violence and excess collaborated with all these newly liberated distempers to impel the different factions to enter the lists in combat. The whole country was quickly torn and fragmented by an explosion of hatred and warfare such as it had not witnessed in generations. In a fit of uncontrollable fury, groups, parties and races fell upon one another.

The government had to face three main opponents: the communists, army mutineers and the Karens.

Like most of the country's political leadership, the communists too were essentially primitive and parochial. Politics was more a question of personalities than it was of programmes. The Burmese communists had never had any intimate contacts with the international communist movement and their understanding of communist principles and practice was of the most rudimentary kind. Russia was too far away and even the Chinese communists did not extend them any considerable assistance in all the years of rebellion. Though they had some contact with the Indian Communist Party they were most reluctant to follow their advice, partly because they disliked them as Indians. Communists and socialists had worked together in the Thakin movement, together they had accepted Japanese aid and then had turned against them. Their subsequent splits and battles had more to do with personal animosities and ambitions than with genuine differences over fundamental political principles. But now, seeing their chance for a bold stroke, they were the first to light the fires of rebellion.

The communists were split into two factions—the 'White Flag' and the 'Red Flag' Communists. The 'Red Flag' Communists, the smaller of the two groups, were the first to take the path of rebellion. They were led by Thakin Soe, who has been described by J. S. Furnival as a 'man of little education but fanatic zeal'. Branded a 'trotskyite' by his party rivals, a term which has no relevance to the Burmese situation, he is in fact an old-style Burmese dacoit, who has furnished himself with barely understood communist slogans. The bigger group was the 'White Flag' Communists, led by the more intelligent Thakin Tan Tun. In 1946 his popularity as a nationalist was exceeded only by that of Aung San. Soon enough, however, the communists under his leadership came into conflict with the dominant socialist A.F.P.F.L. leadership; Tan Tun was dismissed from his post as general secretary; and in October 1946 they were expelled from the organisation. In the national crisis that followed Aung San's murder, there was a temporary rapprochement between the A.F.P.F.L. leadership and the Tan Tun communists, but this collapsed as soon as the agreement with Britain was signed. Disappointed at his failure to dominate the A.F.P.F.L., thwarted in his ambitions, attracted by a life of insurgence and adventure, Tan Tun and his associates decided to change their policy from that of legal agitation to open revolt.

Using the Nu–Attlee agreement as an excuse, they denounced the military and economic concessions granted to the British government and claimed that the proposed independence was a sham, and that the A.F.P.F.L. had become a tool of British imperialism. At this time, too, Moscow had decided on a change in tactics and was now advocating a more militant insurrectionary line all over the world. In Europe, they were determined to use every means to sabotage the recovery programme supported by Marshall Aid funds. In South East Asia, they urged a policy of overt revolution to overthrow the newly formed 'sham independence' governments. Rebellions broke out in Malaya, Indonesia and the Philippines. The Burmese communists, after attending a meeting of the Indian Communist Party Congress in February 1948, decided to go underground and to launch their armed insurrection against the government. The communists, however, decided to rebel not only because they had received instructions from the Cominform; they also moved in that direction because opposition to authority in Burma was traditionally associated with banditry and they felt that only by violence could they hope to secure power and eliminate their opponents.

Even more serious than the communist rebellion was the growing discontent within the People's Volunteer Organisation. The P.V.O. was the para-military organisation, consisting mainly of ex-service men, organised by the A.F.P.F.L. to back up its demand for independence. It was now an integral part of the A.F.P.F.L. and was prominently represented in the Assembly. It had its units in virtually every locality in Burma and many of its members had ideological or sentimental affinities with the communists. Although the government tried to dissolve it, to absorb the fit and qualified into the armed forces and the police and to resettle the rest in agriculture, the P.V.O. refused to leave the public stage and now decided to intervene in the intensified contest between the government and the communists. It felt that it could unite the left parties, save the A.F.P.F.L., and perhaps secure top positions for some of its prominent leaders in the government and the army.

U Nu tried to meet the swiftly deteriorating situation by a desperate effort at conciliation. He announced a fifteen-point 'Leftist Unity Programme' to form the basis for a new 'Leftist Front'. Under this programme Burma would establish closer political and economic relations with the Soviet Union and the 'popular democratic' countries of Eastern Europe; 'mono-polising capitalist undertakings' would be nationalised; the working conditions and social security of labour would be improved; the state would handle all foreign trade; the Burma Currency Board would be moved from London to Rangoon; foreign aid with 'strings attached' would be rejected; the armed forces would be built into a 'People's Army'; land would be nationalised and distributed to the landless peasants; the state would push ahead with industrialisation; in the frontier areas 'people's governments' would be established; the present bureaucratic machinery of administration would be trans-formed 'into a democratic machinery'; and a 'League for the Propagation of Marxist Doctrine', composed of socialists, com-munists, P.V.O.s and others who lean towards Marxism, would be formed 'to read, discuss and propagate the writings of Marx, Engels, Lenin, Stalin, Mao-Tse-Tung, Tito, Dimitrov and other apostles of Marxism'.

This 'Leftist Unity Programme', reportedly drafted by Thein Pe, a communist leader who had not gone underground, was, as can be seen, permeated with communist ideology and ter-minology and was the theoretical price which U Nu was pre-pared to pay in order to convince the P.V.O. to help him against the communist rebels. Its publication created a stir of apprehension abroad and many in Britain already believed that Burma 'had taken the road to communism'. Although the last point of the programme was quickly dropped, the A.F.P.F.L.

at that time still did not reject 'communist objectives' but only the violent methods by which the 'left-wing deviationists' sought to attain them. Despite all these gestures of accommodation, however, the majority of the P.V.O. ('White Band') joined the general insurrection against the government. This was immediately followed by the mutiny of two of the army's five battalions.

But worse was still to follow. While the government was reeling from all these blows, a new and even more formidable threat suddenly loomed large. The Karen minority, which had for long been seeking their own independent state, preferably separated from Burma, now came forward to press their demands. The Karens, about two million in number, lived in scattered villages across a wide strip of central and lower Burma and retained their own language and social organisation. Many of them became Christians under British rule and constituted an important element in the military and police forces which they recruited. The relations between the two peoples, especially since the eighteenth century, had been one of hostility. The Karens had helped the British to conquer the country, they had served them loyally and were now afraid of the consequences of Burman rule. To placate them the new constitution made provision for the establishment of a 'special region' for them. The Karen National Union (K.N.U.) regarded these provisions as wholly unsatisfactory. They and others who were even more ambitious then began to prepare for the creation of an independent Karen–Mon state, to include much of the Irriwaddy delta. Efforts to reach a mutually satisfactory settlement failed. And in January 1949 the Karens, led by some of the most Westernised individuals in Burma, and joined by the Mons, went into rebellion. They were the most disciplined, skilled and formidable military opponents that the government had to face, and soon Rangoon was a besieged city. The A.F.P.F.L. regime was now hovering on the very brink of disaster. Government authority survived only in a number of isolated administrative centres and in the frontier states. And the whole country was practically in the hands of marauding rebel bands. Law and order had collapsed and the guns held sway.

Yet the government survived. This is the greatest miracle of modern Burma. Rebel divisions and lack of military co-operation, heroic perseverance, U Nu's steadfastness and luck all helped to turn the tide. Although the insurgents might have been at first more numerous than the regular loyal forces, they were not as disciplined and did not have a unified command. The communists had not really organised themselves for the revolt but, in typically Burmese fashion, they had acted more on impulse than on thorough preparation. They had, furthermore, greatly overestimated the extent of their support in the country. Except in scattered areas and intermittently, the 'multi-coloured' rebel groups were unable to co-ordinate their efforts or their objectives. Groups which were in temporary alliance one day started to fight each other the next day. Rivalry and personal jealousies further weakened them. The Rangoon government, on the other hand, encouraged by its diplomatic ties with the outside world, sustained by the emergency income from the government's rice export monopoly, was able to strengthen itself by the purchase of new arms and to provide its loyal forces with those few additional aeroplanes and armed naval craft which helped to swing the balance. Above all, in the midst of all this confusion and violence, a new ruling elite was fashioned, made up of the A.F.P.F.L. and socialist leaderships and the top echelons of the reorganised armed forces, and assisted by the higher ranks of the civil service. This new ruling class, though confused and mediocre, and shot through with archaic prejudices, was yet adequate enough to meet the challenge which had been thrust upon it. It was this leadership, fighting for its very life, thrown together by dire peril and now tempered by the fires of battle, which managed to rescue the country from the abyss of anarchy.

Towards the end of 1949 and the beginning of 1950, the strength of the rebels was gradually draining away and the government slowly began its counter-offensive. Key cities were recaptured. The rebels were driven out of those strategic areas where they had achieved an initial successful occupation and thrust back into the countryside. It was precisely at this moment that the A.F.P.F.L. government had to face a new threat from a remnant of Chiang Kai Shek's troops which had crossed over into Burma and begun to live off the countryside and to pillage and kill its inhabitants. And so, having barely succeeded in overcoming its own rebels, the Burmese army had to divert its energies to fight the Kuomintang troops too. This diversionary operation, however, did not change the decisive fact that the central government had more or less established its authority over the whole country.

Although the insurrections had not been totally defeated then, and have continued as a standing threat and as a source of national instability ever since, they had already, at that time, left deep scars upon the life and habits of the country. Besides the immense material damage which they had caused and were still to cause, besides the heavy national outlays on defence which they necessitated (it has been estimated that during the years 1948–50 about half of the national revenue was spent on anti-insurrectionary activities), the rebellions and the fight which was waged against them further helped to distort the character of Burmese society.

The men with the gun were now in authority, particularly in the countryside. The 'cult of the gun' reigned almost unchallenged. Effective power was passing to the thugs and the desperadoes, to the ignoramuses, to the ruthless, to the 'bad-hats' and 'zeros', as U Nu was to describe them later. In their petty domains, these 'strong men' became little tyrants with the power of life and death over the people. The political balance had shifted to men whose knowledge of the outside world was very threadbare, who only knew Burmese (and therefore knew next to nothing of modern ideas) and whose parochialism was only exceeded by their incompetence. One of Burma's leading army officers, a man both genuinely disturbed about the condition of his country and sincerely devoted to it, once said, in a private conversation: 'The only way one can understand Burma is by realising that the country is being governed by ignorant men and that the only way they can maintain themselves in power is by surrounding themselves with subordinates who are even more ignorant than they are.' These were the men, all aflame with zeal and ignorance, who now assumed the heavy mantle of authority at its highest and lowest levels. And there was insecurity and fear in the country.

The rebel bands which survived naturally lived off the land, terrorising all those who came in their way and spreading havoc and murder wherever they passed. But the villages did not only live in terror of these rebel bands; they also lived in fear of the regular army and of the many para-military groups organised both by the government and by local party bosses to fight the insurgents. Local 'peace guerillas', unpaid by the government, customarily collected gate fees from travellers and sometimes resorted to other more direct measures of personal aggrandisement. The regular army in its operations was often almost as indiscriminately predatory as were the local bandits. Organised dacoit bands, at times in co-operation with the rebels and sometimes alone, spread death and destruction. The crime rate climbed to one of the highest in the world. Within a year of the insurrections over 30,000 people had been killed. Total losses since then probably exceed 70,000 victims. The socialists, who were the leading element in the government, were furthermore charged with abusing their power, with arbitrary imprisonment of their political opponents and with preventing the functioning of rival political organisations. And U Nu had already started to recite his recurring litany of complaints against the conduct of the A.F.P.F.L. and begun his long series of declarations that it had itself become corrupt and oppressive. The breakdown of law and order thus did not only have serious material consequences but also had a calamitous effect on the nation's moral fibre. Dr Maung Maung has called attention to this widespread moral decline:

Old values such as kindness and good neighbourliness declined, and greed and lust and selfishness took hold, not in the lower strata of society only but even in the highest places. Just as crimes of violence and lust increased, so graft and corruption and unashamed grabbing for high office and power tended to become a common, and almost accepted thing.[1]

It was against this unhappy background of violence and lawlessness, moral decline and general social and cultural backwardness that the Union Government began to make gran-

[1] Dr Maung Maung, *Burma in the Family of Nations*. Djambatan, Amsterdam, p. 139.

diose plans for the future, which seemed quite dazzling. The A.F.P.F.L. leadership was now ready to move into a new phase of its ideological and political development. There was now no more talk of a 'strong state' and 'one-party rule', and the programme for 'Leftist Unity' was just simply forgotten. Burma was now to become a socialist welfare state, guided by the principles of democracy and freedom and buttressed by a revival of Buddhist values and Burmese social traditions.

This amalgam of socialism, Buddhism and traditionalism was, however, never split up into its component parts and its separate elements analysed to see if they really fitted together. But it did seem to serve, despite its inherent contradictions, as some rough and ready indication of what the Burmese leaders wanted. For the more traditionalist U Nu, Burma's ancient civilisation required very little improvement. Speaking in Washington he discussed Burma's way of life in these terms:

First of all, as most of you probably know, Burma has a long history. We had a great and flourishing civilisation in Burma based on one of the great religions of the world, Buddhism, at the time when William the Conqueror was crossing the English Channel. This civilisation, passed on to us by our forbears, has now become our national heritage. It is our way of life. We prefer it to any other way of life on this earth. We do not say that it cannot be improved, or that it cannot be adapted to suit modern conditions, but we do not wish to change its basis. We are not prepared to exchange it for any other way of life. This is not a matter of conceit. We do not claim that our way of life is better than that of other people. We merely say that it is different, that it suits us better, and that we cannot therefore be induced to give it up in exchange for some other way of life, be that the Communist way, the West European way, the American way, or any other way.[1]

An official government publication, on the other hand, proudly declared that the new Burma saw no 'conflict between religious values and economic progress' and believed that 'spiritual health and material progress were not enemies but natural allies'. In its opinion, Burma was going to become one

[1] U Nu, 'An Asian Speaks', National Press Club, in Washington, on 1 July 1955.

of the most prosperous nations of Asia, living 'consciously and gladly in the twentieth century while yet remaining faithful to our past'. It was blandly convinced that the country could 'blend successfully the religious and spiritual values of our heritage with the benefits of modern technology'. They were nevertheless ready to make the effort, to align their civilisation and way of life to the demand of the outside world and at the same time to preserve their national identity and the 'traditional principles' which they held dear. Socialism and Buddhism harnessed together would be able to pull the country through the tangle of all its difficulties and dangers and bring it safely to the sunlit and luxuriant shores of progress, abundance, tranquillity and spiritual liberation.

Steps were soon taken to fill all these splendid slogans and sweeping plans with some kind of reality. Official Rangoon suddenly became a place of animation, of excitement, of grand dreams and dizzy ambitions. There was an initial flurry of activity that promised well, and that impressed the Burmese leaders as much as it did the conscience-stricken and well-meaning Western world. In the first place, the government redeemed some of its political pledges. It nationalised the land; limited the maximum size of holdings; promised to distribute the land to the cultivators and labourers who would then become state tenants; guaranteed safe tenure with rights of inheritance but not of sale; limited rentals to no more than twice the amount of assessed taxes; cancelled agricultural debts and set as its aim the encouragement of collective or co-operative farming. It furthermore nationalised essential industries and utilities. It acquired an important share in the mines and in the production of petroleum. It nationalised the sale of rice by setting up an Agricultural Marketing Board. The profits made by the board, provided by the wide gap between the price it paid to the cultivators and what it received from sales abroad, have in fact become the major source of assured revenue. The government was also able to improve transport, to realise some degree of physical reconstruction, and achieve some positive results in education and refugee rehabilitation.

While engaged in the implementation of all these measures the government additionally decided to call upon the outside world to provide it with financial and technical assistance. The British government granted a small loan. A technical aid agreement was signed with the United States government in 1950 and an American engineering company and a group of American economists were asked in 1951 to prepare an economic and engineering survey of Burma and to propose a comprehensive development plan. American technical assistance specialists provided practical assistance in such fields as health and sanitation, transportation and housing, and contributed towards the co-ordination of the numerous economic objectives which the government was interested in. A United Nations Social Services Mission came to advise on welfare needs, cottage industries, public administration and labour management problems and statistics. Finally, all these plans were worked out to form a comprehensive Pyidawtha—which means a peaceful, abundant and happy land—Welfare State programme which the government announced in August 1952.

The new Burmese ministers, moreover, began to travel abroad, most of them for the first time in their lives, in order to obtain additional ideas and inspiration for the new society that they were about to create at home. Study missions consisting of ministers, army officers and trade unionists were sent abroad in a steady and unceasing stream, visiting most countries in the East and the West. Wherever they went they were deeply impressed. They were even sometimes overwhelmed by what they found. They wanted everything they saw, practically, for Burma. They began ordering technicians, equipment, ideas, methods of organisation, on a grand scale and almost indiscriminately, like newly rich and entirely inexperienced housewives determined to furnish their new homes from top to bottom with the latest and the best. A shoal of additional foreign experts, from both the West and the East, were brought in who would begin to teach, organise and prepare the plans for Burma's road ahead. State scholarships were granted for study abroad in England, America, Yugoslavia and Australia so that a new indigenous elite would spring up at once in order to set the wheels of industry rolling. Everything needful in science, technology and twentieth-century methods would now be employed in the country, and on a national scale. Thus under-developed and archaic Burma, it appeared, was going to throw off its backwardness in one fell swoop.

While the Burmese were most energetically exploring the outside world, while they were nonchalantly experimenting with modern techniques and ideas, the government, this time under U Nu's direct inspiration, was also making a concerted and most expensive effort to revive and glorify Buddhism at home. The Burmese government became an active 'Promoter of the Faith' and placed a growing emphasis on the revival of Burma's ancient traditions, folk-ways and culture patterns. They decided to continue to wear the *longyi* (sarong) as opposed to European dress. Ancient pagodas were restored; meditation centres were established; and Buddhist teaching was carried to the non-Buddhist peoples of the Union. Under government prompting the schools and university endeavoured to revive the tradition of doing reverence to teachers and elders. U Nu was instrumental in convening the Sixth Buddhist Council at Yegu near Rangoon, from 1954 to 1956, at which an elaborate cere-monial recitation of the sacred Pali texts was conducted. An imitation cave hall was built for this purpose as well as a 'Peace Pagoda', which were later to serve as an international Buddhist university. The government actively embarked on a policy of restoring the monkhood to the position it had occupied under the Burmese kings. Mass Buddhist spectacles were staged, as in pre-British days. Alleged Buddhist relics from India, Ceylon and China were brought back to Burma in state and amidst great popular rejoicing. An impressive indication of the persistence of animistic beliefs and practices was the fact that the Cabinet as a group made offerings to the indigenous Nats on behalf of the nation. Astrologers, numerologists and spirit women sprouted like mushrooms after a heavy downpour. All told, no small pro-portion of the national resources was devoted to the spreading and revival of Buddhism.

Even U Ba Swe, the leader of the Socialist Party, came up with the novel idea of uniting Buddhism and Marxism as his programme for socialism in Burma. Marxism, he claimed, only deals with mundane affairs and seeks 'to satisfy the material needs of life'. The Buddhist philosophy, on the other hand, 'deals with the solution of spiritual matters, so as to give spiritual satisfaction in life and liberation from this mundane world'. He therefore believes that they have found an inherent correlation between these two mutually opposed philosophies. He claimed, furthermore, 'that being a Marxist helps one to become a better Buddhist and that a study of Buddhism must lead one to a firmer acceptance of Marxism'.[1] And Burma's parliament on 1 October 1951 even went so far as to pass a resolution as follows: 'that this parliament declares its firm belief that it is necessary to devise such measures as would help man to overcome greed (*lobha*), hatred (*dosa*) and delusion (*moha*) which are at the root of all violence, destruction and conflagration consuming the world'. The decision of the Burmese leaders to promote the revival of Buddhism was not, however, deliberately taken in order to clothe the naked innovations which they intended to introduce in an ancient disguise, and thus to make them more palatable to the people, but it was essentially the symbol of their return to the old, comfortable, consoling but enervating customs and traditions of the ancient Burma which they knew and in which they found it most easy to operate.

With the consolidation of its authority over the country, the government began to play a more important international role. It established new foreign contacts. U Nu began to travel to the capitals of the world's great powers—Washington, Moscow, Peking, London—and was received everywhere, but especially in the West, as the genial, moderate and deeply religious representative of the new Asia that was arising. Burma was one of the Colombo powers that convened the first Bandung Conference of Afro–Asian states. It became a shining example of neutralism. Burma became an important station on the road of the new perambulating international diplomacy that was now becoming the fashion. Krushchev and Bulganin, Chou-En-Lai and Nehru, Tito and the Emperor of Ethiopia were among the many international figures who visited Rangoon. The First Asian Socialist Conference, which aroused such great hopes—which were, however, soon enough dashed—was held in Rangoon and Burma's capital became the headquarters of the organisation. Caught up in the swim of things, the Burmese

[1] U Ba Swe, former Prime Minister of Burma, in *The Burmese Revolution*.

government felt that it was making a significant contribution to international life and amity and U Ba Swe even went so far as to declare that the most important achievement of the Burmese government was to have helped save the peace of the world.

Burma's socialist government, moreover, developed particularly close relations with Yugoslavia (after it had broken with Moscow) and with Israel. There was a continuous exchange of delegations between Belgrade and Rangoon, and Yugoslav military experts came to advise its army on how to fight the insurgents but unfortunately without much success. The parochial and easily enthused Burmese and the gushingly adolescent Israelis (particularly when it comes to foreign relations) seemed to fall into each other's outstretched arms. Burma was now ready to incorporate Israel's system of agricultural settlements —the kibbutz (collective settlement) and the moshav (small-holders' co-operative village)—ready made and packaged, into its own society and to import many of the hard-won achievements of Israel's agriculture and of its network of labour enterprises. An agreement was signed, according to which one million acres of virgin land would be brought under cultivation by the two countries for their mutual benefit. This was immediately released to the international press by the Israeli authorities and even the greatest Western newspapers, not knowing very much about Burma, but ready to believe anything that sounded plausible, began to write inspired articles about this great pioneering venture in the cause of freedom, right on China's doorstep. Although this whole scheme never left the diplomatic paper on which it was written, Burma at least seemed on the move and stirred by vast projects and human ambitions.

Many world-famous journalists after a brief stop-over in Rangoon could, after having been told of these and other similar projects, then give it as their well-considered opinion that the Burmese government was one of the most dynamic in South East Asia and the hope of the region. And a number of American and British professors of international relations and lecturers on South East Asia were enabled to write books about Burma, quoting all the paper plans without troubling themselves to examine the brute realities behind them. U Nu was described as the 'Serene Statesman' in an article in *Pacific Affairs* and Guy Wint, in his book *Spotlight on Asia*, put forward U Nu together with Nehru, Bhave and Mao as the 'four main figures in Asia in 1955'. And writers and scholars who themselves were not averse to the blandishments of the West's material civilisation, suddenly discovered the great virtues of Buddhism, precisely because it is a religion of withdrawal and renunciation, as a powerful barrier against communist 'godlessness' and as an appropriate incentive for modernisation.

But although many things can be hidden from the eagle eyes of journalists, university professors, diplomats and politicians, and from all those who are the devoted practitioners of the 'conventional wisdom' of their societies, the relentless march of events has an uncanny way of exposing the true realities behind the soothing and bland commonplaces which protect all these experts and professionals from the cold and harsh facts of the world. Slowly, but with gathering momentum, facts and realities came to the surface which shattered the complacent picture which had been painted of Burma. Some of the authentic problems of Burmese society suddenly pressed their way to the centre of public attention and concern. All the naive expectations which had been propagated about Burma, by Burmese and foreigners alike, were quickly enough scattered to the winds.

It soon became apparent that it was easier to draw up vast plans than to realise them. When the time came to prepare a balance sheet of Burma's first forward-thrusting impulse, it was discovered that there was a wide and dangerous gap between promise and performance. The future refused to be born. The plans which had been drawn up were far in excess of Burma's limited capacities. In every sphere of activity there was the same grim and disillusioning story to relate. The majority of the nationalised industries worked at only 50 per cent of capacity (if that), and were usually run at a loss. Their managers were accused of theft, incompetence and corruption. Only those factories functioned efficiently which were under contract to foreign firms and which employed foreign personnel in the leading managerial positions. Large and wasteful investments were made. A steel mill was built though the only raw material available consisted of war-time supplies of scrap metal which was soon exhausted. A modern airport was built at the cost of two. A pharmaceutical plant manufactured vitamins that could not be marketed. Completed housing projects were often without adequate water and sanitary facilities; and road construction languished for lack of experienced engineers and because of unscrupulous contractors and corrupt municipal authorities. Government boards and corporations abounded, but they were more productive in supplying houses, cars and other benefits to their high officials than in translating plans and appropriations into tangible productive facilities. Burmese businessmen, granted import licences, sold them to the more enterprising Indian and Chinese merchants at a fat profit. Burmese students made a mockery of the free education offered to them by turning the university into a shouting ground for communism; by holding protest meetings instead of attending classes; and by fighting for the privilege of being allowed to stay on for three years in the same class instead of hurrying on to finish their studies. The students who returned from overseas study have tended in the main to prefer not to dirty their starched white shirts by hard work, settled comfortably into managerial posts and found satisfaction in the position and status these bring while they disdained the sweat and effort they ought to have involved. The rank-and-file soldiers sold their weapons to the rebels. Even the Buddhist monks, though given a most prominent and respected place in the community, neglected their spiritual duties and tried to impose their views upon the government, when they differed with it, by riot and turbulence, sometimes even in co-operation with the communist opposition. It is an unpleasant truth, generally acknowledged, that very few of the Western techniques and institutions which the Burmese have tried to introduce, function as it was assumed they would. The modern machine which they tried to build broke in their hands.

Although rice production has increased, the land reform programme has only been carried out haphazardly in a few localities. In 1955, only about 575,000 acres had been distributed out of an available 7·3 million acres. Indebtedness was again becoming a problem despite the fact that government loans had in most cases not been repaid. The State Agricultural Marketing

Board became a byword for inefficiency and corruption. Even Burma's rice strain deteriorated. An I.L.O. survey of labour conditions in Burma in 1955 reported that 'cultivators tend to complain about their low standard of living'. And the 'democratisation of local government' remained a pious hope. The 'colonial' system of administration was retained but without its many positive features.

Burma's general administrative structure was, moreover, completely inadequate to handle the vast new responsibilities which had been imposed upon it. Government administration was both inefficient and dishonest. The top posts were staffed, in most cases, with political appointees who were just plain ignorant, untrustworthy, incompetent and refused in most cases to accept responsibility. Even those who were willing to do a job of work suffered from an inability to take decisions and from fear of making them. The civil service became an arm of the A.F.P.F.L. and lived in the overbearing shadows of the politicians who were dominant in their particular district. U Nu's establishment of the Bureau of Special Investigation to fight corruption only aggravated the problem. Although it tended to check some flagrant abuses of authority, its officers, swollen with power and arrogance, only spread fear and stultified initiative. It was, furthermore, used as an instrument in the struggle for power among the leading A.F.P.F.L. politicians. Corruption and graft, nevertheless, continued to flourish.

It was not surprising, consequently, to find that the foreign technicians and advisers who were called to Burma to work (and some of them really felt, at first, that they were genuinely wanted to play an active role) found themselves hampered and frustrated almost from the moment of stepping off their planes. They came to realise soon enough that the Burmese did not want to make use of their knowledge or experience, that at best they only wanted them to help maintain the façade of modernisation. Sooner or later these men had to resign themselves to apathy and disappointment. One would confess, at a cocktail party among friends, that his Burmese staff at the office seemed to look through him as if he were not really there at all. Another might proclaim, cynically, that he was in Burma on a year's paid vacation. Officially, of course, all seemed to be running smoothly; everyone was very busily engaged upon some great and important project. People began to play up to this situation and this was a game that was rather pathetic to watch. Pretending to do more than one knew was really the case shaped the mouth into a wry twist of a smile, made the voice boom out with unnecessary vigour. It was essential, above all, to write long, thoughtful and well-sounding reports—though one might mock oneself a little for them afterwards, in private. For the Burmese ministers had, and still have, a great liking for reports and for far-reaching plans. They sound so excellent on paper. Thus the era of the report, of the cyclo-styled document and, in consequence, of the file, has been flourishing in Burma. All these papers find their final resting place, too, in one or other of the innumerable government offices behind the imposing red-brick façade of the Secretariat in Rangoon where the ministers work. But one has to do something.

There have, of course, been experts in Burma whose competency could be called into question and whose understanding of the country's problems left much to be desired. It would not be true either to condemn all the top Burmese civil servants, managers, or foreign-trained technicians, both past and present, as unable or unwilling to work well. But there is no doubt that some of the things that are lacking could at least have been supplied if the Burmese leaders had genuinely decided to make use of the experts from the advanced countries. But here, too, the Burmese have shown themselves too proud to admit to their own terrible weaknesses and flaws. Instead of meeting the challenge these men presented when they arrived, the Burmese shirked from measuring up to it. All their old feelings of inadequacy and inferiority came to the surface. Instead of using the power which they now had to exploit the knowledge and experience which they had summoned, they drew back in fear and incomprehension. They turned away from the demands of learning and assimilation which the experts brought to them. For most of the ministers, to have an expert attached to their ministry was a sign of status and prestige. Admiration and a show of deference, not advice or the valuable transmission of experience, was called for.

Burma's democracy, like every other sphere of national life,

THE BURMESE DILEMMA

also suffered from the same cankerous afflictions. Although some of the forms of democracy were maintained, the reality was in sharp opposition to them. Shaped by a history of despotism and violence and of strong men struggling for power, the masses of the people have no understanding of the meaning of democracy and are ill-prepared to make the choices which democracy presents to a mature electorate. Intoxicated by the heady fumes of power, animated by a Messiah-complex, some A.F.P.F.L. leaders even began to proclaim that it would rule for forty if not 400 years. Reared by a country wracked by lawlessness and disorder, the A.F.P.F.L. became a quasi-military political organisation, employing strong-arm tactics and intimidation to uphold its supremacy. It was, furthermore, not only a political organisation. It was also active in many other fields of national life. Through the All-Burma Peasant Organisation it reached out into almost every village in the country. There it was in the position to control and influence the day-to-day interests of the humblest cultivator in ways that he could easily see and understand. Land allocations, crop loans, small and large favours, purchase of the harvest—all these were controlled by A.F.P.F.L. officials. Local 'peace bands' and other para-military formations were their ostensible protectors against insurgents and other dacoits. In the towns the A.F.P.F.L. had its own 'headmen' in every ward and constituency to 'control' and 'guide' the population and to serve as their link with the government and its considerable powers of patronage and coercion. Workers were controlled through the Trade Union Congress of Burma, which was less a trade union than an instrument of party rule. Licences were in its power to grant or refuse. One of Burma's leading army officers once said that the Pyidawtha programme was not really a welfare programme in the Western sense, based upon the country's productive capacities and exertions, but a mere form of undisguised political bribery. During election time both the civil service and the army were mobilised to 'organise' the voters. An indication of how elections were managed and won was given to me in a private conversation. The junior minister involved had received the largest majority in the general election of 1956. When asked to explain how he had achieved this he replied:

In my constituency, all rebel and criminal elements are beaten to death by the villagers themselves, without waiting for the police or the army. I have my own militia in every village. No strangers are permitted to move around without my permission. My motto is: If there is any shooting to be done then it is always best to get in with the first shot. The people did not vote for the A.F.P.F.L., they voted for me because I was there to protect them and to look after them.

The two elections that were held during that period (1951–6) were accompanied by acts of terror and coercion committed by both the government and the opposition (which was mainly communist-inspired). Voters in many instances were brought to the polling booths at gun point. The election campaign was interspersed with gunfire, kidnappings and killings. Although the A.F.P.F.L. now used the language of democracy, they in fact employed the methods of the 'strong state' but without being able to build up a structure of strong and effective government. It was, in fact, both oppressive and incompetent.

Abroad, however, Burma was hailed as a democratic socialist society, as an inspiring example of bold and successful democracy in action. Professor Trager, a leading American 'authority' on Burma, predicted with rare scholarly restraint and understanding that Burma's economy would approach that of 'Britain under Labour or more closely that of the Scandinavian countries'. Unblushingly, he wrote that most of the Burmese intellectuals are committed to a form of 'humanistic socialism' (nothing less than this would do, of course), and 'that Burma will move towards what both the Scandinavians and the Buddha have called the Middle Way'. Even Richard Lowenthal, a sophisticated commentator on international affairs, could write in *Encounter* (Sept. 1960) 'that the regime of the Thakins in Burma' was 'perhaps the most tolerant and democratic of the intelligentsia regimes'. But even sophistication is unfortunately not enough. It has to be married to knowledge.

The atmosphere and state of Rangoon perhaps symbolised more graphically than anything else the condition of the New Burma. In pre-war days it had been known as one of the jewels of the East, as one of its cleanest and most attractive garden cities. The British had built Rangoon in their own image. Their skill had constructed heavy, granite-like buildings along the waterfront, built imposing government offices, paved streets and laid out broad avenues. Stately houses and flowering lawns grew up where tropical profusion had held sway before. But for all that, Rangoon has never really been an urban metropolis in the European sense, to which men of talent or ability are attracted, where they are made welcome, and which develop a distinct culture of its own that in the course of time and movement leaves its mark upon the whole country. It is not that today either. One has the feeling in Rangoon that something unexpected, something formidable, hovers in the air; that the full battle against the surge of nature has not been won completely and that the jungle, in fact, could still return and claim possession over it.

Rangoon, despite its asphalt and concrete European heart, is an Asian town, full of an ancient, all-accommodating passivity. It is at best an unsuccessful mixture, a jumble. There is a seedy and corroded core that is European, and its buildings have been spat upon and stained with red betel juice by totally indifferent passers-by. The lovely houses remain, but tend to grow unkempt with neglect. A few new showpieces have been built, like the architectural college, the polytechnic school, the Broadcasting House and the airport terminal. These (being new) still maintain their gloss for the outside world and the Burmese to admire. Streets are a-bustle with speed and motion too, as in any other city. But the asphalt is cracked and corroded, and the work of patching them up is only intermittent. An extraordinary number of vehicles flow over them nevertheless, consisting mainly of old jeeps, held together literally by a shoe-string or a complicated web of wires, flying like flocks of careless birds in every direction. New buses bought with Japanese reparations, and old ones ready for the scrap-heap, are loaded to the brim with passengers and tear with no regard for safety through all the main streets. There are bullock carts and trishaws and a multitude of bicycles and pony-carts. Crowds throng the pavements, anonymous as everywhere else. Large shops display their choice of wares behind plate-glass show-cases and the cinemas attract attention with raucous and gaudy posters advertising the latest American westerns, long-winded Indian musicals or plain Burmese melodramas. There are lights, shops, banks, offices, taxis, hotels and trains. And yet Rangoon is more like an ancient Asian market place than a European city, for nothing really seems to happen there to mark the passing of the years, except decay.

Rangoon is the modern heart of Burma, the government centre and the commercial centre, but the buildings which symbolise these European elements fit, one feels, only rather flimsily into the town. The European-created core looks solid, exists and functions. Business is transacted, the ships of foreign nations lie in the docks and telephone communications keep Burma, if only ineffectively, in touch with the world. The Burmese are still pulling the switches which the British introduced. But because of the weight of old, slow-moving Asia that is everywhere, what belongs to the modern world seems to have merged with the general, interminable stagnation of the old. The activities of modern civilisation go on, but they have lost their inner drive—their inner life. There are no modern men to sustain them. One feels, after a time, that one has stepped into limbo; into a state where nothing really moves. It is like living in a dream, where everything is unreal, where all the mainsprings of action have stopped; all the motors and engines that impel a modern city into motion merely keep on ticking, without actually driving the whole mechanism forward.

What was far better understood by the Burmese, termed deplorable sometimes, but still apathetically accepted, were the thousands of huts teeming with men, women and children, set up in *kwettits* (townships) which arose and vanished and returned on every vacant plot. They were impermanent, unsafe and wretched. Sudden pillars of fire razed them to the ground and left a blackened char of dust in their place. They were cleared away, either overnight when state guests had to pass along the broad avenues where they spread, or were even entirely eliminated and their squatters moved out of town (as the army officers did in the General Ne Win interregnum). Yet somehow they always began to appear again, and their people filled the pavements once more and the same old indifference, the same squalor—all those symptoms of the languid, timeless, all-pervasive East—also returned. And so the jungle in this way returns, too, with the large rats in the houses, the black crows hovering on the tree branches, the dogs covered with sores roaming about everywhere, the smallpox and cholera and typhoid that come with the hot season, and the cases of plague.

A clean sweep of all these things was made, and even successfully carried out, for a time by the army administration, but this attempt was doomed to failure, because it did not solve the basic problem. The element of determination to eradicate many of the prevailing evils is lacking on all sides. For, towering over the city is not the sense of technological or cultural achievement or ferment, but rather the magnificent bell-like dome of the Shwe-Dagon Pagoda, flaunting a coat of gold against the sky. Under its broad umbrella the images of the Buddha repose, splendid and blissful and remote, evoking the Master's teaching of the worthlessness and vanity of human life and calling upon his followers to liberate themselves from all human desires, efforts and passions. For only by following these austere but essentially inhuman doctrines will they be able to escape the eternal cycle of birth and rebirth and find release from the sorrowful wheel of existence, which can bring only suffering and distress of soul.

This is Rangoon's spiritual core and one feels it in the morning, when the steady clamour of gongs greets the ear, inducing the pious to contribute their alms to the monastery or the pagoda; when in the morning or towards evening the yellow-robed monks go out with their black lacquered begging bowls. Rangoon only really comes to life during the Burmese festivals. Then the languor suddenly lifts and everything is in merry commotion. Every man, woman and child is suddenly busily engaged in building silver-tinselled arches across the streets, in sending Chinese fire-crackers flaring skywards. Whole streets are blocked off from traffic in these times, so that stages can be erected across them and all-night *pwes* (shows) commence with the audiences squatting sleepily around while agile dancers and tumbling clowns amuse them through the sedentary hours against the lively thrumming of gongs and drums and amateur orchestras. There is a multitude of festivals throughout the year. One, the water-festival, lasts for three days. Everything of course closes down. The people then feel they have really come into their own at last; they are no longer impaled by modern society—they can go back into a dim and fairy-tale past, into an ancient, uncomplicated existence.

Rangoon and the whole of Burma lives in the rhythm of an older time and at a pace that is out of step with the twentieth century. Burma has gained independence but this victory was not designed to place the country as a modern nation on an equal level with other modern nations. Victory, it would be rather more true to say, has meant in Burma that ancient Asia has wrenched its original domain from the alien West and that it is endeavouring to reimpose itself once more in all its indolent and unyielding oppressiveness. The dirt, the squalor, the decaying buildings of Rangoon; the continued sense of the permanence of brute nature in the country as a whole, are but the tangible symptoms of the Burmese state of mind. The old Burma, yearning to reject the hated presence of modern commerce and industry, dreaming of an isolated, mythical and golden time when men enjoyed a so-called 'peace of mind' behind impenetrable jungle and mountain fastnesses, is returning once again.

This is the dominating theme in Burma. There is, however, another equally potent one. The Burmese would like to go back to the past, but they have also felt the magic touch of the present, of the modern world. They have become aware that it has attractions to offer which they would like to accept, mixed though these desirable things are with dangers against which they would like to guard. And they realise grudgingly that the outside world is hammering at their gates and that they will, in one way or another, have to come to terms with it.

To live with one open and one obstinately closed eye to reality brings no solution and is not a state of affairs that can last forever. The Burmese are not a race of empty or passive dreamers and they can show courage, decisiveness and practical ability in certain situations. In order to end British rule they openly welcomed the Japanese invasion. They stopped the multi-coloured insurgents at the gates of Rangoon and managed to thrust them back, if only into the deep countryside. They demanded independence and got it. In fact, of all the new countries there are few which can compare with them in toughness, courage and ingenuity. If India had had to face the same desperate situations which confronted the Burmese, it is almost certain that it would have collapsed. Nevertheless, if the Burmese are dissatisfied and disappointed with the results of all their efforts and exertions, it is not because they regret their freedom but because their souls are so deeply divided when they have to decide upon what to do with this independence they have so painfully gained.

Unable to move forward, then, and unwilling to engage themselves or their country in the Darwinian struggle for existence, the Burmese leaders found themselves stymied and hemmed in. Not really ready to adapt Burmese ideas and civilisation to the necessities of modern times, unable to get rid of all the absurdities and inhibitions which hampered their efforts, beset by a mass of difficulties, their original momentum petered out for want of a binding and valid community of aims, and all the centrifugal forces of factionalism, personal antagonisms and disruption within the ruling party itself suddenly came to the surface. The A.F.P.F.L. split at the seams—and nobody seemed to know what principled differences or what great issues of state divided its leaders, least of all, as they frankly admitted, the leaders themselves. The battle began, in the words of U Nu, as a political boxing match, adhering to the Marquess of Queensberry rules, it continued as a 'Fairbanks–Pickford divorce case'; and immediately degenerated into a savage free-for-all.

In a struggle for personal power and nothing else, the leaders of the nation accused each other of having committed all the crimes under the sun and of suffering from a frightful miscellany of defects and weaknesses. U Nu accused his mainly socialist opponents of having turned the A.F.P.F.L. into a Kuomintang-like organisation and declared that some of their leaders were lazy, corrupt and dissolute and that their followers were guilty of murder, theft and rape. The A.F.P.F.L. had become, in his words, 'filled to the brim with thieves, racketeers and opportunists who were in politics to make their fortune'. The socialists (U Ba Swe and U Kyaw Nyein) hurled the same charges back at U Nu and his followers and, furthermore, accused them of being power-drunk, incompetent, primitive and superstitious. In a pathetic exchange of letters between U Nu and U Kyaw Nyein, the latter accused U Nu of having surrounded himself with rich merchants who, by flattery and 'ostentatious offerings of charity and religious works', had incited him against the socialists. He furthermore wrote that U Nu had become a Stalin, autocratic, suspicious and vindictive, who resented all criticism and who was ready to use the Bureau of Special Investigation to punish and liquidate his opponents. U Ba Swe in a later statement said that 'U Nu has not been effective (in the fight against corruption) because he is just a stunt man who makes a lot of noise and gets nowhere because he acts wildly'. U Nu in his reply to U Kyaw Nyein accused the socialists of having behaved disrespectfully towards him, of not having stood up when he entered the room in the presence of foreign guests, of not having commended him on some of his achievements (U Kyaw Nyein had even said on U Nu's return from the Soviet Union: 'We are afraid that you might have turned communist') and of having shielded corrupt elements in the organisation and the civil service.[1]

As the split developed each faction began to organise its own private para-military organisations and there were open clashes in the countryside. No organisation was found to be based on popular support with its own indigenous leaders. The Peasants' Organisation turned out to be the personal property of one; the Trade Union Congress the personal spoil of another. Nothing remained untouched or existing in its own right. From the Burma Translation Society to the Socialist Party, to the smallest A.F.P.F.L. branch in the most remote country district—everything was a glittering prize to be wrested from or held by the one leader or the other. It soon came to light that a fair election would mean driving the peasants to the polling booth at the point of a gun, bribing supporters and threatening potential oppositionists. When he felt that his faction might be defeated, the Buddhist U Nu had no qualms about ruling in parliament with the aid of the communist above-ground opposition. The farce of democracy was then abruptly brought to an end by the intervention of the army. Exasperated by U Nu's collaboration with the communists, fearing that he was going to make a deal

[1] *The Nation*, Rangoon, 10 May 1958.

with the communist insurgents and alarmed by the danger of a possible civil war, the army, it appears, forced U Nu to resign and decided to take over the government.

The question then posed was whether the army officers would be able to do better than the politicians.

The rise of the colonels to power on 28 October 1958 was greeted with naive enthusiasm by many Western observers and journalists. It was claimed that at last the country was in the hands of a dynamic group of reformers, determined to 'discipline Burma into tidiness and efficiency'. And at first it appeared as if the army was going to renovate the country and not alone the city of Rangoon, which they began to clean up with great energy. It seemed that they would really raise Burma, by swift and effective action, to a more modern level of awareness and sustained effort.

The positive impact of General Ne Win's regime was quickly felt. Army units, government employees and civilian volunteers were mobilised to clear the refuse and garbage of the streets of the cities. Hordes of miserable and often disease-infected dogs were destroyed. The incompetent Rangoon City Corporation was dissolved and its management taken over by an army colonel. Monks were moved from the steps of the Great Pagoda. The marshy ground outside Rangoon was drained. Illegal hutments within Rangoon were demolished and the displaced persons living in them were made to build their own houses in a new township outside the city. Consumer prices on staple items were reduced sharply and more than 1,130 fictitious and irresponsible import firms (mainly Burman) were de-registered. The army scored new successes against rebel and bandit gangs. Communist agitation was outlawed on the university campus and their student leaders were jailed. Burma's offshore Coco Island group became a well-populated penal colony holding scores of communist leaders, U Nu supporters, commercial racketeers and corrupt civil servants. Many of the too-ambitious economic development programmes were cancelled and for a time at least it looked as if the orgy of incompetence, extravagance and corruption would be put to an end.

But then, towards the end of 1959, General Ne Win suddenly announced that elections would be held early in 1960 for a new parliament and that power would be handed back to the politicians.

It was rather difficult to fathom the reasons for this precipitous move. For it was more than obvious that the army had become unpopular with many sections of the people, despite the number of tangible improvements which it had introduced; that its attempt to shake up the country, even if only superficially, had not, in the very nature of the case, won it greater popularity. (This, incidentally, is the main justification for the establishment of an authoritarian regime in the newly independent territories. For it is only by severe and unpopular measures that an archaic and stagnant society can be made to change its ways of life and thought, which it is not otherwise able or willing to do, and to adapt itself to the needs of the modern world.) What was even more surprising was their decision to reliquish the power and perquisites which many of the colonels had aspired to possess after only a brief period of office and responsibility.

The mystery can, however, be cleared up if one is familiar with the character of these officers, if one knows who they are, how they live and think and what their capacities are. We can only understand a society by knowing what sort of people undertake what sort of functions in that society. Kingsley Martin, in his usual inimitable and misleading fashion, has described General Ne Win as one who is (no more and no less) '. . . of all the soldiers I have ever met, the most conscientious and sincere in his democratic faith'. General Ne Win may be a sincere democrat but he also gives top priority to gambling, horse-racing and cocktail parties. His lack of ambition does not spring from his democratic faith (which in so far as it exists at all in Burma is a rum enough thing), but from the fact that he feels himself incapable of leading his country and from his lack of deep or enduring commitments to any captivating ideology or cause.

The answer to the puzzle is as simple as it is illuminating. General Ne Win himself, wearied by all his great exertions, wanted to return to the less arduous tasks of social life. Although the army officers—and a few of them were the most capable and dedicated patriots in the country—who had pushed him into politics stepped into power with a show of reforming enthusiasm, they did not offer a new and dramatic programme of change to go with it. They became the rulers only because the A.F.P.F.L. had disintegrated and not because they were imbued with any desire to lead the nation in a new direction, out of the old, recurring cycle of Asian conservatism.

Having no coherent goal or capacious vision, their social programme comprised a number of emergency measures and consisted of a disconnected series of short-term operations. Once they had effected all the things which have been enumerated, the poisons of corruption began to seep through their ranks too (and the dogs and the dirt began to return too) and quickly and disconcertingly they discovered that they did not know what to do with the power they had acquired. Having given the country an intermittent taste of their physical energy they came face to face with the startling poverty of their intellectual and spiritual resources. They had nothing further to offer the nation. And because the officer group was not a united body determined to retain authority, they permitted the holding of an election which would give one of the contending parties the opportunity of returning to power.[1]

Despite reports of army threats and brutality and the open help which some army officers extended to U Nu's opponents,

---

[1] The above analysis was confirmed in a private conversation with one of Burma's leading officers. He said: 'The basic aim of the army regime was to clean up the mess created by the politicians and then to hand the power back to them and thus give them a better base on which to operate. Some of us, however, understood what was necessary for Burma. We knew that we could not move forward without separating religion from the state (and making it a private affair of the individual) and without liquidating the old leadership of the A.F.P.F.L. But unfortunately we were too soft and too weak. We could not muster the necessary strength to act ruthlessly against our old comrades with whom we had worked together for over twenty years. We did not want to become dictators. General Ne Win himself was quite satisfied with his present position and status. He was, moreover, filled with the idea of going down in history as the general who had taken power and then handed it back. Western Socialists and liberals by their uncritical advocacy of democracy for Asia have helped to confuse and bedevil the thinking of the new Asian elites and of the socialists among them. If Tan Tun [the leader of the White Flag communists], had the courage to come out of the jungle, he could take over power within five or six years.'

it was U Nu who scored a landslide victory. The political group which had been associated in the public mind with army rule was overwhelmingly defeated.

U Nu's victory can be attributed to a number of factors, some positive and some negative. On the positive side was his promise to make Buddhism a state religion, the support, both political and military (rebel gangs threatened to burn down houses in the villages if they did not vote for U Nu), which he received from the communists and other rebels, and the fact that he managed besides to rally around his person all the forces of tradition and conservatism which want to maintain the old Burma against the challenge of the modern world. Buddhist monks threatened not to attend the funerals of their followers if they did not vote for U Nu. U Nu also succeeded in convincing the people that of all the politicians he is the least ambitious, the only one who is in politics because the dangerous state of the nation demanded it and not because of his will to power. His highest aim is either to write plays (which show that his talents lie elsewhere) or to retire to a monastery. Many people have come to believe these oft-expressed intentions. But all this is of course a complete deception. It is true that U Nu is not really interested in political ideas or problems, but without the pomp and illusions of power his life would become shrivelled and empty. Although he is a sincere Buddhist, his espousal of Buddhism is essentially a political trick and weapon. U Nu can be as tough and ruthless a politician as the next man, and perhaps even tougher. And his constantly reiterated threats to leave politics and to devote himself to Buddhist study and contemplation is a wonderfully effective form of blackmail.

On the negative side, U Nu's party gained strength from the revulsion against army rule which took hold of large sections of the population.

Exploiting his great personal charm, captivating the nation with his vast and intimate knowledge of Burmese folk tales, playing upon the simple hopes, dreams, superstitions and fears of the people with infinite skill and guided by his primitive peasant cunning and astuteness, U Nu, who has suggested that he may be on the way to becoming a Buddha himself, once again became the prime minister of Burma. And to set the tone for the new regime, one of U Nu's first acts was to travel to Maymyo, the former summer capital of British Burma, perched above the country's dry zone, and there, in the animistic tradition of ancient Burma, lead his people in prayers to the Nats for rain.

U Nu's victory, however, was short-lived. Forced to witness his continued dilatoriness and ineffectuality; his growing policy of adjustment to Chinese pressures; and his fumbling approach to the demands of Burma's minorities for greater autonomy or secession, the army's top command after much hesitation took over power in March 1962 for the second time in four years. But on this occasion they did not define their regime as a 'caretaker' one but clearly indicated that they meant to stay in power for some time. The Revolutionary Council, furthermore, arrested most of the prominent leaders connected with U Nu's administration and made it very obvious that they considered the parliamentary system as unsuitable for Burma. They now openly declared that they saw a 'strong dictatorship' tinged with Marxist slogans and following the 'Burmese way to socialism' as the only solution to the country's problems.

Burma's recent history has thus, after many fruitless and disillusionary meanderings, returned to the political system envisaged by Aung San under the Japanese occupation. However, it is not enough to establish the outward trappings of a 'strong government', one must also know how to rule, and be ready to assume all the heavy responsibilities and burdens which governing in this time of crisis and disturbance demands.

Burma's future, then, is highly uncertain and problematical. The present Burmese elite has not only failed to reform or modernise its society, it has not even been capable of maintaining a united ruling class or of achieving a durable political equilibrium. It has, moreover, so far failed to come to grips with the real problems of its country, not only because of its basic lack of knowledge (which could easily be remedied), but decisively because it has been unwilling or unable to understand the intimate and organic connection that exists between modernisation and the essentially Western spirit and values that make it possible. It has seen the products of industrialism and has wanted them, but has not even attempted to understand the complex and arduous processes which have produced them. It has wanted to build Israeli kibbutzim and moshavim in Burma but it was not prepared to undergo the severe training or assimilate the new habits and beliefs that have produced them, nor was it aware of the almost inexhaustible financial resources that have supported them. It has wanted the ends of industrialisation and modernisation which it took European civilisation many a revolution to achieve and failed to realise that to make them available to their own society it would have to bring about the same revolutions in their own ways, habits and customs. It did not want to accept the fact that there is no easy, painless short-cut to modern civilisation and that to travel this hard road would entail sweeping away many ancient and customary traditions and changing the society itself and everything about it. It was confronted with the need to painfully learn new ways and to make extraordinary exertions and sacrifices.

Factories have been built in Burma, machinery has been brought and installed and men have been hired to run them and managers to plan and organise production. The factories—and even a steel mill—are there. But the Burmese still have to learn about the importance of the clock—they must still fashion industrial workers who have a sense of labour discipline and who are imbued with a feeling of pride in their work. Machines and an indolent, submissive peasant community simply do not go together. Neither managers nor workers are impelled by those economic virtues and habits which make modern industrial production possible. According to the Burmese ethic of respect for elders, subordinates or juniors are prohibited from expressing any judgement—much less from acting upon it in opposition to, or even independently of, an elder or superior. There is no conception of the dignity of labour in Burmese society. Manual labour, in fact, is looked upon as something degrading; as something to escape from. The Burmese ideal is to become a *min*—a government official—to be surrounded with all the pomp and circumstance of power and to be in a position to rule for personal profit and prestige over others. And for them it is the holding of the position rather than any particular achievement in it which is satisfying. Economic development furthermore is virtually impossible in a society where there is little respect for the person and property of strangers and where lawlessness has become a national pastime.

The Burmese are by no means unaware of the presence of the demanding and pushing modern world, but they have not really felt that they must accept the necessity of going to learn in the strict and highly disciplined school of modern civilisation. And things have been made easier for them because no strong, critical world opinion has condemned them for not doing so. The world, on the contrary, has been treating them, as it has all the Afro-Asian countries, with condescension and flattery. It has been much easier for the Burmese, therefore, to join the Afro-Asian camp and feel themselves a power to be courted abroad than to provide answers to their own problems at home. Playing a role in international affairs, without having to pay any price for it (except the opening up of their country to communist penetration), is a far from unpleasant game, even if not a very rewarding one. And Western sentimentality and guilt feelings towards these countries has helped to exalt the international role of all the weak, unreformed and irresponsible Asian and African states and to leave them unprepared to face all the consequences of their folly and their flight from reality.

For a voice in international affairs cures not a single dilemma at home. Because they have done nothing about their own problems, the Burmese, while garbing themselves with old traditional clothing and new modern slogans, have only created for themselves frustration and neurosis.

It has led to a deep-seated discontent, not only among the army officers, the handful of intellectuals and other professional elements, but even the man in the street feels the same uneasy dissatisfaction. The old, carefree happiness does not exist—and perhaps it never did. Going back to some golden past is only one kind of yearning. It is balanced by the knowledge that the nation has to go forward, into a better future. The past and the present thus clash ruinously in Burma and the Burmese feel ground and crushed between its millstones. Because of these contradictions and mutually antagonistic impulses, the Burmese have become a nation of divided souls and of split personalities.

Faced with the choice between independence and civilisation, Burma has always, in the past, chosen independence. This choice no longer exists. For if Burma still wants to maintain her independence she should now also bind herself to choosing, whole-heartedly, the modern civilisation that goes with it—the necessity of lifting herself up to the level of the outside world, which she has always managed to evade in the past. She should substitute a forceful, dynamic and active life for the old, slow bullock-pace of the present one. This, of course, calls for a radical change of soul, a real revolution in depth. It will not be engineered by men who are rooted to the past, or by those who waver between past and present, but by a new kind of spirit— by new men who desperately want to belong to the twentieth century. Burma's leaders (both civilian and military) so far have been appalled by the difficulties of this task and by the enormous demands made upon them. They ought now to try to develop a new kind of leadership, which will be ready to make change the centre of its ambitions and policy and which will strive to remove every psychological and social block that stands in the way.

If men of this type come to the fore in Burma, who are single-mindedly, puritanically and even fanatically intent upon taking their country out of the circle of a frozen and enervating history that is over and done with and into the mainstream of Western civilisation, with all its splendours and miseries, the Burmese will lose their reputation for gentleness and softness, but they will have something a good deal more vigorous to look forward to. The modern world might appear to be coarse and hard and demanding in Asian eyes, but the old Burmese gentleness and softness has, in most cases, covered a multitude of oppressions and corruptions. It has been a blanket for despotism and for accepting one's fate of backwardness and poverty with reasonable cheerfulness as inevitable; it has served as a cover for man's inhumanity towards man and has chained human individuality and vitality. What is called for now is the creation of a hard core in Burmese society and this work can only be done by men who place a hard centre within themselves, who will subject every sphere of Burmese life to critical examination and questioning and who are ready to make all the necessary transformations. Before Burma can move forward into our revolutionary age and forge the social, economic and human vigour and resilience necessary for a stable democratic existence, she has to pass through a reformation in her national conscience and an entirely new deal in her emotions. Something drastically new is required to arouse the people, to release their energies; to concentrate their will. Burma will not even begin to move forward until its elite will have begun to question the fundamental tenets of Buddhism and until it will have brought about a religious reformation.

In this, then, lies the Burmese dilemma. For there can no longer be any question of continuing as an archaic, agrarian society, steeped in worn-out and lifeless traditions and ornamented with a few ceremonial Western forms. Burma is faced, rather, with the inexorable necessity of choosing either to be conquered and reshaped by the violent and blood-strewn methods of Communism or to be made free and strong by a new and radical force coming from within her own society, which will break with the past while not necessarily renouncing it and which will lead the nation with a strong, strict, yet humane hand towards fulfilling itself in the contemporary world.

Chapter 4

THE IRRELEVANCE OF
ASIAN SOCIALISM

i

As we have already seen, most of the leaders of the newly independent countries regard themselves as socialists of one kind or another. We therefore now have assorted types of Arab socialism, of African socialism and of Asian socialism. In Asia in particular, socialist sentiments have become almost universal. It could even be said that socialism has become the predominant ideology in South East Asia. Almost everybody is a socialist. Kings and maharajas, wealthy landlords and rich merchants, princes and playboys, saints and sinners, students and their teachers, illiterate peasants and workers, all have declared themselves to be socialists. And even those regimes which do not call themselves socialist and which are considered as most reactionary by 'advanced opinion' (as in Formosa, South Korea, South Viet Nam, Thailand and Pakistan) are in practice not much different from those governments which regard themselves as socialist or are looked upon as such by the majority of Western socialists.

Socialist parties exist or 'socialism' has triumphed in countries which have barely emerged out of the late Iron Age, in simple, primitive and agrarian societies, in Himalayan mountain fastnesses, in societies which still practise animism, and in Moslem, Hindu and Buddhist countries encrusted with millennia of inhuman traditions and superstitions. But one crucial fact characterises them all—these are all pre-industrial, pre-scientific, pre-rationalist and pre-democratic societies; some are even societies which are pre-Hellenic and pre-Biblical in their essential mental make-up. None of these countries have passed through all those profound revolutionary transformations—the Renaissance, the Reformation, the Enlightenment—which have shaped and tempered the outlook and character of modern Western man. Their socialism is therefore by its very nature of a completely different kind from the classical socialism of Europe. The social realities which have given birth to European socialism hardly exist in any of these countries.

In Cambodia the socialist party is called the Popular Socialist Community Party, and is led by the former king, Prince Norodom Sihanouk, who voluntarily abdicated in order to form and lead this party. This party is the only organised political body in the country and 'won' all the 91 parliamentary seats in the last general election. In Nepal, the socialist party is the Nepali Congress, led by P. B. Koirala, who was the prime minister of this country until he was placed under arrest by the king in December 1960. Its chairman is one of the biggest landowners in the country. In Ceylon, the present 'communalist' government calls itself a socialist government. All these parties are connected with the Asian Socialist Conference, which is the already moribund 'international' organisation, formed by the democratic socialist parties of Asia. In India, Burma and Indonesia, 'socialistic' governments are in power. In Singapore a militant socialist government is in office. Opposition socialist parties also exist in India, Japan, Indonesia, Burma and Malaya.

The basic issues which agitate the advanced socialist parties of Europe are, however, completely irrelevant in Asia. No significant capitalist class exists anywhere. The industrial proletariat is extremely weak. The most pronounced form of property is the tiny plot worked by a primitive and hopelessly inefficient peasant. Asia, moreover, is not so much faced with the problem of redistributing wealth as of creating wealth. In all these countries the question is not how to raise living standards but how to make the initial investment that will initiate the process of self-sustaining growth across the threshold of stagnation and growing misery. One of its main contemporary tasks is to create a modern society, not a welfare state. It is not faced with the need to civilise an existing industrial system but with the need to lay the foundations of an industrial civilisation. Poor in capital, poorer still in entrepreneurship, private and public, government planning and state ownership of key resources of one kind or another are inescapable necessities everywhere, for every regime, no matter what it calls itself, if these societies are to be held together at all, not to mention their necessity if those countries are to implement a wide-ranging programme of development and modernisation.

The Formosan government, for example, has thus carried out an agrarian reform, has implemented a number of four-year development plans, and it has been estimated that government enterprises produce about 50 per cent (by value) of industrial goods. South Korea's constitution, which was drafted when Syngman Rhee was still in undisputed control, provides for government ownership of public utilities, financial institutions, transportation and communication facilities and mines. The government is additionally responsible for many other industrial enterprises as a result of nationalising property left behind by the Japanese. Government enterprises, furthermore, play an important role in all the newly independent countries. In Pakistan government planning and state encouragement of industrialisation is almost on as extensive a scale as in India. In Franco Spain, to take a current European example, the government is a weighty factor both in the country's economic life and in the labour field. Nationalisation or government planning in themselves, therefore, do not determine the character of a society, and do not convert reactionary dictatorships or hopelessly corrupt and obsolete regimes into socialist ones. In Asia, the Middle East and Africa, in any case, the problems are of a different nature and although some of the institutions and some of the methods might look alike, they basically serve a different purpose and assume a different complexion.

The problems of Asia, moreover, are of a different order of magnitude and call for a different set of priorities. The most fateful decisions which the leaders of the newly independent countries must take, no matter what label they have assumed, lie not in the political, economic and social fields, but in the larger and more momentous fields of culture and of basic human values and aspirations. For the real conflict in Asia (as in all the other underdeveloped countries, wherever they might exist) which so many Westerners find it so difficult to comprehend is the conflict not only between different political philosophies and economic systems or rival power blocs, but between the fundamental assumptions of Western civilisation and of Asian civilisation. Asia is today a separate world of violent contrasts, painful tensions and exasperating instability, not because its people are inherently dissolute or deficient in human capacities, but because it is caught in the imperious grip of an acute and inescapable conflict of fundamental ideas of civilisation at war with each other.

It is only against this background and within this context that the relevance or irrelevance of Asian socialism can be judged. These preliminary remarks should, furthermore, make it clear that the old labels and concepts which might conceivably still illuminate political and social realities in the Western world, where they were first articulated and cultivated and fought over, undergo a violent sea-change when they are transplanted to a completely different environment. Yet if non-Western politicians and intellectuals want to call themselves socialists, one can do very little about it except to accept this designation of themselves and try to understand the distinctive framework in which they live and the genuine problems they are trying to solve. To delineate the specific nature of Asian socialism, then, we must attempt to trace some of the leading ideological influences which have shaped some of its parties and leaders over the past few decades.

At the end of the second world war a number of political parties calling themselves socialist appeared in South East Asia. They differ from one another in many respects. Each was shaped by the particular national characteristics of its own country and by a diversity of ideological and political influences. But they have a great many features in common and because of these common features they can be classified as belonging to a distinct political species.

In South East Asia, socialism arose as an ideological and political current inside the various national movements against Western rule, which sprang up in that whole region between the first world war and the end of the second world war. It was not, like communism, organised from abroad, but evolved out of the process of nationalist revolt. Originating in the nationalist movement, it formed, at first, only its left wing. But when these countries achieved sovereign statehood their socialist groups asserted their own independence. This was the case in India, where the socialists had been a minority group inside the

Indian National Congress and then severed their ties with that body and formed an opposition party to it. In Burma and in Indonesia, the socialists, who had played the leading roles in these countries' nationalist movements, afterwards formed their own distinct political parties.

The common experience of foreign domination and of fighting for national independence, therefore, constitutes the very scene and sphere within which Asian socialism found itself and developed its own unique characteristics. One cannot begin to understand the inclinations, the prejudices, the inspirations and the impelling motives of Asian socialism without taking into account its heavy entanglement with the forces of colonialism and nationalism.

Nationalism was and still is the pivot, the most meaningful and the most overwhelming compulsion in the lives of the Asian socialist leaders. Their concern with the issues of nationalism has moulded and influenced all their political activities. It is the axis around which revolves their whole universe of values, passions and ideas. For the majority of Asian socialists, to champion the cause of nationalism and to denounce colonialism is the beginning and the end of political virtue and wisdom. Even for the minority whose political horizons extend beyond nationalism, the reality of foreign domination and the struggle against it still touch deeply buried cords of instinctive sympathy which overrule every other consideration. Out of this searing experience ideologies have been woven, national policies contrived and personalities have grown and been formed.

Their concern with nationalism has, moreover, made them cling to the immediate past of opposition, to the memories of struggle rather than to the fact of victory and has dangerously limited their ability to move forward to meet the pressing problems of the post-independence era. Many of the former embittered and deprived revolutionaries have now assumed control over their own national affairs and have very tangibly realised their ambitions for power, position, authority and status. Some rule at home and all are respected and honoured abroad. This dramatic change in their fortunes has not, however, rid them of their old feelings of inferiority and of hurt national pride. In these backward countries, where audacious enterprises of innovation are called for and where a wrenching national renaissance is demanded, the Asian socialists have been unable to purge themselves of their old humiliations and resentments in order to fit themselves for the immense efforts which await them. Nations, like individuals, can only be—as far as that is possible, and then, at best, only precariously—at ease and secure in the world, neither militantly arrogant nor tormented by their own sense of inadequacy, when they feel and know themselves to be creative. Only in the crucible of monumental efforts, of great national and individual achievements, will they be able to forge that necessary self-confidence and self-respect which will enable them to face the world on more equal terms. But that has not yet even so much as begun to happen.

In conflict with an imperialism which they identified with capitalism, many of the more radical elements within these national movements turned to socialist ideas, both as aids in their struggle for freedom and as the nebulous image of the future society they hoped to create after independence was attained. In those early formative years Marxist ideas played the predominant role in fashioning their conceptions of socialism.

They were attracted to Marxism, however, not because they understood or accepted its radical critique of Asian civilisation, or its rational approach to life, or because they saw it as one of the movements—heretical and utopian as it was and wrong-headed as were many of its analyses and predictions—generated by the development of a Western, secularised industrial civilisation. And they were very far from accepting the Marxist, which was also the general, nineteenth-century liberal assumption, that the strenuous and energetic Western industrial civilisation which was their common meeting ground was the most revolutionary and creative society, despite all its flagrant blemishes and injustices, that mankind had ever known. The Marxism to which they responded and which they were ready to imbibe was something much less complex or provoking, and more conservative. Their approach to Marxism was very selective and discriminating. They borrowed from it only what suited their immediate interests and tastes and incorporated only those ideas which they could readily and without too much

THE CHALLENGE OF MODERNISATION

friction assimilate into their general nationalist outlook. The
heady wine of nineteenth-century Marxism, or for that matter
of liberal civilisation, had to be watered down considerably
and made a much thinner brew before they could even begin
to taste it.

But Marxism provided a few good props which had their
uses. In the more primitive form of Leninism-Stalinism, it gave
them a very convenient and psychologically satisfying absolutist and simplistic analysis and critique of the imperialism
against which they had declared open war and which held
them in its grip. Its militant and extremist sentiments, its calls
for uncompromising mass struggle, its emphasis on mass
agitation, boycotts, strikes and even insurrectionary actions,
answered their spiritual needs for a more violent rejection of
their foreign rulers. Its militant and extremist sentiments were
like new ideological weapons thrust into their hands, which they
could use to oppose the more moderate elements in their own
nationalist movements. In Marxism they found 'a hard edge to
the struggle for freedom'. It gave their anti-imperialism a radical
and revolutionary hue and offered them a fleeting sense of
greater strength and confidence. Marxist ideas provided a new
direction to their political energies, prompting them to organise
trade unions and peasant organisations as reinforcements to the
national struggle and as additional sources of strength to
support it.

Once they came into contact with the 'masses' in these
organisations they were brought face to face with the 'social
question', and this forced them to see their own people's terrible
poverty and to try to find the means of overcoming it. In this
context, their own form of primitive Marxism came to be
an emotionally charged message, containing both prophecy and
promise. It predicted disaster and ruin to the rulers as retri-
bution for the power that they had wielded for so long. At the
same time it promised a utopian future of social harmony,
peace, justice and material prosperity, all of which would
automatically follow (as some seemed to have believed) the
triumph of their national revolutions and thus they would be
recompensed for all the degrading and inferior conditions
which, they believed, had been imposed upon their societies.

Finally, they identified Marxism with the Russian revolution and with the growing strength and successes of the Russian state and this proved a great source of encouragement to their own aspirations for independent statehood.

Although they greatly admired Soviet Russia, they never, however, accepted its guidance in formulating their programmes. This (as well as significant differences in personal psychology and temperament) was their main difference with the communists. They never had any organisational or financial ties with the Comintern but the various socialist groups did, in the beginning of their political careers, attempt to collaborate with the local communist parties.

Gradually, however, their contact with the local communists and events in Russia itself began to make deep inroads into their admiration for communism and finally led to their disillusionment with it. In India their break with the local communists came after the socialists admitted the local communists into their party, in an effort to realise 'socialist unity' at the time when the socialists were still operating within Congress. This experiment, lasting for four and a half years, taught them an unforgettable lesson. They experienced, at first hand, the communist's utter unscrupulousness and grasped the political fact that the communists had been using the slogan of socialist unity as a mere manœuvre with which to undermine the socialists and to take over their organisation. In Indonesia, a united socialist party was established in 1945. Within this party, two distinct groups soon became noticeable. One consisted of nationalists with left-wing socialist views. The other was made up of communists who had infiltrated the party in order to capture it from within. The conflict between the two resulted not only in a split within the organisation but also in the socialists taking the lead in suppressing, after several weeks of fierce and bloody fighting, the communist-organised rebellion against the Indonesian Republic of 1948. It was only after this extremely costly, but highly enlightening experience of communist treachery and rebellion that the Indonesian socialists could re-establish their own independent party in 1949. And in Burma the socialists and communists have been locked in violent struggle since 1948.

Their ardent admiration for Soviet Russia also began to cool as the true nature of the Russian regime began to reveal itself to them. For some, the first great shock which upset their trusting confidence in Russian communism were the purges of the late thirties, in which the old guard of the revolution was liquidated. This influential event opened their eyes to the regime of terror by which Russian communism maintained itself in power. For others, there were additional shocks to produce disappointment and disenchantment. Stalin's pact with Hitler; the twists and turns of the local communists as they had to follow every new zigzag of Russian policy; the communist sabotage of their nationalist movements during the second world war; Russia's expansionist policy at the end of the second world war; Stalin's peremptory expulsion of Tito from the Cominform; the ever-growing mass of information showing and exposing the totalitarian character of Russian society, the brutal Russian suppression of the Hungarian revolution—all these factors contributed to their final ideological rupture with Russian communism. On a different level, a further important factor in their disillusionment was their recognition that Soviet communism represented only a variant of modern technological civilisation, more inhuman and threatening than the original Western model but clearly tainted with the same basic motivations and constituting the same kind of challenge to their own native traditions. Much nearer home, all the non-communist regimes of South East Asia have come to feel in recent years the tremendous and ever-growing threat which the extravagant and restless ambitions of Chinese communism presents to their independent national existence.

Although they all, without exception, fully understand and fear the danger of Chinese expansionism (even if this might not always find clear and bold public expression), yet this menacing knowledge has not incited them to that level of effort and critical self-awareness which this peril calls for.

All these disturbing and dismaying experiences, as well as the new knowledge of Russian and Chinese communism which they acquired, sharply changed the direction of their thinking. They became more clearly aware that their differences with the communists were not limited to practical or minor doctrinal issues, but concerned much more fundamental matters than they had, earlier, thought was the case. They were forced to rethink and to re-evaluate many of the ideas which they had formerly firmly believed in and to look about for new ideological foundations on which they could build their own structure of Asian socialism.

Although this search for new ideological foundations has nowhere yielded any basically satisfying new synthesis, it has led a number of the representative figures of Asian socialism to formulate ideas and perspectives which more directly give expression to the indigenous Asian environment in which they live.

Repelled by the inhumanities of communism, by its totalitarian excesses, Asian socialists have vaguely defined their general political objectives as that of democratic socialism. Within the last few years, however, important voices have even begun to call into question the validity and relevance of Western democracy to Asian conditions.

Unable, unwilling and perhaps incapable of integrating themselves into the framework of Western socialism, they have come forward with the dogma of a distinctive Asian socialism, differentiated from Western socialism not only by its anti-colonialism, its policy of non-alignment in world affairs, but also by its basic cultural values and by the massive fact that they must operate in peasant and underdeveloped societies of 'teeming millions and low technology' and must, therefore, pursue their own path of socialist development and their own pattern of industrialisation. Now that they have attained national independence, many of them are becoming impelled by the desire to discover, within their own national traditions, the ideological and cultural inspiration for their political conceptions and social programmes. As a result there is a movement in many of their parties to return to ancestral symbols and traditions, to more indigenous ways of thinking and living, and to 'go back home'—from where they had only temporarily strayed in the heat and press of their struggle against foreign domination.

For those who are in power, the immense difficulties in governing, in raising the level of their backward societies and in achieving quick and dramatic results have made them much more cautious and restrained in their internal policies. This cautious spirit has, however, in compensation been eloquent by its absence in their foreign policies. For the others, particularly in India, the Himalayan scale of the problems which face that country, the immense efforts which are needed to stir into action the inert, passive, change-resisting mass of the Indian people, have made them retreat to simpler, less risky and less demanding programmes of national development. But everywhere, appalled by the difficulties of initiating development, let alone realising prosperity and welfare, there has been a narrowing of horizons, a fatalistic yielding to circumstances and a precipitous drop in ambitions and hopes. Over the whole movement there hangs a cloud of discouragement and a feeling that they are living, perhaps, on borrowed time.

All these emotional and political currents, coalescing, have brought about a general reluctance to meet the tremendous challenge produced by the Asian encounter with Western civilisation. All these influences, jumbled together, have produced political parties, programmes, ways of thinking and a general approach to the problems of their own societies and of the world which constitute a separate though highly fragile political movement and a local response to the conditions of their own region.

The following, then, is a brief survey of some of the 'rethinking' that has been attempted.

INDIA

In India, the major drift of socialist thinking is in the direction of merging socialism with Gandhiism. The leading exponent of this new tendency is the well-known, highly popular and immensely respected socialist leader, Jayaprakash Narayan.

Unlike some other socialist leaders, whose advocacy of a specifically Asian socialist path of development springs from a fierce spirit of revolt against the West, Narayan's brand of Indian socialism stems rather from his recent complete identification with the Indian way of life, and from his recognition, quixotic and utopian though it may be, that contemporary India cannot and should not follow any other pattern of social development. Implicit in his whole approach, however, is a total rejection of Western economic, cultural and social values. At the heart of his creed there is a desire to freeze the development of Asian civilisation; a quest for the certainties of a static type of society; an attempt to escape from the harsh choices which history so often imposes; and a conception of man which deprives him of his tragic grandeur, of his pain and suffering and of his sense of joy and exaltation in life's unfathomable and open possibilities.

Narayan starts off from the premise that there is a great similarity between the Russian and the Western economic systems, in that both of them are based on 'big concentrations of production, industrial development represented by huge machines, very high productivity and much investment of capital'.[1] He believes that this form of economic life is not suited to a human culture that is to include freedom and that its heartless conglomeration of machines, its frenzied pursuit of an ever-rising standard of living, has a deadening effect on the individual caught up within it. Man becomes enslaved to institutions and to technology, his humanity is forgotten and his freedom is limited.

Proceeding from this he advocates an economic system which would be based on the small economic unit, guided by the ideal of converting the home into a workshop. He particularly lays stress on the need to abolish private property in land and to transfer all property rights to the village, constituted as a co-operative. A redivision of the land, together with the development of cottage industries, is his solution to the economic problems of India. Only in this way, he believes, can the people be rescued from their abysmal poverty. And only thus can his aim of making every village as self-sufficient as possible be realised.

Although he recognises that this programme could not be universally accepted, he yet believes that on balance 85 per cent of the economy would have to be decentralised in the

[1] *Cultural Freedom in Asia.* Charles E. Tuttle Co., Vermont and Tokyo, p. 217.

fashion above described and the remaining 15 per cent would have to be given over to centralised industries like metallurgy, power and railways. But his ideal is a society where every village would be a

community—a direct community, a face to face community; of people living together, knowing each other, a kind of enlarged family; producing all the food and all the clothing it needs, its building materials. In such essential matters every village should be self-sufficient, so that life is not interfered with by people sitting in some far away government office.[1]

Only communities thus organised can realise and fulfil the great ideals of Asian religion that

. . . we are living in order to achieve our deliverance, whether we call it Nirvana with the Buddhists or Mokshe with the Hindus— deliverance from the limitations of time and space, from the limitations of life and death—from bondage. This was regarded as the noblest effort—the noblest ideal for human kind to follow— deliverance.[2]

Asia has, therefore, not to search for any new path—or any new idea to guide it in its present period of transformation— but must try '. . . to build on the foundations that already exist . . .' The task of Asian leaders is to persuade the peoples of Asia to practise the religions that they profess, to work with the existing formulas and to practise what they believe here and now.

Rejecting the idea that socialism might be equated with mere economic growth, or that the dynamics of social change must be based on a conflict of 'self-interest', he advocates the need for the individual to voluntarily '. . . subordinate his own interest to the large interest of society'. He is therefore not in favour of distributing wealth, but of sharing wealth. 'Equality does not consist in taking from the rich and distributing it to the poor. But in the poor setting an example to the rich by practising equality first of all among themselves.' To achieve this, however, requires the '. . . construction of a new type of

[1] *Cultural Freedom in Asia.* Charles E. Tuttle Co., Vermont and Tokyo, p. 218.
[2] Ibid., p. 19.

human being . . .' And this movement of human reconstruction, removed from the vicious circle of party politics, indifferent to the political goals of the capture of state power by parliamentary or other means, is the great need of the hour.

Having, as he has stated, tasted both the ashes of independence and of socialism, he has decided to withdraw from 'party and power politics' and to devote himself to the Bhoodan movement of voluntary land reform. He feels that the parliamentary democratic system which India has borrowed from the West is 'something foreign, implanted from the outside' and bound to fail under Indian conditions. He therefore recommends that a political system should be developed which is more Indian, 'more suited to the soil' and one which the people themselves will be able to understand and practise. This new 'communitarian' system will have to be based on the villages, which should become the 'primary brick' of the new structure. And these villages 'do not require the party system' but should take their decisions on the basis of a 'general consensus of opinion'. He believes that the political and economic tyranny of the nation-wide political parties should be broken.

The state that he envisages for India is to be a confederation of self-governing communities. It would form not a bureaucratic but an organic hierarchy, from the village community through regional district and state councils, all elected, except at the village grass-roots, by indirect vote based on the personal merits of the candidates.

Without entering into the merits and defects of this kind of political structure, it is only relevant to point out that this kind of system is also being advocated, with minor variations of terminology (but without the same moral fervour), by such disparate figures as General Ayub Khan of Pakistan and Colonel Nasser of Egypt.

A more violent and astringent advocate of Asian socialism is Dr Lohia, who at one time served together with Jayaprakash Narayan in the leadership of the Praja Socialist Party, but is today the leader of a 'more militant' splinter group within Indian socialism. More than in most other Asian socialist leaders, there is to be found in Dr Lohia a deep feeling of rebellion against the most prominent features of Asian society, but this feeling of rebellion is unfortunately allied with utopian and naive notions of the role of Asian socialism which vitiates his whole approach. He is also animated by a spirit of hatred of the West and of violent opposition to the civilisation of the 'pink-coloured peoples'. In his case, a violent form of rhetoric is allied with a pathetic form of practical impotence.

Returning from a trip which he had made to Europe and America, he wrote bitterly and scathingly of an Asia of 'teeming millions, of dirty and impotent millions, of ill-fed and diseased children, of fouled humanity sprawling on roadsides, prostrate with the common disease of poverty'.[1] In the hungry two-thirds of the world, he believes, man has been reduced to a beast of burden, homes more often than not are pig-sties and man is listless. In his view, Asia suffers from the following five major diseases:

(1) The existence and growth of politics based on religion, caste or race; (2) the prevalence of government by repression or terror and opposition politics by armed rebellion or assassination; (3) the rise of a new middle class or bureaucrats and politicians with expensive European habits; (4) the undisputed leadership of phrasemakers or stage-actors whose deeds are negligible; (5) the absence of a social philosophy and comprehensive policies and programmes. The fifth disease is the root cause of the preceding two diseases and also gives powerful nourishment to religious and terroristic politics.[2]

Although he too believes in the necessity for a specifically Asian path of socialist development, he has yet realised that Western civilisation has great achievements to its credit in the fields of revolutionary technology, rising standards of living and social equality and that

. . . it has been the active element in human history for the last three hundred years.

. . . Asia and Africa have not been that active and in the last 300 years have been slothful. I am not an Indian who speaks of the past spiritual glories of his country. Whatever the past or the future, our

[1] Rammanohar Lohia, *Aspects of Socialist Policy*. A Socialist Party Publication, July 1952, p. 3.
[2] Ibid., p. 10.

present is muck. The most dominating character of my part of the world is sloth and indolence.[1]

To meet this kind of situation, to stir into activity the moribund peoples of Asia and Africa and to harden the 'world's soft belt from Egypt to India', Lohia advocates the adoption of an Asian socialist programme, which will be drastic instead of gradual, unconstitutional though using peaceful methods of non-violent resistance, and one that will have to emphasise the problems of production which in the advanced countries have already been solved.

But his approach to the problems of production is to be radically distinguished from that of Western capitalism and democratic socialism on the one side and that of communism on the other. For he sees 'no difference between Ford and Stalin'. In his view, they both ultimately produce the same kind of civilisation. The three qualities of modern civilisation—revolutionary technology, rising standards of living and social equality—have run into trouble. The anxieties, tensions and general emptiness arising out of the insatiable hunger for increasing living standards and output are becoming unbearable. The tensions and emptiness of modern life, he believes, seem too difficult to overcome, whether under capitalism or communism, '. . . as the hunger for rising standards is their mother and common to both'. The individual has been reduced to a mere number.

He is a number not only when he is a prisoner, but also in practically all walks of life. Starting out with the glory of individualism, this civilisation seems to have gone full circle and come to a stage when the individual is nothing but a cog in the machinery of the collective. It is now breaking under its own weight. . . .[2]

Although he does admit that the social and economic equality which have been attained by the white peoples of modern civilisation should make previous human civilisations feel humble, he yet believes that the original sap which made this possible seems now to be drying up. For him, collective life

---

[1] *Lohia Meets America*, p. 10.

[2] Lohia, *Wheel of History*. Navahind Publications, p. 96.

has become callous and modern man is but the object of an experiment.

In his view, man must therefore move away from existing civilisation in both its capitalist and communist aspects. Their kindred qualities and drives have made them both equally irrelevant to the venture into a new civilisation. When a civilisation flickers the torch generally passes 'into the hands of the outcasts'. The outcasts of the present civilisation, he believes, are the underdeveloped two-thirds of the world. But they will be worthy of that torch only if they make a break with the old and devise their own forms of thinking and living.

He admits that Asia needs more tools and machines, new industries and occupations; that it needs to cultivate new lands and make the old yield more. But all this can only be done by a new technology in the shape of the small machine and tool, driven by electric power or by oil or even by atomic energy. He does not believe that the spinning-wheel can be a solution to Asia's poverty, but the spinning-wheel run by electricity —like the cottage power-loom invented by Japan—can be. Too little land and too many men and too few tools are the mark of Asia, so that the application of the techniques of mass production are utterly impossible there.

This small unit machine, however, can be made available to hamlet and town and must be built on the principle of immediacy in production and output and will therefore not require a large investment of capital. This machine will not only solve the economic problems of the underdeveloped world. It will also (no more and no less) enable

. . . a new exploration of and achievement of a society where man will be at peace with himself, enjoy a decent standard of living, live a life of poise and relaxed activity, without hunger for ever-rising material standards, where political power will be decentralised and where everyone will govern himself peacefully at all levels from the village to the world parliament.

Asoka Mehta, another one of the top leaders of Indian socialism, has also been trying, during the last few years, to formulate a more coherent ideology for the P.S.P. He has tried to construct a socialist home of many mansions, containing elements of British Fabianism, of Nehru's brand of socialism, of

Ghandiism, of Utopianism, all co-existing precariously, without any integral unity or fruitful tension between them, and with some of the occupants not even on speaking terms with one another. Asoka Mehta has, furthermore, not been able to make up his mind whether he favours a peasant or industrial form of socialism or whether he belongs to the government or the opposition. Perched uncomfortably between all these clashing alternatives, his ideological and political posture is indecisive, vague, and productive only of well-meaning confusion.

Following Dr Lohia he too, at one time, spoke about a distinctive Asian path to economic development, a path which would lay its main stress on agriculture and deliberately renounce the aim of catching up with the more advanced countries. 'Apart from the inclinations of the peasant, the fact remains that for Asian countries to achieve the visage of the West is just not possible.' [1] He therefore advocated the creation of a balanced economy, based on small-scale industry, 'diversified farming and family economics', and state control of the commanding heights of the economy. He favoured a

many-levelled structure with appropriate links and locks. . . . In the peasant sector of economy, land distribution, village oriented economy and voluntary labour for rural public works, would provide opportunities for full employment. . . . In handicrafts, better tools, adequate raw materials, co-operatives for credit and marketing and protection against developed industries would provide increased and secure employment. . . . In development industries, in so far as that sector is concerned, the Keynesian multiplier would work. Each level has to seek its appropriate 'full employment'. [2]

This was in 1953. At the end of 1955, at the Gaya Conference of the P.S.P., he had realised that this picture of Indian development was far too simple and idyllic. There he advocated a socialist programme which would lay its main stress on industrial production and which would welcome increases in production as advances along the road to socialism. In a private conversation he even went so far as to say that India need only produce 18 million tons of steel per annum to scatter to the winds all the notions of Gandhiism and of 'peasant socialism'.

[1] 'Can Asia Industrialise Democratically?' *Dissent.* Spring 1955, p. 158.
[2] Ibid., p. 159.

In 1959, however, in his *Studies in Socialism* he again presented a confused picture of mutually opposed intentions. Aware of the inhibiting effects of Asian traditionalism, yet unprepared to face the consequences of this knowledge, Mehta engaged himself in a search for irrelevant ideological positions. He went back to the leaders of European revisionism (Jaures, Bernstein and Fabian socialism) for ideological guidance, but he then attempted to apply their recommendations in an Indian context, which had nothing in common with the situation that they had faced in their own countries. You cannot reform a capitalism which does not exist. And to affirm your belief in democracy does not make it prevail.

However, he not only rediscovered revisionism. He also exalted Utopianism as the 'only hopeful avenue of progress'. Recognising that the ancient 'social fabric of Asia survives at many places', admitting that the 'covenant between man and nature is the core of Asian culture' and that 'contemporary western ideas, the dazzle of their achievements, divorced from the brooding void and want they produced (!), proved a lag, a serious handicap in effective understanding and amelioration of Asia', he yet announced that 'Asia is big with the dream of Utopianism'. By Utopianism, he means the teachings and example of Gandhi, the Bhoodan movement started by Vinoba Bahve, the Marxist Buddism of U Ba Swe, the example of the Israeli kibbutz and the teachings and efforts of men like Robert Owen, Proudhon, Kropotkin, Landauer and Martin Buber.

Utopianism in this context means the creation of 'free villages', the 'self-sufficiency of a person, of a village, of a region', and 'it involves a person wearing his own cloth and using local goods'. Instead of sharpening antagonisms, Utopianism breeds solidarity and 'unlocks humanity from every heart'. To compensate for the 'gaping scarcity of capital', Utopianism encourages a 'loving care of ravished land'. Its whole approach has to be 'intensive, small in area, but deep in effect'. Although he admits that the 'village communities have generally broken down' and that they 'present a picture of economic debris and social decay', he nevertheless feels that these communities can be revived by a new spirit which will yet have to be 'ethical, non-militant, essentially Utopian—that is—idealist-missionary'.

Having made obeisance to the prevailing sacred cows of Indian socialism, Mehta yet understands that the problem is much more serious than he has admitted. Discussing the problems of economic growth, he states that the real task facing the underdeveloped countries is to transform the traditional economy and to construct a modern and efficient economy. This has been made even more urgent by the long period of neglect which all these countries have suffered from and by the pressure of population. He admits that stagnation and stability cannot go together.

For industrial development to commence on a large scale, many conditions have to be fulfilled. The most important condition, however, is that priority should be given to such productive activities as would help to improve and revolutionise tools and techniques. That means that iron and steel, coal and power industries should receive precedence. Therein is the core of the growth-inducing sector.[1]

The introduction of new and better tools and techniques, however, demand 'new skills, new attitudes and rhythms of work, new social disciplines'. He quotes with approval the statement of Sir Denis Robertson, a British economist, that 'the sacrifices necessary to achieve growth consist not only in passive abstinence from consumption, but in something which is much harder . . . namely, consent to being disturbed in established routines of life and work'. Asian socialists must, furthermore, cease to frown on profits, must learn how to channel profits into investment and accept the fact that the 'production oriented economy is a harsh system' and that the motive force for economic development comes from those who have 'the urge to innovate'. But how then is this 'harsh system' to be reconciled with the sentimentally vague effusions of Utopianism and its practical ineffectuality?

Asoka Mehta, furthermore, believes that there cannot be socialism without democracy in Asia. He is yet aware of the fact that a multi-party system, with the possibility of frequent changes of government, would make long-term planning and development extremely difficult. Development depends on 'the

[1] *Studies in Asian Socialism.* Bharatiya Vidya Shavan, Bombay, 1959, p. 233.

acceptance of equality, austerity and hard work'. It is thus easy for an opposition party to oppose the sacrifices that are demanded in the interests of development and by its constant challenge to the government in power encourage a situation where there is 'an all-round reluctance to embark upon bold policies'. He therefore argued (in 1953) that the 'political compulsions of a backward economy' demand the maximum co-operation of the people. While rejecting totalitarianism, he still felt that 'parliamentary democracy is not much helpful'. A parliamentary democracy in a backward country is often enough faced with the fundamental alternatives of 'stagnation versus disruption'. In his opinion:

the compulsions of backward economy tend to push towards totalitarianism or timidity. The dilemma can be resolved by (1) so broad-basing the government that it gets power to move forward, because opposition is driven to the fringes, and (2) strengthening the forces of pluralism in authority and initiative. In such a re-organisation, democratic rights—of speech, press, assembly and association—have not only to be cherished but strengthened. Only frequent changes in government, that parliamentary democracy assumes, would be replaced by a broad-based government holding power on a long-term tenure—in effect though not in law. Criticisms would be expressed through the usual democratic channels, the opposition, as distinct from criticism, would be confined to those irreconcilables who are opposed to the fundamentals of the State.[1]

Although Mehta's solution to the grave problems raised by the 'compulsions of a backward economy' does not go beyond the conventional framework of Indian society, yet the very fact that he raised the issue at all shows that he has a more than vague premonition that the existing arrangements are unsatisfactory.

SINGAPORE

The group of young men who at present rule Singapore constitute probably the most able, educated and vigorous government to be found in non-communist Asia. Before coming to

[1] P.S.P. Report of the Special Convention held at Betul, Madya Pradesh, June 1953, p. 169.

power their party, the People's Action Party, was even accused of being a front for the communists. Most of them are of Chinese origin and therefore possess a store of native energy and vigour which the other nations of the region seem to lack. Some of its leading members had studied at Cambridge or had been taught by Harold Laski at the London School of Economics. The People's Action Party was described by most observers as a radical socialist party of extreme views and militant policies. An illuminating insight into the real thoughts and feelings of even this vigorous group was given to me in a private conversation with one of its leading members.

Discussing some of the problems connected with the process of modernisation in non-communist Asia, he said that perhaps Asians should not even attempt to modernise their societies. He felt that Asia did not have the means for it, did not have the leadership for it, and that the mass of the people were not yet ready for all the sacrifice that this demanded. Asians should, therefore, not set themselves goals which they cannot achieve. To do that is to assume a mere pose which it seems everybody is adopting because it has become fashionable. If the West is too far ahead of us, if the Chinese path demands too much of us, then perhaps Thailand can serve as a model for the rest of Asia.

He then went on to say that the cohesive, united oligarchy which rules Thailand has succeeded in maintaining the country's independence and that the Thai people are happy and well fed (if only on rice) and are not too oppressed. The peasantry works for only a few months in the year and spends the rest of the time in play, festivals and idleness. This oligarchy, having come to the conclusion that it could not modernise the country, that this task was beyond it, decided to keep its people isolated from the modern world. This should be the pattern for Asia. It also knew how to manœuvre between the imperialist powers which attacked Asia, between Britain and France, between Japan and the United States, and how to always side with the victors. Although this oligarchy loots the country it has yet set limits on its appetites and this, too, helps to maintain the stability of the state.

This Thai policy, he believes, should be followed by the other

Asian countries. Their ideal should be to withdraw from the modern world with all its demands and cruelties. Asians should not indulge in all the dangerous experiments of industrialisation, education and emancipation. In order to implement all these explosive goals, we need a secular priesthood, absolutely devoted to its vocation and ruthlessly determined to compel the people into the twentieth century. Without compulsion, without sacrifices, without ruthlessness, he thinks all these things cannot be done. Western democratic socialism and parliamentary democracy are irrelevant to Asia's problems. To modernise you have to change a people drastically, in two generations or not at all. It can't be done gradually, slowly, by evolutionary means. Unfortunately we do not have the secular priesthood to carry out these tasks. He feels therefore that they are not in control of their own destiny. The future belongs to communism.

The communists are everywhere attracting the best, the most idealistic, people. And they are beginning to feel that they can do anything, that nothing is beyond them. Although many overseas Chinese are repelled by the grimness of communist China, they cannot be anti-communist. The 'Chinese Resurgence' brought about by communism has even given pride and self-respect to Chinese millionaires. While the Chinese are hard, dynamic and industrious, the Indians are soft, lethargic and incapable of the hardness that the situation demands. Looking at the Asian scene, he saw on the one hand a steady process of disintegration, a universal feeling of uncertainty and a general lack of direction, and on the other, the fact that the communists were not yet ready to march and to take over.

INDONESIA

Of all the Asian socialists, only the top leadership of the Indonesia socialist party has tried, though unfortunately unsuccessfully when measured in practical results, to confront the genuine and fundamental problems of Asian society. Only they have realised that the basic decisions which they must take concern not only political, economic and social questions but revolve around the more fundamental issues of human values and aspirations.

Soetan Sjahrir, the Indonesian Republic's first prime minister and leader of the Indonesian Socialist Party, is one of the few Asian leaders who was aware of this fundamental challenge even before the second world war. Writing in *Out of Exile*,[1] which consists in part of letters that he wrote to his former wife in Holland during his years of exile and internment (1934–8) in 'Bovendigoel, New Guinea', Sjahrir went straight to the heart of this problem.

Already in 1937, Sjahrir had rejected the concept of the East '. . . as a promised land of peace of mind and spirit . . .' which attracted many Europeans. He sees the East, on the contrary, with its 'carefreeness' and 'moral superiority', where 'people can sit for hours thinking about absolutely nothing', as a society of feudal servitude, that shows none of the stimuli of modern life. This world of squalor and indolence, with its eternal fear of evil spirits and permanently haunted by malevolent ghosts, has been moulded and nourished by the hierarchical relationships of a feudal society in which a small group possesses all the material and intellectual wealth and where the majority have been made acquiescent by religion and philosophy in place of sufficient food.

The Eastern outlook is therefore based on the negation of the world and of life. Notwithstanding the fact that this 'art of life' exemplifies the virtues of endurance and adaptation, it is really only an adaptation 'that makes an unbearable life bearable'.

As against the 'servile East' Sjahrir holds up the example of a Western world which is forceful and dynamic and accepts the 'active life'. He says openly that 'it is a sort of Faust that I admire and I am convinced that only by a utilisation of this dynamism of the West can the East be released from its slavery and subjugation'. He makes his general approach even clearer by claiming

that the West is now teaching the East to regard life as a struggle and a striving, as an active movement to which the concept of

[1] The John Day Co., New York, 1949.

tranquillity must be subordinated. Goethe teaches us to love striving for the sake of striving and in such a concept of life there is progress, betterment and enlightenment. The concept of striving is not, however, necessarily connected with destruction and plunder as we now find it. On the contrary, even in Faust, striving and struggle have the implication of constructive work, of undertaking great projeçts for the benefit of humanity. In this sense, they signify a struggle against nature and that is the essence of struggle: man's attempt to subdue nature and to rule it by his will.[1]

He feels, furthermore, that what the East now needs

. . . is not rest—or death—but a higher form of living and of striving. We must extend and intensify life and raise and improve the goals toward which we strive. This is what the West has taught us and this is what I admire in the West despite its brutality and its coarseness. I would even take this brutality and coarseness as accompanying features of the new concept of life that the West has taught us. I would even accept capitalism as an improvement upon the much famed wisdom and religion of the East. For it is precisely this wisdom and religion that make us unable to understand the fact that we have sunk to the lowest depths to which man can descend: we have sunk to slavery and to enduring subjugation.[2]

Sjahrir therefore recommends that 'every vital young man and young woman in the East ought to took toward the West, for he or she can learn only from the West to regard himself or herself as a centre of vitality capable of changing and bettering the world'.

Sjahrir admits that he has sometimes been called 'a half Westerner', and that he has often been distrusted by those who are fanatically inclined towards Eastern civilisation and culture and who reject Western materialism. This is in fact the tragedy of Indonesian socialism. For although it has been conceded on all sides that the party contained some of the most capable men in Indonesia it has been steadily losing support since independence and today constitutes a mere handful of leaders alienated from the life and thoughts of their people and practically without influence in the country. It has been outflanked not merely by a mountebank like Soekarno, but also by the more energetic and ruthless communists. This has happened not only

[1] *Out of Exile*, pp. 144–5.   [2] Ibid., p. 145.

because the Indonesian socialists have demanded that the country's leadership should be honest, hard-working and devoted to the real interests of their people and that it should assume the arduous task of teaching the nation 'better methods of production, enlightened self-interest and, above all, more rational ways of thinking'. Perhaps the main reason for their failure lies in the fact that, though they have thought and think in Western terms, they have not shown themselves strong and determined enough to act, or to be accepted by the nation, as the bold Westernisers or modernisers of Indonesia.

Yet, in spite of the failure of Indonesian socialism in its own country, and in spite of the pathetic gyrations of Asian socialism as a whole, the grand issues which Sjahrir has raised remain the central and inescapable problems of South East Asia and of all the poorer countries of our world.

Chapter 5

THE CHALLENGE OF
MODERNISATION

i

I T has become a commonplace of world politics to describe the changes that have taken place in the Afro-Asian countries as a revolution. The international atmosphere is absolutely clogged with slogans, speeches and books extolling the 'Great Revolution' that has supposedly been brought about in all these populous territories. Some glibly announce that these countries are already involved in a 'Revolution of Rising Expectations'. President Kennedy has spoken of the 'Revolution of the Rising Peoples'. Liberals, socialists and conservatives alike mobilise all the stale clichés of a simple-minded but heart-warming 'progressivism' in support of the 'Afro-Asian Revolution' and thoughtlessly bend to the 'Wind of Change', without really understanding what kind of wind it is and where it is blowing and what has been changed or what will have to be changed.

But the distressing fact about all the changes that have taken place in the Afro-Asian lands is that they do not in any way add up to a revolution. No revolution has, as yet, taken place anywhere. There has been a political change-over, political power has been transferred to new ruling elites, new flags have been designed and unfurled, the number of nations represented at the United Nations has gone up by leaps and bounds, but neither the men who now rule nor their societies have been revolutionised. They have neither acquired new virtues nor removed old vices. The present-day regimes are mere synthetic substitutes for the genuine revolutions that will still have to be made. What we are witnessing in reality is a colourful masquerade, a sort of superior political orgy, superficially exciting but essentially undermining, and leading only to a process of dissolution.

All these countries have achieved their independence not because they were ready for it, or had adequately prepared themselves for all its consequences, but only because two destructive and fratricidal European wars have demolished the material, political and moral foundations of Europe's world authority, and because the growth of liberal and democratic ideas within the Western community has made the business of dominating others both unpopular and unrewarding. The decline of colonialism in the West is due much more to the spread of liberal and socialist ideas among their peoples than to any increase in Afro-Asian strength. The importance of these countries, moreover, does not stem from their inherent capacities but only from Western weakness and gullibility and from its disturbing loss of confidence in itself and in its civilisation. The Afro-Asian camp has been exalted because the West has systematically been degrading itself.

Our very brief analysis of some of the leading ideological and political currents within the Afro-Asian world should, we hope, have shown the parlous condition in which all these countries find themselves. The old social forms which they have inherited are in a process of disintegration: the new forms which they have taken over from their former imperial masters have either been twisted out of all recognition or are in ruins. All these old societies are machines worn out by the wear and tear of use and abuse. Most of their peoples are socially and politically at sea. Their elites are generally not at home in their environments, torn by conflicting impulses, and though they vaguely know what they want they do not know how to get it. In spite of a number of achievements in different fields—some economic development, a considerable expansion of educational facilities, and the extraordinary level of international prestige and status they have attained—all these countries are, in fact, in a state of melancholy bewilderment, living in fear of what tomorrow might bring, and without an appropriate or vital philosophy of life to guide them. The turgid energy of their eloquence is only exceeded by the langour of their ways and thoughts.

The elites of all these countries have not yet found a language in which to express themselves. Attracted and repelled by the modern world (both by the democratic West and by totalitarian communism), compelled to perform a task which they are incapable of undertaking, these elites are tragically split in their very souls. These men still feel stunned and hurt and ravaged by petty pathological emotions, despite the freedom which they have acquired. They are, besides, filled with fear and foreboding. They are afraid that they might be re-subjugated. They are aware that they do not possess the necessary moral and military strength to safeguard their independence. They therefore live in even greater terror and anxiety in freedom than they did under foreign rule. They have not yet discovered a new cultural home where they can find sustenance and inspiration for their torn hearts and minds. They are still very badly prepared for the immensely difficult part to which blind fortune has called them.

But the outstanding fact about the elites of all these countries is that they are not in possession of that system of live ideas which represents the superior level of the age. All of them live at a lower level than the age demands, on a mixture of archaic ideas, and have stepped down to a lower life, with all its wounding embarrassments. This state of affairs, as Ortega y Gasset has written, constitutes the plight of all backward peoples and individuals. All these peoples and individuals, therefore,

ride through life in an ox-cart while others speed by them in automobiles. Their concept of the world wants truth, it wants richness, and it wants acumen. The man who lives on a plane beneath the enlightened level of his time is condemned, relatively, to the life of an infra-man. . . . It is a life crippled, wrecked, false. The man who fails to live at the height of his times is living beneath what would constitute his right life. Or in other words, he is swindling himself out of his own life.[1]

More than a decade after the liquidation of the Western empires in Asia, the main trend among the succession states is to dismantle their parliamentary systems. In Africa it took only a few short years for most of the parliamentary regimes to assume an authoritarian form. In the Middle East, except for Israel and the Lebanon, the military have uneasy power. Even a country like Israel, from which more could have been expected, shows all the signs of political and even social backsliding. Its democracy is shot through with abuses and aberrations; an insidious 'mystic cult of the personality' around Ben

[1] *Mission of the University*. Princeton University Press, pp. 83 and 85.

Gurion has been systematically cultivated and spread by all the numerous organs of propaganda both at home and abroad; and a former prime minister described the regime in Mapai, the dominant democratic socialist party of Israel, as resting 'not on honour and justice' but 'on fear and expediency'. Corruption is on the increase. Instead of critical thought, there is archaeology; and in place of making a determined attempt to assimilate advanced Western values (and not only in the material sphere), there are enthusiastic bible quizzes. Pretentious 'Messianic' phrases have become a substitute for ideas. The archaic elements in Jewish life, allied to the invidious habits of the small eastern European village or town, are coming to the fore and tend to contaminate the whole society. And after almost thirteen years of uninterrupted and unchallenged Ben Gurion rule, the country is still without an alternative government. If this is the position in Israel, the most advanced, the most 'Westernised', the most successful of all the newly independent states, what can the position be in the other more backward countries?

Instead of striving with all the strength at their command to make the titanic effort to 'catch up' with the Western countries, the underdeveloped lands are falling behind in the race for economic expansion and modernisation. The advanced countries, even without the benefit of their former colonies, are today moving towards levels of economic prosperity and general well-being which their peoples have never known before, while the newly independent countries are becoming poorer both materially and spiritually. For them, national independence has not led to substantial economic development, nor has it produced any noticeable improvement in the material welfare of their peoples. And it has not generated as could have been expected that sense of national rejuvenation that drives a new country forward.

On the contrary. Their faltering attempts at modernisation have only added new social stresses to the old. The existence of all these societies is marked by unrest, violence, and a turbulent emotional thrashing about as men search for new identities and for new ideologies around which to organise their loyalties and aspirations. Everywhere, too, there is a desperate attempt to protect oneself against unpleasant truths and to evade and deny painful realities. Traditional and modern values and groups clash in every field of national life. The conservative countryside feels threatened by and opposes the new economic interests of the city. Entrenched and routinised civil servants resent the influx of young administrators and technicians. The professional classes are torn between their attachment to the past and their desire to belong to the modern world. Corruption and nepotism blight the best of intentions and make a mockery of even the most progressive policies. The haphazard and superficial nature of their planning produces university graduates without jobs; elegant hospitals run by inadequate and poorly trained staff; factories without trained managers or technicians; modern programmes without capable modern-minded administrators and giant irrigation dams which the primitive peasantry does not even know how to make use of. All these societies are more concerned about forms and appearances than about substance. Their vanity is stronger than their misery. They all want the fruits of modern progress but without being willing to suffer the pain and to engage in the toil necessary to produce them. And on top of all this most of the Afro-Asian countries live under the threat of a population explosion, which if not drastically controlled will nullify even the most ambitious programme of economic expansion.

The artificial attempt to imitate the West is, moreover, everywhere breaking down. It can now be seen that the wholesale borrowing of Western forms of government, administration and ideas without making an effort to understand the spirit and ferment which have shaped them has only proved, as one writer puts it, the 'futility of facsimiles'. The new elites have amply revealed that they are incapable of governing in the foreign style which they have adopted. The political and social habits of the past have, therefore, everywhere begun to reassert themselves. Personal rule has become the common form of leadership in almost all the new states. The Western party system has split up into personal cliques, regional rivalries and tribal and linguistic divisions. Intimidation replaces consent. People follow the local 'political boss' rather than his party. Officials rule by fear and enrich themselves by graft. A romanticised 'nativism' takes the place of a desire for Westernisation. Traditional rituals, customs and myths have been pushing their way to the centre of national life. Individual rights or the rights of minorities are again being subordinated to the traditional 'servile solidarity' of the community. Opposition is either muzzled or suppressed. The pseudo-parliamentary regimes that were set up after independence are either discredited or in ruins. A former president of the Indian National Congress once said that 'India does not have democracy so much as a system of weakness and lameness'. He too, who had been a close friend of Gandhi, and who is a fanatical believer in 'non-violence', was prepared to welcome a military dictatorship for India as 'not a bad thing because it would at least hold the country together'.

The failure of Western forms of rule and the breakdown of the government systems left behind by the former Western rulers should not have come as a surprise to those who knew anything about the character of these societies. What is both surprising and comical, however, is the naiveté with which the Western governments, who pride themselves on their political sophistication, assumed that they could spread their own forms of government over societies which differ in every way from Western society. It was the epitome of wishful thinking to imagine that institutions which are the products of great revolutionary transformations and which even then only evolved slowly and haltingly over centuries in the compact industrial societies of the West could be grafted on to all these archaic agrarian societies with all their ingrained habits, very high rates of illiteracy, and crushed as they are by oppressive and irrational tribal religions. It is absolutely amazing that highly educated officials and intellectuals could ever believe that the strong, wiry but very sensitive plant of democracy which, given the right kind of deep and rich social soil to nourish it, can sink such powerful roots and sustain the historically exceptional experiment of representative government, could be expected to grow in the shifting sands and rocky wastes of societies which are still either primitive or, at best, rooted in the habits and values of oriental despotism. Yet these are not the only illusions the West suffers from. And these are not the only examples of its naiveté. Even today, after everything that has happened during the last fifteen years, very few people in the Western world have an adequate, realised image of how the peoples of Asia and Africa really live, what they really think, and what their real problems and needs are.

However, even the dictatorships, either military or personal, which have already emerged lack strength or solidity, and are devoid of any radical programme of national transformation or reconstruction. The officers who have come to power do not represent that new revolutionary force which all these countries so urgently require. Although many of them are superior to the incompetent and corrupt politicians whom they have replaced, they are still connected by a thousand threads to the basic values and assumptions which shaped their policies. They are undoubtedly more disciplined, more competent, more efficient than their predecessors, but all these commendable qualities are being harnessed to run the old system more efficiently, not to change it. The authoritarian regimes now in power in most of these countries are essentially of a stop-gap character, contrived in desperation, and having no sense of the urgencies or the opportunities of the situation which has pushed them forward to a temporary prominence.

Neither the former parliamentary regimes, nor the present dictatorships, nor Nehru's experiment in 'democratic socialism', nor the impotent and juvenile Asian socialist parties, then, have even so much as begun to come to grips with the authentic problems and dilemmas of their societies.

ii

The central fact about all these countries is that during the last 300 years and more, they have come under the disturbing impact of the West. This pressure of the West upon them, superficial and restricted though it has been, has come to be the paramount social force with which they have to come to terms. What Toynbee has called 'the Western Question' has become the mighty challenge to which they will have to respond sooner or later.

It is, of course, much more comfortable and, in a way, all too human to shrink from accepting this painful challenge and to flee from the disorder and the evil and the opportunities of history. Stark existential alternatives of this kind are always extremely difficult to accept, whether they are placed before an individual or presented to a whole society. And if only they could somehow evade having to choose between them and be able to continue with their present, shadowy compromises, moving on the surface of life while shying away from the fierce subterranean problems, both they and the rest of the world would be spared a great deal of trouble and upheaval.

For to look this challenge in the face, to find and to choose a path through this welter of tensions and conflicting pressures, requires a degree of resolution and of strength of soul which only the truly creative are capable of. But unfortunately this is precisely the response that is demanded of the present elites of Asia and Africa at this stage of their historical development.

Viewed in the broadest historical perspective, the countries of Asia and Africa are caught in a period of history when the rhythm of their development demands that their 'cake of custom' should be broken, when the disrupting and innovating energies necessary for accomplishing this act of renovation should be given the freest opportunity of expression. This basic conflict within all these societies, between the forces of renovation and the forces of tradition, between the call to build a new life and the drag of the past, comes to a head in the problem of modernisation or Westernisation. It will, therefore, have to be accepted that every impulse, every challenge of the present situation, leads to this central goal. As with every advance in civilisation, the way will at first be thorny and forbidding, and hedged about with almost insuperable obstacles. But if these societies want to renew themselves, to realise the creative potentialities they possess, they will have to travel along this thorny road of liberation. Once this 'take-off' into modernisation has, however, been successfully launched, the forces of social tradition whose task it is to refine and stabilise social institutions, to contain and sublimate the excesses generated by the process of innovation, to give the society a sense of style and dignity, will come into their own. It is only with this counter-movement which requires for its effectiveness an equal measure of reforming energies that these societies will develop and learn to use the whole range of democratic institutions necessary to humanise and civilise the relations between its various classes and groups. But at this particular moment the forces of innovation should be regarded as the instruments of emancipation.

This does not in any way mean that a new 'heaven on earth' is going to be built. Many of the old problems will be removed, but formidable new ones will spring into existence. Many of the old inhibitions will be purged, but new modern frustrations will take their place. There will most certainly be new triumphs, but new failures as well. Humanity will be released from ancient thraldoms, but new evils and miseries will surely come. One can only approach the task of forging a new civilisation by accepting the inescapable fact that the tragic in human life can never be exorcised. For one of the elements of tragedy is this cruel need for change, this irksome need for man always and in every generation to refashion his time, when and as it gets out of joint, without ever really eliminating the 'primordial pain and contradiction' at the very heart of things. And this is why Asia and Africa, which have prided themselves on the static and quiescent nature of their societies, have really had no understanding of the complexity, ambiguity and anguish of change, nor of its liberating effects. But if they want to move forward towards a higher level of existence and endeavour— and there seems to be no way of avoiding this—they will now have to accept the harsh necessity that the old, with all its virtues and vices, has to give way to the new, with all its vices and virtues, and that the new has to transcend the old before the backward nations can truly become an active part of our modern world.

It should, furthermore, be clear by now that this challenge cannot be met by the expedients which have been devised by those who, in one way or another, want to retain and perpetuate the ancestral forms of thought and action which have outlived their day. The wish to retain them is, in itself, a tangible sign of failure. Nor can it be faced by all those who attempt to create some brittle synthesis of the new and the old. These attempts at synthesis between incompatible values and aspirations have seldom been successful. And it most certainly cannot be confronted by those who are animated by a 'messianism of backwardness'.

THE CHALLENGE OF MODERNISATION

To begin moving towards the goals of modernisation, how-ever, does not mean that the nations of Asia and Africa are going to lose their identities or that they are going to become mere carbon copies of the West. Nor does it mean that these countries are going to attain a Western standard of living and civilisation (with all its benefits and defects) tomorrow or even in the next few generations. Nor does it mean that they will have to become mere replicas of the West in every form and pattern of their lives. Many of the old forms and patterns, both the valuable and the degrading will, for good or ill, not only remain, but will stubbornly resist all the efforts at their trans-formation for a long time to come. But what it does mean is that these unreformed, pre-capitalist societies which have now been more or less stagnant for centuries have to infuse a new revolu-tionary principle into their lives. If they want to remain within the orbit of civilised life, then all will have to create an Asian or African or South American version of Western civilisation. And it should be clearly understood that though the desire to avoid all the mistakes and excesses of the West is a praise-worthy one, it yet appears that there can be no forward move-ment in human affairs without mistakes and excesses and that all these countries will have to endure them and try to over-come them as all other mature and virile societies have to do.

The scope of the present book does not permit me to enumer-ate all the steps that must be taken (many of the economic steps have, in any event, been discussed *ad nauseum*) to effect this transformation, the greatest and most comprehensive that they have ever undertaken, but the bare outline of what is involved can at least be suggested.

A whole ancient mode of sociological functioning, burdened as it is with an overwhelming historical heredity, of past glories, myths and legends and past diseases, is in the process of coming to an end in this whole torrid zone of the earth's surface. New social forms of life have therefore to be created and the multi-tude of the underdeveloped lands must be pushed forward by a new thrust of social development, sufficiently powerful to enable them to adjust themselves to the imperatives of the modern world.

The overpowering natural environment which has shaped

and stunted the lives and thought of all the countless peoples of the region from time immemorial, can only be reduced to human proportions with the aid of mechanisation on a grand scale. A predominantly agricultural society must be transformed into one significantly engaged in industry, communications, trade and services. Incomes above minimum levels of consumption must be shifted into the hands of people who will spend it on roads and railways, schools and factories, rather than on country houses and servants, personal ornaments and temples. To provide a higher standard of living for all, to lift the crippling yoke of poverty, economic growth will have to become an organically built-in feature of each of these societies. A new technological civilisation, to be shaped by the combined forces of science and industry, must consequently be fashioned. And this new civilisation will be launched, not by the inert and archaic villages with all their 'ancient wisdom' but by the creative cities, despite all their commotion and disorder. Without cities and city life, without its heresy and unrest, without its ardent enterprising spirits, no civilisation of whatever level is, in fact, possible.

Now this new technological civilisation, once it is built, will for many, many decades continue to differ in many significant respects from the high quality of civilisation which exists in the advanced countries of Europe and America. It will not be as urbanised as Western society is, nor will it be as industrialised, nor will it be driven along by the same intensities of aspiration and ambition. The majority of its peoples will still continue to live in their villages and to be engaged in agricultural pursuits, supplemented by cottage industries of one kind or another. It appears that the industrial societies which these countries will have, or will want to create (even under the best of circumstances), will function on a lower level of vitality and on shallower bases. But it is also clear that even before this more modest type of industrial society can be built, all these countries, without exception, will have to move beyond the social and cultural limits which they have at present set for themselves and will have to prepare themselves for changes of such magnitude and asperity in their lives that not even those very few of their leaders who do contemplate change have yet imagined.

And even if most of these societies remain predominantly agri-cultural, they can only meet their problems of agrarian poverty, backwardness and overpopulation by revolutionising their methods of production and their basic social relations and, above all, their whole mental outlook.

All these countries are, in fact, faced with three main tasks:

(1) to produce a new elite of reformers and innovators, ready and willing to assume the hardships and risks of modernisation, and nerved with the courage to overhaul their societies and to change the ethos of their civilisation. (Within this innovating political elite, the entrepreneur, the captain of industry, the bold economic pioneer, will have to occupy a place of the highest importance);

(2) to develop a new ideology with the power to bring about a cultural revolution; to make people work-minded and develop-ment-minded, to sweep away the countless barriers to discip-lined, rational effort, resulting from traditional habits and superstitions, and to achieve what the Reformation and the Enlightenment combined attained over the centuries in the West;

(3) to organise the state in such a manner as to impose col-lective savings far beyond the limit of what individuals would be likely to save if left to their own devices and to invest these forced savings in an all-round development programme.

It should be quite obvious by now that this new elite, if and when it arises, will find it impossible to carry out all these tasks in a liberal democracy, because to implement them requires the concentration of a great deal of economic and social power in the state, the taking of a great many unpopular decisions and an attack on the people's most cherished beliefs and traditions. The economic tasks of development, moreover, cannot be realised by the methods of a liberal economy. The country is backward precisely because one of the basic conditions for a liberal economy—a private class of entrepreneurs—is absent. Capital can only be accumulated out of the abstinence and deprivation of the poor and economic development requires the taking of decisions which will hurt many vested interests. This cannot be done within a democratic framework. Democracy unfortunately is not a panacea for every situation, is not suitable for every country and is not even desired by every people. And at some stages in human development, a form of absolutism is needed to clear the ground of the accumulated debris of centuries and to impose unwelcome but necessary changes upon the 'unenlightened' people. Before any kind of economic transformation can take place, however, there must be the indispensable non-economic conditions for the take-off. What all these countries need above all, therefore, is the emergence of a new elite, capable of assuming all the burdens and risks of leadership and ready in the very depths of their hearts and minds to break with the enervating customs of their traditional societies and to accept the immense sacrifices necessary for taking their peoples through all the unsettling but liberating upheavals and innovations which the West had to go through before it could become modern and dynamic and prosperous and democratic.

The new elite that will develop, if at all (at the present moment there is no sign of it apart from the communists), will consist of exceedingly unattractive specimens. Whether we like it or not, this will be an elite of 'hedgehogs', consisting of men who, in the words of Isaiah Berlin, will 'know one big thing', and very little else, and who will relate everything, every aspect of their lives and thoughts, to a single, central vision. They will be narrow-minded fanatics, half-educated, crude and primitive, without sophistication or wide interests, full of an unscrupulous self-confidence and organised and tempered by one idea—how to modernise and strengthen their societies and drive their peoples by 'forced marches' into the modern world.

This new group will at first be stern and harsh and will cast aside the pretence of ruling by democratic means. Their political thinking will be determined by two pressing essentials: the need to turn their society upside down and inside out and the need for discipline and order. They will accept the fact that rapid change is more desirable than the partial gradual change of traditional institutions and wisdom. Instead of patching, grafting, clipping and altering this or that branch of the national society, and thereby only creating new discrepancies and discordances, the new, purposeful elites will seek to transform the whole pattern in one sweep, break with the familiar past and develop a more or less consistent set of new habits. They will, therefore, organise an authoritarian (if not totalitarian) state and will be quite ready to sweep away the last vestiges of the traditional order, to jolt the people out of their ruts, and to attack their most ancient beliefs and practices. The rights of the individual will be overruled, traditional safeguards will be rejected, and no class or interest will be permitted to stand in the way of modernisation. This group will be as hard as nails, organised for governing, and they will be the inflexible servants of an idea. It will be moulded by the slogans of an oversimplified ideology, and sprung out of the most energetic and virile sections of the 'intelligentsia' and the 'people'. In spite of its many defects, in spite of its many ugly features, it will have the necessary strength of character and self-confidence to destroy most of the traditional obstacles to modernisation.

Before this new elite, however, can even begin to wrestle with the ponderous and sluggish social forces with which it will have to contend, it will have to absorb the spirit generated both by the Reformation and Enlightenment. Without assimilating these Western values, emotions, virtues and drives, no development of any sort will be possible. And unless these new qualities are transmitted to the society as a whole, in the course of a prolonged process of change and innovation, these countries cannot become rational enough to confront their problems. To build a new civilisation, irrespective of the speed of its development, is an arduous work that must, in the very nature of things, stretch over centuries and can never really be finished. But as a beginning, a new ideology has to be developed, forceful enough not only to effect a revolution in their traditional scale of ethical values, but powerful enough to create a new type of character. It can only live in a series of individuals who are capable of intellectually and morally incorporating it in themselves. It must not only stand for new ideals of social conduct but also have the strength to fashion and fertilise souls. It must, in short, be capable of injecting a germ of such powerful potency into the society that it will at once be able to act as a stimulant to sustained and energetic enterprise and as an acid dissolving many of the obstructing customary relationships. And this potent germ of innovation will have to affect every department of life and it will have to penetrate every nook and cranny of the country. Starting with the top layers of the society themselves (and there everything will have to begin) it will have to seep down to the civil servant in his office, to the student in his classroom, to the worker in his factory or small workshop, to the peasant and agricultural labourer in his village, field and cottage. And from this first circle this new spirit of life and movement will have to be communicated through all the spheres of the nation. But before such a new momentum can draw the society together and drive it forward, millions of people in every walk of life are unfortunately going to experience the dislocations, the pains and ferment produced by that leaven of change which they have for so long tried to resist. But if they want to enter this new age of increased opportunities and benefits and of new problems, troubles and anxieties, they will have to pay the high price that it demands. No society can become richer without emphasising hard work and thrift, without developing a high propensity to innovate and without revealing a high level of willingness to accept and initiate change. And the hard work will not only have to be done by the working classes of the society, but the example will have to be set by the elite itself. The poor countries have remained poor for so long because their values have not emphasised becoming rich and because they have given too high a place to stability, tradition and the other-worldly values of religion.

Now this new ideology which they will have to develop can assume different forms although it will have to serve the same central purpose: to break decisively the powerful and unreformed forces of religion and tradition and to clear the ground for the building of more rational societies. In its search for this new ideology, it can either try to go back to the past, though it is irretrievable, or determine to leap forward into the bravest and most dazzling future, though it is unrealisable. It can invent a completely novel idea or seize hold of an ancient superstition. It can aim at creating something new or at restoring in a new and modern form something that existed many centuries ago. This ideology can be naive or sophisticated; it can extol the beauties of nature or the superior virtues of urban life. But it must have one supreme and indispensable quality: it must call for a sharp break with the nation's predominant traditions and call into question its most cherished beliefs. It must create a new type of man, strong and ruthless enough to revolutionise himself and his society. Unless it has the force to make people change themselves and to break with all those traditions that have clogged their minds and frustrated their energies, it can never serve as that instrument of liberation which is needed.

To take a few examples: The European Protestants and Puritans believed in an unyielding form of predestination, but encouraged individual initiative; they wanted to re-establish the simplicities of primitive Christianity and helped to fashion our complex urban and secular industrial civilisation; they employed the methods of absolutism and helped to shape our modern tradition of dissent, emotional independence and personal freedom; they were firmly convinced that they were the ardent servants of God but in truth they became the worshippers of the idolatry of wealth. The Russian Marxists, when they made their revolution, firmly believed that they were the vanguard of a new, classless and stateless society, without exploiters and exploited. But they in fact only prepared the conditions for the growth of a 'state form of capitalism' or a 'bureaucratic form of collectivism' (the term is not really important) and established, at the beginning, the most ruthless regime of exploitation that mankind has ever known. Instead of a socialist revolution, they brought about an industrial revolution, with all its suffering and exhilaration. In Israel the country has been modernised and industrialised by a 'pioneering elite' which believed in the priority and superiority of agriculture as a way of life, in the evils of urbanism, and in a utopian form of classless socialism. Yet all these beliefs did not prevent these 'revolutionary farmers' from becoming not very efficient factory managers, tough army officers and the determined organisers and builders of an essentially urban society, dominated by a parvenu new ruling class, and marked by some of the abuses that they had originally declared to be anathema.

The important thing, then, is not so much the ideology as the spirit behind it. If the particular ideology has the power to produce a sudden crisis of thought and to generate a revolution of feeling, then the nation will be able to move from a static to a dynamic state, and a vital impulse will have been given to the more rapid development of the individual and his society. Man will again be plunged into the current of evolution, of invention and freedom. The fixities and rigidities which have held the society prisoner will be broken. New roads and new perspectives will open. Bound energies will then be liberated, ancient mental interferences removed, innumerable and hitherto unsuspected powers unlocked and the energies of loyalty, courage, endurance and devotion awakened. However, if the new ideology will be incapable of generating this movement of change and creation, enterprise and effort, and will be incapable of arousing the forces of energy and courage, then, no matter how revolutionary it sounds, it will in reality be hollow, stale and unprofitable, a mere dark shadow over the land.

Technology has been described as always concerned with setting energy to work. The new elite that is insistently demanded will have to concern itself with the primary task of setting liberated human energies to work. A whole society will have to be set to productive work and organised to create wealth on an immense scale. Without such a cult of work, an almost religious sense of the importance of working for human improvement in this mundane world, no modern industrial system can, in fact, be built. Once this combination of qualities, however, is present, once the vitalities of dynamic enterprise have been unleashed, once the new principles of change and experimentation penetrate the very subconscious layers of the human psyche—and there to effect an inner-psychic transformation—then only will the society suddenly come alive and pass from one stage of culture to another—from a more primitive condition to a more advanced one. Without the assimilation of these 'heroic' Western qualities of change and effort, all the backward societies of our world will continue to live in a fever of dissatisfaction and instability, restlessly lurching between the West and communism, between Westernisation and 'Asianism', between modernism and tradition, and tilting fretfully between complacency and panic, from flabby parliamentary systems of government to unguided military dictatorships, from expedient to expedient, which no mere rearrangement of its superficial features will be capable of overcoming.

It will continue to remain impoverished and miserable, both economically and spiritually, even while some steel mills, irrigation dams and nuclear reactors are being built. For all these essential elements of modern society can only serve, within the present context of its arrangement, as pyramids in the desert—or as troubled and fragile superstructures resting on the cracked foundations of fossilised institutions, outworn beliefs and impoverished and backward humanity.

iii

It is only against this backdrop of backwardness and disintegrating archaic societies that one can begin to understand the role and significance of communism. It is not, as its propagandists and apologists claim, a new post-capitalist civilisation. It is not a creative answer to the genuine problems and difficulties generated by a mature, industrial, urban and democratic society. Its imposition upon the advanced and mature societies of Western Europe and Northern America would not only constitute a monumental historical setback but a human and cultural disaster of the first magnitude. It is anything but a new start in human life. It has basically nothing to do with socialism or with the best ideals of the democratic labour movement. And in the process of appropriating Marxism to serve its own power interests, it has distorted and vulgarised it beyond recognition. Communism fulfils quite a different historical role. The greatest historical significance of the Russian Revolution lies in the fact that communism now represents an alternative way of industrialisation to the 'slum countries' of the world.

Communism today is the patently effective twentieth-century substitute for the 'bourgeois revolutions' which have failed to take place in those traditional societies where these were both a necessity and a possibility. It is an inhuman, totalitarian but highly successful instrument for industrialising, modernising, and, in its economic, educational and scientific fundamentals, 'Westernising' those underdeveloped societies which were ready for this momentous historical transformation. And because it has the ruthless courage to reject the most deeply rooted traditions of its environment, it has managed to release the formidable energies necessary to build a new industrial society. It has, besides, the 'barbarian strength' to set a whole nation to work, to turn its society upside down and inside out and the 'barbarian insensitiveness' to disregard the claims of every class or group that stands in its way, and to shut its eyes to the suffering and misery that it is causing all around it.

Communism has, furthermore, been able to fashion out of its ranks a 'state bourgeoisie' or 'a state bureaucracy' with the necessary 'Western' qualities and virtues to plan, run and manage a new industrial economy. The creation of this new 'state bourgeoisie' constitutes its greatest achievement. For it is only through it that it succeeds in its programme of industrialisation, and in building up the material and human strength necessary to support its other ambitions, to realise its 'grand design' for the world. There is therefore no such thing as an 'agrarian communism'. Communism may first develop in the countryside, it may organise and exploit peasant discontent to gain power, but its essential goal, if it is at all a serious political movement, is to organise the energies and ambitions of its adherents for implementing the tremendously difficult tasks of industrialisation and modernisation. It is a modern, a more cruel, a more powerful and a more concentrated version of the 'primitive' bourgeoisie of the early nineteenth century. And because it duplicates the essential work of the bourgeoisie in countries that have never known all those fertilising movements which have created the conditions for Western liberty, and because it telescopes into a few decades a process of change and transformation which it took the Western bourgeoisie a few centuries to accomplish, its work must, in the very nature of things, assume a much more brutal and savage character and must take place on a much lower level of civilisation than existed in the West in the same period.

Communism, in fact, in its internal operations, is a highly contradictory phenomenon. It fights barbarism with barbarian methods. It liberates millions of people from ancient superstitions and traditions and subjects them to a system of unprecedented ideological and political despotism. It 'Westernises' a society and cruelly seeks to estrange it from the West. It rules at all times through a regime of personal insecurity and in its early phase through a regime of terror, and yet provides vast opportunities for all who have talent, ambition and the will to work. At the beginning it creates new wealth for the nation and impoverishes the people. It subsequently, slowly prepares the material conditions for a more advanced and humane form of society and tries to prevent this more advanced society from coming to birth. One of its fundamental goals is to 'catch up' with the West, and to imitate it, yet it does this by declaring open war against it. It educates and enlightens and at the same time does everything in its power to place the mind in a mean pigeonhole of inflexible and primitive dogma. Its spiritual and cultural poverty marches hand in hand with its vast and well-defined ambitions. It is, as G. L. Arnold has described it, both 'autocratic and dynamic' and 'represents revolution and counter-revolution in one, the ideology of the October rising and the practice of despotism, socialist slogans and techno-cratic reality, slave-labour camps and industrial progress, imperial conquest and world-revolutionary rhetoric'.[1]

On the international level, Russian and Chinese communism in absolute control of two super-states, represent two essentially separate centres of national power, driven along by vast 'mes-sianic' pretensions and imperialist ambitions. Communism's early utopian phase of internationalism is a thing of the past, and has not only no influence on the policies of the two major powers but does not even affect the policies of the minor and subordinate regimes and parties. Communist states, as much as any others, have divergent and even clashing interests. The Eastern European countries feel themselves to be the captives of Russian imperialism. The communist parties outside the com-munist sphere of rule do not belong to a 'communist inter-national' but are, while in opposition, either the supporters of the 'Russian camp' or the 'Chinese camp'. And once these parties occupy the seats of power they begin to develop their own interests and ambitions which, in many respects, begin to conflict with those of their more powerful communist neigh-bours or with those of the more powerful communist states or empires.

In both Russia and China, communism has not only effected,

[1] *Pattern of World Conflict.* The Dial Press, New York, p. 112.

or is effecting, a vast internal upheaval, but it has also awakened the intense nationalist passions and ambitions of both these countries. The communist ruling class of Russia has already fashioned a new Russian empire to gratify its aroused national appetites and visions of glory and to mirror the new power which it has so grimly been accumulating and moulding out of the blood, sweat and tears of its own people. The Chinese communists are, at present, in still an early phase of 'primary accumulation'; they are still not strong enough to play a leading role in international politics. But even today, Chinese policies are not dictated by such abstract considerations as that of 'communist internationalism' nor even by the needs of its present alliance with the Soviet Union, but are shaped by distinct Chinese national interests and by their desire to revive the imperial glories of China's ancient past and to improve upon them. The basic aim of Chinese communism is to build up China as a great imperial power in Asia, to make it the leader of the communist camp, and thereby to influence and perhaps to impose itself upon the Western world too. The Chinese drive for industrialisation and modernisation at home and empire and influence abroad are the two sides of its communist medal.

The drive for empire of both these countries is thus neither surprising nor out of character. This has happened before in history and the same drive and ambition will, most certainly, stir and dominate other countries in the future. Here we have two populous, proud and energetic nations with great resources, which for centuries have been kept retarded and depressed by their own inadequacies and anachronisms and which have, especially during the last one hundred years, not played that role in international life which their position, resources and inherent strength make it possible for them to play. China, in particular, became a semi-colony and felt itself to be humiliated and despised by the Western powers, which intervened in its affairs. Now under communism, a powerful electric current of awakening and renewal has been shot through both these societies. In Russia a poor and ruined nation has become a nation of immense power, and Moscow is now one of the world's greatest capitals. In China they are desperately and most energetically trying to follow this forceful example. A feeling of increased power and self-confidence, of released energies and new ambitions, has naturally as a consequence stirred within them. The power elites of both these countries do not only want to raise the status and prestige of their respective nations, but also see immense possibilities of extending their power abroad, especially among the weak and disintegrating states of Asia and Africa. No wonder they are so aggressive and zealous, and confident that the levers of the future are in their hands.

Russian and Chinese ambitions are so formidable, however, their challenge to the rest of the world is so effective and comprehensive, because they have managed to disguise their naked imperial ambitions in the cloaks of a new secular religion, full of insurgent hope and desire. To all those small groups of the intelligentsia in the backward lands (and this includes South America, Spain, Portugal, Greece, etc.) which are in the process of tearing themselves away from the stifling traditions of their antiquated societies, they are the only ones who seem to offer an effective programme of modernisation and of a radical reconstruction of society. In some of the more unstable and flawed countries of the West (Italy in particular, and to a much smaller extent France), they have been able to organise and capture considerable pockets of discontent and to threaten the integrity of the national community—although this is already a receding threat. But they are, above all, so dangerous because in both cases we confront two young, lean and hungry elites motivated by a ruthless will to power, professional to the core, unafraid to face the realities of world power and to shoulder the heavy burdens of leadership, and extravagantly over-confident in their mission.

In both these countries, moreover, political purposes, political aims, rule every sphere of national life. Economics, education, science, foreign policy, all are resolutely subordinated to the sovereignty of politics. Through their systems of centralised national planning, despite all their shortcomings and failures, they are able to organise their national resources to serve the overall global aims of their elites. Russia has thus already succeeded, on an even more meagre economic base than America disposes of, to challenge it in military might, scientific skill and international prestige and even to surpass it in the more restricted field of military science. And though the Chinese communists, when they came to power in 1949, took possession of a country which in many respects was even more backward, poor and intractable than India, they have already far surpassed the latter in economic growth and their general impact on international life is much greater than that of India's. The spectacular rise of China to the status of a world power is not only the most significant political development in Asia since the war, but it also portends the growth and expansion of the most disrupting and menacing revolutionary power that mankind has perhaps ever known.

To implement their seemingly unlimited hopes and ambitions both these communist powers have devised a diplomacy which it appears the Western powers, still dominated by the traditional and conventional methods of the nineteenth century, and by even more sentimental and ineffective twentieth-century ones, are finding it extremely difficult to match and sometimes even to comprehend. Russia in particular, as the more experienced and advanced power, has contrived a diplomacy which is active, confident, highly inventive and skilled in using a considerable variety of weapons. It has achieved world influence by an aggressive and consistent policy, which employs fear, cajolery, seemingly logical propaganda and the conviction that history is on its side. It is as ready to use military force as to attend an international conference to settle 'all outstanding problems'; to encourage revolution as to organise a 'peace rally'; to resume nuclear testing as to call for 'complete and total disarmament'; to export culture as machinery; to send astronauts whirling into space as to send its blown-up leaders rampaging all over the globe. Krushchev is as capable of banging his shoe on the table at the U.N. as he is of threatening the world with nuclear destruction. Russia is not afraid of ruthlessly crushing all opposition in its satellite countries, as in Hungary, despite the disapproval of public opinion, despite the condemnation of the United Nations and in the face of the displeasure of the 'uncommitted nations'; and yet somehow, perhaps even because of it, it can still retain the support and respect of all those 'sensitive' and 'progressive' nations and groups which it should have lost by its cruel and challenging action.

Everywhere it probes for the weak spot in the enemies' armour (and it regards every other regime as its enemy) and, once having found it, it moves with alacrity to widen it for penetration and exploitation. It is as capable of creating a crisis as of dampening it down. It knows how to blow hot and cold at once, in an almost dizzying alteration of moods, so as to keep its opponents off balance. It is always on the alert, always on the move, ever restless for the promising risk.

Russian diplomacy is as ready to provide aid as to promote and support a revolution against the very country it is extending this aid to. It knows how to maintain diplomatic relations with the established government, how to engage in all the complacent cant and protocol of formal diplomacy and at the same time how to sustain and inspire the communist opposition in that very same country, or how to search out and cultivate new revolutionary elements which can be used against the powers that be. It is active in the countries of Asia and Africa not only to encourage the forces of neutralism against the West but to transcend them with its own programme and leadership wherever it can. While supplying President Nasser with arms and aid, Krushchev was not deterred from openly declaring before a high-ranking Egyptian delegation that the Nasserite regime was a failure and that communism would sooner or later triumph in Egypt too. It talks of 'peace' and of 'peaceful co-existence' but never for a moment does it lower its guard, or relax its efforts to strengthen its military, economic and political power and to prepare its regime for every challenge and opportunity. For Russia, 'peaceful co-existence' is in fact synonymous with all those conditions of menace and challenge and competition which the West understands by the 'cold war' and which it finds so disturbing and frightening and does not know how to handle. Russian communism appears to the rest of the world as an event-creating movement, which forces its opponents to respond to the events which it has set in motion. Guided by a long-term political perspective, impelled by a coherent sense of purpose, aware of the true situation and prospects in the underdeveloped lands, Russian and Chinese communism represent a political force of immense potency and danger.

The West, however, is not only menaced by Russian and

Chinese ambitions and designs. Its general position in the world is also being challenged and undermined by the rise and growth of the new states of Asia and Africa. For on another level of meaning, 'the world revolution of our time' is a revolution clearly directed against the world hegemony formerly held by Western civilisation, and this includes America, no matter what anti-colonial position it may adopt or what kind of anti-colonial rhetoric it may practise. A former president of the Indian National Congress once said in a private conversation that if India had to industrialise on a Western scale, it would have to dominate the world in order to obtain the raw materials and secure the markets that it needed. Although given a 'materialistic' justification, the unconcealed enunciation of this possibility shows more than an unconscious aspiration for world power on the part of as 'pacific' but as potentially important a country as India could become. And it would be ludicrously naive to believe that this 'natural ambition' for power and influence, which all other rising states have so far amply revealed, should by some sort of strange alchemy stop at the frontiers of India or of any other Asian or African state. Those who deny these possibilities continue, in fact, to regard the Afro-Asian peoples as some kind of inferior specimens, unmotivated by these (as historical experience has shown) normal human passions and appetites.

The Afro-Asian desire for 'self-determination' is, in fact, in no way the innocent liberal objective which so many simple-minded liberals and socialists assume it to be. Egypt's fight for 'self-determination' does not prevent it from wanting to swallow all the lands of the Arab Middle East (particularly the oil states), and from wanting to 'organise' and 'unify' even the Arab and Moslem lands of North Africa and the rest of Africa. Pan-Arab nationalism would not only like to drive out the 'imperialist exploiters' but also reduce Western Europe to a state of dependency by seizing control of its oil supplies. The Algerian F.L.N. nationalists, in the course of their savage struggle for independence, are not above regarding their Maghreb partners of today as their possible satellites of tomorrow. Ghana feels that its desire for 'self-determination' should embrace as many of the lands of West Africa as could be annexed or incorporated into its sphere of leadership without too much trouble or fuss. While missing no opportunity of advocating 'Pan-Africanism', it is, in fact, only interested in Ghanaian expansion and in the growth of its power and pomp. Nigeria is today on the side of the 'moderates', for the simple reason that its own future as a 'federal' state is still in grave doubt, deeply divided as it is between its northern, western and eastern provinces. India's attitude to Kashmir, and its actions in Hyderabad and Goa, showed no particular regard for 'national self-determination' nor a 'moralistic' horror of imperial considerations. The Indians have besides taken over Britain's 'advisory role' in Nepal and the other smaller Himalayan states, and like all advisers they are not too welcome. Behind the tension between India and Pakistan there is patently present the competition between Hindu and Moslem as to who is going to dominate the Indian sub-continent. The Indonesian government has repressed native insurgent forces demanding local autonomy in Sumatra, Celebes and the South Moluccas, sometimes even with great ferocity. Burma has had to suppress a series of local nationalist rebellions—the Karens, Mons, Shans, etc. It appears that already today a new line of division is being drawn within the Afro-Asian camp, not so much between so-called true nationalists and 'neo-colonialist stooges', or between progressives and traditionalists, or between revolutionaries and reformists, but simply between states that are territorially satisfied and those with programmes of national expansion.

All the states of Africa and Asia want to be free and independent, a desire which is both legitimate and justified. But they would also, quite naturally, like to become strong and influential. They would, however, not only like to be the makers and shapers of their own history, but also of the history of other countries, including the West's. Of course, this ambition is beyond their reach at present. But it is quite possible that in the future, once they will have built up sufficient national strength and power, whether on a communist or some other revolutionary basis, the most ambitious, powerful or aggressive states will, in the process of working out their own national destinies as they understand them, and not as Washington,

London, Paris, Moscow and Peking understand them, attempt to increase this national power by one form or another of foreign aggrandisement.

It is only too true that the older Western empires are disappearing and that nothing can recall them to life. Yet their disappearance has not removed the conditions for the emergence of new non-Western empires. Imperialism is definitely flickering out in the West, but it is clearly reviving outside the West, unctuously rejecting the name but realistically fulfilling the substance. Asian and African ambitions and aspirations and the new conflicts resulting from national rivalries between them will thus not be quelled or satisfied by the mere change of masters. Instead of entering a new period of 'universal sweetness and light', of 'universal co-operation and peace', we might only be entering a period marked by a new and complicated world power struggle. The world, unfortunately, is not one grand community and it may never become one. Although many of the same ideas, the same slogans, the same institutions and the same machines are now found the world over; and although the world has achieved a degree of unprecedented diplomatic unification; humanity is still today as sharply divided as it ever was in the past, if not more so. The epoch of Western contraction could quite easily be followed by an epoch not only, as it has already, of communist expansion and of communist empires, but also of new Asian, Arab and African empires. It is highly probable that mankind will, in the future, still continue to be shaped and determined by the customary forces of history with its perennial 'drama of empires, armies and heroes'.[1]

During recent years both communist and Afro-Asian nationalist mythology have come together to propagate the fiction that imperialism is a special vice of the white Western capitalist nations. The truth, of course, is that this form of Western imperialism is an invention of the last few hundred years and that throughout the longer part of recorded history it has been the West that has been attacked by the more formidable and massive Asian empires. Starting with the Persian wars against Greece, the West has been threatened by one wave

[1] Raymond Aron.

after another of Asian aggression. In the early Middle Ages it was besieged for about 300 years by the Arabs from the south. Only an accident—the death of Ghengis Khan—saved Europe, except Russia, from Mongol domination in the thirteenth century. Later the Ottoman Turks overran southern Europe and pressed up the Danube valley for three centuries; and they and the Berbers enslaved Christian Europeans until well into the nineteenth century.

Imperialism has, however, not only been in history an issue of Western peoples against non-Western peoples. The non-Western countries have experienced their own, indigenous forms of oppression and domination, as have the Western countries. Asian and Middle Eastern history in particular is saturated with the history of predatory and tyrannical empires which, in the course of their careers of conquest, blindly destroyed not only the laboriously constructed foundations of civilisation but also the precarious independence of all those countries which stood in their way. Asians and Africans fought and exterminated each other, enslaved and exploited each other, before and after the arrival of the white man to those continents. The Mongols under Ghengis Khan, the Turks under Suleiman the Magnificent, and on a much more primitive level the Zulus under Chaka, were all famous empire-builders and conquerors. There have been Persian, Chinese, Indian and Arab empires. Burmese conquerors repeatedly invaded Thailand, destroyed the Thai capitals and led part of the population as slaves into captivity, from the twelfth to the eighteenth centuries. Nor did the Thai kings refrain from retaliation whenever they found an opportunity or deny themselves the prospect of military conquests in Laos. Japan built up its own Asian empire in the thirties and early forties. And these imperialist and national conflicts among Asians and Africans will, in today's different context, continue and perhaps even increase after the last vestiges of the relatively brief period of Western rule will have completely disappeared.

Nor are racial superiority complexes anything peculiar to the white race. Although these are ethically objectionable and politically oppressive wherever they raise their heads, it yet appears that superiority feelings, in different forms, are a general human defect. The Manchu conquerors of China enforced strict racial segregation and forbade all intermarriage. The caste system of India is the petrified perpetuation of indigenous racial conquests and discrimination. The people of southern India who speak Dravidian languages, of which Tamil is the most important, have today formed their own Dravidian Federations to work and agitate for their liberation from 'north Indian imperialism' and from 'Brahminism' which they claim has kept them for many centuries on the lower rungs of the social ladder. India's post-independence history has been characterised by numerous agitations raised by one 'subnation' against another (the Maharatis against the Gujeratis, the Bengalis against the Biharis, the Assamese against the Bengali minority and the hill tribes, the Punjabi Sikhs against the Punjabi Hindus, the Christian Nagas against the Central Government, etc.), and by bloody riots and indiscriminate police shootings. The forty-two million strong Moslem minority has claimed that its legitimate rights are being disregarded by the Hindu majority. The Mohammedans in China's northwestern territories participated in many uprisings for independence until the terrible repressions in the nineteenth century drowned all their efforts in a sea of blood. Japanese colonial administrators copied and even exceeded the racially arrogant practices of the Western colonial administrators whom they briefly replaced during the second world war. Western racialism is, besides, being replaced in many areas by a new form of bitter and revengeful Afro-Asian racialism, compounded of a moral superiority complex, fear, insecurity, resentment, envy, and a desire to humiliate and pay back old scores.

iv

This far from complete analysis of some of the major forces at work in our world should have shown that we are all caught in an immensely complicated and many-sided intellectual, technical, economic and political revolution, which, almost like some vast cosmic force, is carrying us all towards strange and unknown shores. Empires are collapsing, old cultures are disintegrating, the balance of power is shifting, peoples are being broken and remade, there is a global agitation and uncertainty and mankind's familiar landscape is being violently rearranged by horny and powerful hands. Never have things been so fragile, so protean, so subject to sudden and dramatic alterations as they are today. We are, in fact, caught in a cycle of history which is drastically transforming our world; the actors, inspired, mediocre or indifferent, in a long epic, the outcome of which no man can foresee. We live, in the midst of a revolutionary epoch comparable to those which saw the passing of the city-state, the collapse of the Roman empire and the breakdown of European feudalism. Destiny has placed us in a dynamic world of challenge and response, a world of forces and counter-forces, of conflicts and struggles, where all institutions and all life are mortal and subject to death.

This is a world in which nations, empires and civilisations rise, flourish and decay in ever-fluctuating relationships of competition, conflict and alliance. The conditions of success and failure, of strength and weakness, are incessantly changing so that no static or enduring balance is possible for too long. No nation, no system, no party, no ideology, is exempt from the consequences of the iron law of change, the relentless impact of competition and the inroads of decay and corruption. Nothing is absolutely secure in human life and history. Those whose power was supreme, weaken with age, luxury and the loss of confidence and energy; and others with the hardy strength of youth and the fierce drive of unfulfilled ambition, rise up to claim their place in the sun and to call into question the old certainties and menace the old arrangements. The virtue, the strength, the security, of any one nation can thus only be the painfully won result of its own arduous efforts and sacrifices, of its powers of adaptability and change and of its ever-nurtured vigour and vigilance. Apart from this all passes, all changes. It is in this world of incessant change and challenge—which we must bravely accept rather than find cowardly distressing— that we have to exist and it is to this environment that we have to respond.

The outstanding and irreversible fact of contemporary history, then, is that Western civilisation is now under concentrated attack and on many fronts. It is being attacked not only by communist imperialism, but also harassed and blackmailed by Afro-Asian nationalism and neutralism. The long period of its expansion and hegemony is obviously nearing its end, and no amount of propaganda or economic aid, not to speak of military pacts with inefficient, corrupt and obsolete ruling groups (if they can at all be dignified by that name), can halt this seemingly irresistible historical process. Too many signs of weakness and disintegration within the non-communist sections of our world point to the certainty that unless the West is ready to bring about significant changes and innovations in the heartlands of its own Western civilisation—North America, Britain, France and the rest of Western Europe—and more drastic ones within all those peripheral societies which are willing to ally themselves with it or to remain within its orbit of culture and influence, the West's area of influence and support will shrink even further in the future. More and more a general impression is spreading that the Western countries lack that generosity of endeavour, that force of thrust and initiative, that sort of daring and faith in its own powers and that mercurial and buoyant spirit that are the true marks of a civilisation at the height of its strength and energies. Western civilisation may, therefore, if this is true, as it seems to be, increasingly become a small, gravely threatened numerical minority surrounded by millions upon millions who are either openly hostile to its ideas, beliefs and way of life or else contemptuously neutralist.

Taking a broad view of recent history, it becomes clearer and clearer that the liberal experiment has shown pronounced signs of flagging outside the Western world proper—the world of Western Europe and North America. Only those countries which have been tempered by that complex of social, economic and industrial revolutions which have shaped the Western world and which have been actively participating in the great and liberating discourse of reason and enquiry, of sensibility and imagination which began in Jerusalem, Athens and Rome and which has been going on, in fits and starts, in dramatic leaps forward and in periods of relative stagnation in the West ever since, have shown enough resilience to defy and survive the cataclysms and tempests of the age. All those other societies which have only been touched by superficial Western influences or disturbed by purposeless Western interference have been and are in no position to sustain and cultivate the liberal institutions which they have either inherited from their former Western masters or acquired from desultory Western contacts.

The West, moreover, does not, in this day and age, offer that revolutionary programme, which it itself originated and developed, necessary for modernisation. It unfortunately does not stand for a radical reconstruction of society for the world at large. It cannot offer, or is incapable of offering, those sweeping solutions or drastic rearrangements that the backward countries require. Its ruling elites seem to be more suitable for an epoch of concentration but are out of place in our own age of revolution and disturbance. Although they possess many admirable qualities—self-restraint, good manners, politeness, tolerance and a sense of humanity—they are basically inaccessible to ideas and show no great aptitude for seeing how the world is going. They are more often than not bewildered and helpless in this troubled world of flux and change, of crisis and catastrophe, of sudden breaks in the course of development and of unexpected changes of fortune. It has been remarked that the 'pragmatic' Anglo-Saxon peoples in particular, influenced as they are by a rather shop-worn and shallow philosophy of 'common sense', find it very difficult to grasp the 'dialectics of revolution' at this point in their history. The Western world as a whole gives the distressing impression that it has no plan, no 'grand design', but only an ill-digested set of improvisations.

One of the strangest spectacles is to see so conservative a country as the United States is (in terms of social institutions and attitudes, not of technology) try to line itself up with the 'anti-colonial revolution' without in any way understanding what is involved in this whole process and what is demanded to bring this movement to fulfilment. A conservative British prime minister, whose greatest dream for his own country (as I was once told by someone who had worked with him) was to have a population of five million, with its ruling elite spending most of its time in trout fishing, is yet not debarred from claiming that his party and the country under his leadership have the necessary experience and wisdom to deal with the 'wind of change' in the underdeveloped lands. While clinging to almost mid-Victorian ideas and values in its own way of life, the United States blandly encourages its public representatives to indulge in a hollow and inconsequential form of revolutionary rhetoric. But it is impossible for present-day America, worshipping at the shrines of the religion of self-enrichment, to really conduct a policy of social revolution abroad while remaining as smug, as conventional, as addicted to material comforts and as tied to the established fact as it is at home.

The Western countries, furthermore, have still not grasped the true realities of their situation in the world; have not yet come to terms with the world's changed power balance; and have not yet come to understand where the authentic centre of their interests and purposes lies.

America thus oscillates between a European orientation and an orientation to the 'awakening masses of Afro-Asia' without, however, realising the inherent opposition between the two. It wants both to strengthen Nato and to forget it, if not humiliate it, at the United Nations. Sometimes it seems that America is European-minded until just that crucial moment when Europe needs to have its full and unconditional support; and anti-colonial, just fervently enough to encourage but not to satisfy Afro-Asian aspirations. The American Odyssey has been described as a contradictory and erratic movement away from and back to civilisation, away from and back to Europe.

One could thus, on the one hand, write a post-war history of American policy in terms of the Marshall Plan, the North Atlantic Treaty Organisation and German reconstruction— the most creative and redeeming aspects of American policy— which would place the main emphasis of its efforts on Western Europe and almost make it the exclusive pivot of its diplomacy, interests and hopes. But on the other hand, there is also to be found a powerful countervailing tendency which seeks, under both conservative and liberal leaderships alike, to break loose from 'Old Europe' and to cut its crippling ties with it. This latter tendency is based on the hallucination that it is possible for America to turn its back on Europe with its ostensibly 'ill-famed' imperial and colonial past and all its compromising interests and claims (as happened at the time of Suez, in particular), and to join hands with the rising new 'underdeveloped nations' and together with them build a new, free and prosperous world, without conflicts or complications, and under American inspiration and on the 'optimistic' American model.

But even its attitude to the Afro-Asian nations remains highly ambivalent. It moves from one kind of over-simplification to another. At one time it could see no political role for these new nations except as members of high-sounding (Baghdad Pact, SEATO, etc.) but ineffective military pacts. This has now been replaced in part by a policy which not only welcomes neutrality and non-commitment but enthusiastically exalts it. A new cult of neutralism has, therefore, been permitted to grow up. And this has been accompanied by the false premise that the cold war is essentially a struggle for the political control of the uncommitted areas of the world; and that the heart of Western strategy should be concerned with the contest for their allegiance and with the necessity to win their support at the United Nations. When the full force of this policy is at work, the contest between the West and communism assumes the dimensions of a ludicrously simple popularity contest with the inexperienced, weak, fumbling and presumptuously backward neutral nations placed in the role of moderators or arbiters. (This policy, by the way, is also supported by the dinosaurs of left-wing socialism and of some forms of liberalism in Great Britain and Europe.) But even here it is only necessary for America to perceive that its blandishments, sympathy and its readiness to offer large monetary prizes to all those among the neutrals who are ready to give a friendly nod to the West, do not produce substantial results, when it will on the rebound, in dazed disappointment, make another desperate grab at Europe's coat-tails. Both these tendencies have, however, not only not constituted a single coherent and purposeful policy but have at all times conflicted and interfered with each other and reduced their overall effectiveness in either direction.

What is true of America, the most powerful country of the Western world, is also true in varying degrees of Britain and France. Britain, it seems, can't make up its mind whether it feels itself closer to India, Ghana or Nigeria, or to France and Holland; whether it is a European country or the illusory leader of a heterogenous, mainly Afro-Asian, Commonwealth. Its grandiose belief that Britain, Canada and Australia and India, Pakistan, Ceylon, Ghana, Nigeria and Cyprus, etc. can form a viable political community, a great world-wide force, which is almost the equal of the United States and far superior to Western Europe, is a mere hangover on all sides of antiquated and fanciful colonial habits of thought. It belongs with much else in British life, to the snows of yesteryear. Britain's continued attachment to this mesmerising fiction has helped, together with many other internal flaws—above all, an obsolete and constricting class system—to inhibit the dynamic development of British society and to wrap it up in its present dreary cocoon of dispiritedness, insularity, traditionalism and aimless anger. It has sometimes looked as if Britain's two main parties were moved by only one desire—to turn the country into a quaint, charming and gentle museum of antiquities, controlled by languid, not very bright, impeccably accented, world-weary attendants.

And France has depleted its material and human resources; has been thrown into a grave political and moral crisis; and has been brought to the verge of civil war, because it has been seized by the self-defeating dream that it could build a Greater France, sprawling across the Mediterranean into the Africa of the Maghreb and of French Black Africa and thus become a great 'Eurafrican' power and attain some form of empty, meaningless and irrelevant grandeur.

Faced with the immense problems involved in the modernisation of the underdeveloped nations, the West has only been able to devise a policy of economic aid which in almost every case has not really helped to solve the problems of these countries but only to aggravate them. Economic aid in this context is the equivalent of pouring oil into a motor with ruined cylinders. The oil is quickly burned up but the machine remains a wreck. This policy has fostered the vulgar, 'materialistic' fantasy that it is possible to defend or to expand the area of freedom by the wholesale purchase of allies or of neutrals; that it is possible to buy immunity from the dynamic laws of change by extending economic bribes to the erratic and inherently unstable countries of Asia and Africa; and that it is possible to civilise nations by merely providing them with machinery, technicians, dollars, pounds and francs, wrapped up though all these offerings might be in vain and vague appeals for 'social reform' and 'social justice'. As serious and sophisticated a journal as the *Economist* even went so far as to suggest that public aid and private investment could 'go a long way towards giving the new black elite of Africa the kind of self-confidence it needs'; and that to put money into Africa would help to develop the 'African personality' and provide it with self-assurance ('Money for Africa?' 14 Jan. 1961). A civilisation which believes in these patent medicines; which seems to have forgotten the profound spiritual truth that history is not made by financial outlays but by human beings, by men and women armed with the necessary wisdom, courage, strength and stamina to meet the challenge of their problems and predicaments, is not only inviting disasters but actively preparing them.

From everything that has been written here it should be evident that the issue before the West is not 'the creation under its leadership of a universal community in which free men make their own laws and live by them in peace',[1] or whether 'Western (or European) civilisation will maintain its ascendancy or will be destroyed'.[2] It is in any case beyond the power, resources and political skill of the West to create a 'universal community'; and 'Western ascendancy' can neither be maintained nor restored at this late hour of the day. Moreover, both past experience and the ever-fluctuating realities of power and empire show that it is almost impossible for any power system, whether it be Nazi, communist or democratic, to achieve world supremacy in our highly complicated, restless and fiercely nationalistic and competitive world; or to retain it for long in the unlikely event of its succeeding.

No, the great issue before the democratic peoples is not the political unification of the globe; the fateful question is not whether Western democracy or Russian or Chinese communism are going to establish a future planetary order. The basic issue of world affairs, the axis around which revolves all

[1] Robert Strausz-Hupé.   [2] James Burnham.

the tumult and menace of the cold war between communism and the West is, rather, whether Western civilisation itself can and will survive, or more correctly, whether it has the resolute will to survive, in a world increasingly dominated by anti-Western forces and tendencies. This is the great question which confronts the West, and to which it will have to find an answer; and it is upon this fundamental issue that its policies, measures and imagination will have to be riveted and focused.

For the West is not only under attack, it is also in retreat. External pressures, internal conflicts and weaknesses, and an unwillingness and inability to continue to rule over others are responsible for its general retreat from its imperial positions and traditions, and consequently, from its former position of world ascendancy.[1] No possible military devices, no novel strokes of policy or diplomacy, no economic bribes on however lavish a scale, can stem this process; nor can they prevent the West from being driven back upon the realities of its European and Western existence. The steady shrinkage of its influence in the underdeveloped lands will more and more force the West back upon itself, upon the still unplumbed power and resources of its own civilisation and upon the energy and vitality of its beliefs, values and enterprises. After having sought glory and treasure in all the far-flung and exotic reaches of the earth, only to see it crumble and explode in their faces, the Western powers will now have to rediscover their own treasure-house of potentialities and glory that lies waiting to be unlocked and exploited in the heartlands of their own civilisation. Ruthless facts will now impose on the West the inescapable obligation to be self-

---

[1] The only way the West can maintain its present position within the backward regions of our world is by developing an active and vigorous policy of 'interventionism' towards them. It would have to discard its present demoralising policy of 'aid without strings' and enter these territories with an unambiguous and purposeful programme: to recruit, nurture and sustain in common partnership that revolutionary elite, the character of which I have already described, which is the only force capable of preparing these societies for life in our highly demanding modern world. A policy of this kind, carried out under the aegis of the West, might well retain these countries within the orbit of Western influence and assure their independent existence. But to merely suggest this kind of programme is to simultaneously indicate how impossible it is for the Western elites, as at present constituted, to carry it out.

consistent and to decide whether they authentically believe in what they profess to believe. The West will now have to be really, literally Western. From now on the West will either have to merge itself into the unifying landscape which its own history, over the centuries, has been fashioning, or else face irretrievable decline and decadence, and see all its virtues and higher capacities vanish into thin air, or be buried under the debris of an atomic war.

The West will, therefore, have to forget all the grandiloquent talk of its world mission; gradually cast off its over-extended world responsibilities in Asia and Africa; systematically make itself independent of the raw materials (such as oil in particular) and the bases which some of those countries now supply, and accept the unhappy fact which both Walter Lippman and George Kennan have discovered, that Rudyard Kipling is dead, and that the 'white man's burden' is far too heavy for its shoulders. Not only is this burden too heavy for it today; but even when it was in a position to bear it, the West was not too effective in the handling of it. The democracies cannot thus now organise or run a new, viable world political order; but they still have the inspiring possibility of organising all those countries clustered around the Atlantic basin into an 'Atlantic World', into an 'Atlantic Federation', which could form the metropolitan heart and core, the powerful arsenal and creative laboratory of Western civilisation.

Besides, the need for unity has become crucial because one of the blatant consequences of contemporary developments has been the breakdown of the self-sufficient nation state. In the West, in particular, the creative force of nationalism has long been exhausted, and has in recent years only proved destructive. Not even the most powerful country is today in a position by itself of maintaining security or of realising the true potentialities of its people. Nationalistic defence policies are, in fact, now no longer possible for the Western peoples; and are irrelevant when tried. Economic self-sufficiency can only produce stagnation and impoverishment. The idea of cultural autonomy is an anachronism; both Europe and America live in the same cultural ambience. To want to remain a mere American, Englishman, Frenchman or German is to condemn oneself to an obnoxious form of provincialism. In defending national interests, in exalting national particularisms, the Western countries are merely defending their yesterdays, not their todays or tomorrows. The vital possibilities of every Western people are out of proportion to the size of the collective body in which they are enclosed. Everywhere there is thus a crippling disproportion between the West's great potentialities and the narrow form of political organisation and the restricted political horizons within which they have to act.

The West's long and splendid past and its recent defeats and disasters have, therefore, brought it to a new stage of existence: where the national state in particular has become dwarfed and a ponderous obstacle to further development. Everything has now increased—the tempo at which things move, the force and energy with which everything has to be done, the scale of its problems and the magnitude of the challenge which bears down upon it—and the West is now compelled to excel itself. It it wants to survive, to live, to retain its place in universal history, it must seek its future beyond the frontiers of nationalism. This is the setting of the immense drama to be staged in the coming years. Will the Western nations be able to move beyond their present limitations and frontiers, will they be able to transcend their particular national interests and traditions, or will they remain in essentials their prisoner?

The only way the Western countries can meet the challenge posed by communist ambitions, enmity and competition—a challenge which will persist, in all its ups and downs, for many generations—the only way they can respond to the collapse of their empires and to the global revolution in the balance of forces, is by actively working to create a new balance of power in the world. This should, however, not be difficult. The West is not as bereft of tangible power and resources as its leaders sometimes appear to think it is. Western Europe's economic recovery has been one of the miracles of the post-war world; its movement towards unity has been one of the most positive and constructive enterprises that Europe has ever undertaken; and it now constitutes one of the high spots of civilisation. Great Britain and France, in particular, despite many apparent weaknesses and flaws, still possess an accumulation of power—political, social, intellectual and moral—which has not yet been squandered and can yet be augmented, if only the will to do so is there. And America, notwithstanding the obvious defects of its over-commercialised civilisation, still disposes of enough intellectual and cultural energies, of sufficient economic and military resources which, if wisely husbanded, distributed and developed, could make it not only the shield but the impressive champion of Western civilisation as a whole. Even if all Asia and Africa were to go communist, the West would not have to feel much less secure than it is now. Western Europe and North America, combined and united, are, and are likely for still a long time to remain, as powerful and wealthy as the rest of the world put together.

However, economic power, material affluence and military strength are not sufficient by themselves to constitute the binding ingredients of a great political undertaking. To hammer into shape a vital historical enterprise, the hopes, dreams and the will of man have to be mobilised. A collective programme for the future has to be devised. New stars have to be discovered to guide the life of man. The deeper energies of his personality have to be aroused and stimulated. A powerful will for unity and renewal has to be fashioned. The only way it is possible to give new life to the pulses of the West and to dispel the growing lack of confidence, the disarray, the mediocrity which now mar its collective life is by inventing something new, some great enterprise—the establishment of a Federated Atlantic Community. History is a field of action where possibilities are sometimes converted into actual realities. But these possibilities do not become realities of their own accord. It is only by an adventure of thought and action, it is only by labour and self-sacrifice, that realities are made of them.

Of course, the creation of such a community, which in itself would represent a decisive break in Western development, a crucial turning point in its history, a genuine revolution in international life, will not be the work of a day or of a year. At first the federal arrangements will remain loose and untidy. But gradually, with the proliferation of federal institutions and their functions—military, economic, political and legislative—

and their combination in ever larger complexes, the grand design of unity and of a shared destiny will take shape and become more and more deeply rooted. However, even if the rate of its development will be rather slow and gradual (not too slow and gradual, it is to be hoped), and the whole enterprise will proceed by trial and error, the guiding impulse behind it must be firm, purposeful and sufficiently forceful to stimulate ever-increasing confidence, daring and tenacity. Whether we like it or not, human life is a preoccupation with the future. As soon as man turns away from shaping the future, he becomes degraded, grows slack and slovenly, his soul is paralysed and human history loses all the sinews of risk, adventure and drama. Thus living is always ceaselessly, restlessly a doing, and doing involves bringing the future into being; imagining it, shaping it and conquering it. And this is what the West has to do if it is to preserve and fulfil the promise that it has so arduously been forging during the last six centuries.

This then is the great challenge of modernisation that faces the Western world. Only by creating this larger unity to transcend the self-defeating, parochial interests of the West's provincial nationalisms will it be able to lift itself up to the vital level of our time, and confront with growing confidence and strength our modern world of reality, and all its profound, dangerous, unforseeable and inexhaustible possibilities. Western unification, by providing immensely fruitful new sources of power and new and inspiring political goals, could serve as a valid substitute for the idea of empire which provided some sense of purpose to the Western imperial powers in the past. Its realisation would outweigh by far the economic, military and prestige losses which it has suffered in Africa and Asia and which, under present circumstances, it is still fated to suffer there. Western unification would inevitably, by the very force of its momentum, cast into obscurity all those archaic elements within Western society (in both the conservative and socialist or liberal camps) which still stubbornly refuse to accept the existence of the twentieth century.

It could provide a new and gigantic framework within which all the vigorous and creative forces of Western society could begin to spread their wings, to manœuvre, expand and grow; within which all those groups and interests which are authentically modern—the new generation of government planners and technocrats, some of the more sophisticated groups within the business, military, labour and professional elites—which have felt the peril and potentialities of our times throbbing under their hands, could come into their own. It would enable the West to begin to tackle, with energy and a glowing sense of purpose, the development of its own backward areas—Spain, Portugal and Greece, southern Italy, parts of France, the southern United States, etc. In place of trying desperately to buy disintegrating allies in the non-Western parts of our world, it would integrate and stand guard over all those countries—Australia, New Zealand, Israel—which form islands of Western civilisation in alien seas. Instead of trying unsuccessfully to solve the problems of Laos and India, America would devote its energies and resources to revolutionising (if it can), and thus saving, Latin America—which at least shares a common religion and some common values and beliefs with the West—from communist conquest. And in place of trying to save Ghana, the Congo, or an Algeria dominated by the F.L.N. for democracy and freedom, the West would devote its resources to reforming, improving and expanding its educational systems at home, which is probably its most urgent internal task; to tearing down and rebuilding its cities, so that they could once again become the exciting metropolises that they once were; and to raising the quality of its public services and public life in general. It should support only those non-Western countries, like Turkey and Japan, for example, which are determined and committed to saving themselves. Instead of trying and in the main failing to develop the 'slum countries of the world', the West should really try to get its own civilisation 'on the move' again, to stir and excite it with a new vision of greatness. Nothing reveals the mettle of a civilisation so clearly as the height of its objectives.

No great civilisation can thus exist for long without an encompassing and inspiring vision of greatness. The greatness that the West must aspire to, however, can no longer be the greatness which comes from empire and from ruling over others. It must, and can only be, a greatness which emerges out of its own endeavours and strivings, and which can only rest on the superior quality of its civilisation, the vibrant quality of its inner life and mind and on the strength of character of its citizens.

The West is thus basically not engaged in a crusade against communism or against Afro-Asianism or against any other bloc or ideology. It is waging a sustained, long-term war of survival, not trying to impose some set of fixed values or pre-conceived ideas or unsuitable or unviable institutions upon the rest of the world. Its essential task and mission is to defend Western society against all the dangers that threaten it and to carry out all those changes and innovations which will make it possible for it to survive and to fulfil all its potentialities. In order to implement both these tasks the West will have to remain militarily strong for as long as we can see ahead: ever ready to defend its crucial interests and to repudiate all threats; and at all times on guard against the danger of being dragged into a thermo-nuclear war. While always ready to probe for negotiations, it will yet reject with scorn the methods of appeasement and of unilateral concessions as making war more likely rather than less.

If the threat of a war waged by nuclear weapons can some-how be averted, then it is quite possible that the politics of the future will not be as inimical to Western interests as they seem to be today. The same forces of overweening pride, competition, corruption and decay which helped to bring about the disinte-gration of the Western empires are, in their own mole-like fashion, preparing a similar fate for the communist empires in all their forms. The communist system is as mortal, as filled with contradictions and conflicts, as subject to human frailties and weaknesses as every other. Public magnificence versus per-sonal poverty, bureaucratic corruption and arrogance versus the simple human interests of the population at large, economic progress versus spiritual starvation, a vast increase in material resources in collision with the class and ideological frameworks in which they are being contained, official lies versus the need for free, individual inquiry and judgement, lip service to democratic aspirations versus the systematic denial of genuine democratic rights—all these and many other conflicts and contradictions will undoubtedly in time come to the surface and bring about significant changes and alterations within the more Europeanised sections of the communist system. Who can argue with absolute certainty that the present uneasy alliance between Russia and China will have to continue for all time, and that it could not break up into a sharp conflict of ambitions and interests between the two in the future? Who can claim, with absolute confidence, that Russia will always have to remain the leader of, and the source of inspiration for, all the anti-Western forces which are now so angrily swirling around the shores of Western civilisation; that it will, for all time, have to remain the semi-civilised country that it is; and that it will never seek to rejoin the Western camp for protection or for alliance or even perhaps for human aspiration? And one may even hazard the guess (supported in a way by recent events in Poland, Hungary and Yugoslavia) that after having attempted to revolutionise and modernise their societies, democracy and individual liberty will once again appear as attractive causes to the more sensitive and advanced elements of the elite and of the masses, especially in those countries which have in some form felt the creative impact of the West in the past, and that it might be possible to really put these aspirations into practice.

But no matter what might happen in individual cases, it is clear beyond any doubt that the world will not become frozen in some Orwellian nightmare; but that we shall all experience new surprises, unexpected developments and transformations, sudden changes of pace and revolutionary dislocations. The world will inevitably continue to change, for good or for ill: seemingly firm alliances might crumble, implacable threats might recede only to be replaced by new ones, the partners of yesterday might change sides, and a grand reshuffling of allegiances, of interests and of orientations might take place. And mankind might even, if it is stout-hearted and iron-nerved enough, be able to avert all the dire catastrophes which now appear so imminent.

As I said at the beginning, events, in all their mechanical force and momentum, have not yet taken charge, and responsibility still rests in human hands. The future can still be fashioned by the magic and freedom of human genius and leadership and by the simple but abiding virtues of courage, solidarity and tenacity.

INDEX

A

Acton, Lord, 13

Africa: 8, 10, 28, 29, 33, 47; sub-Saharan, character of, 98–107; basic defects of, 99–101; religions of, 100; achievements, 101; Western impact on, 50, 56, 57, 103; form of socialism, 106; 213, 215, 227, 229, 230, 231, 232

Afro-Asian Revolution: nature of, 206

Afro-Asian world: parlous condition of, 207–12

Age of Discovery, 48

Algerian F.L.N., 230, 247

All-Burma Peasants' Organisation, 143

All-Burma Trade Union Congress, 143

Anant, Victor, 64

Anti-Fascist-People's Freedom League (A.F.P.F.L.), 143–4, 146–50, 152–3, 161, 162, 163; split of, 169–70, 173

Arabs: history of, 94–5; flaws of, 94–6

Arnold, G. L., 225

Aron, Raymond, 232

Ashanti, 101

Asia: 8, 10, 28–37, 47; contact with West, 51–6; 213, 215, 226, 227, 229, 230, 231

Asian civilisation: geographical environment, 29–30; nature of, 44–6

Asian socialism: parties of, 180–181; tasks, 181–3; specific nature, 183–90; relation to Marxism, 185–6

Asian Socialist Conference, 157

Asiatic mode of production, 30, 44–5

A

Ataturk, Kemal, 69–70

Atlantic World: need of, 243–6

Australia, 48, 155, 247

B

Ba Maw, Dr, 133–4, 139, 140–1, 143

Ba Swe, U, 140, 158; combining Buddhism and Marxism, 156; A.F.P.F.L. split, 169–70

Baelz, E., 68

Bagehot, Walter, 18

Balance of power: changes in, 9, 244

Bandaranaike, S. D., 91

Bandung Conference, 157

Ben Gurion, David, 208–9

Benin, 101

Berlin, Isaiah, 218

Bhare, Vinoba, 98

Bose, Subbhas Chandra, 133

Brecher, Michael, 75

Britain, 49–50, 155, 239, 245; industrialisation of, 49; rule in India, 50; rule in Burma, 125–31; attitude towards Europe, 239–40

Buddhism: in Ceylon, 91–2; in Burma, 114, 117–21, 127, 133, 134–5, 156–7; Theravada school of, 117–21; connection with nationalism, 133

Burma: natural environment of, 108–10; population of, 110–111; Pagan dynasty of, 111; ancient political system of, 112–13, 115–17; religious beliefs of, 117–23; British rule in, 111–12, 125–31ff; national character of, 123–5; nationalist movement of, 132–7; Marxism in, 135–6; under

INDEX

H

Hazard, Paul, 18
Hazoumé, Paul, 105
Hegel, 39, 43-4, 98
Hinduism, 39-43, 73, 77
Hourani, Albert, 86
Hungary, 188, 249

I

India: 30, 31, 32, 33, 35, 45, 50, 52, 59-68, 108, 111, 147, 247; nature of society, 39-44; nationalist movement in, 59 ff.; present social structure, 78-83; main cycles of history, 83-5; socialism in, 190-200; ambitions of, 230; power-politics of, 231; communal strife in, 234
Indian intellectuals, culture of, 63-5
Indian National Congress, 54, 59, 72-3, 77, 132
Indonesia: 54, 187; post-independence history of, 86-91; the 'Indonesian Way', 88-9; repression of rebels, 231
Israel: and Burma, 158, 176; condition of, 208-9; modernisation of, 221; 247
Italy, 247

J

Japan: 33, 132, 133, 247; process of modernisation of, 68-9; conquest of Burma, 137-43; imperialism of, 233
Jaspers, Karl, 19
Jones, Richard, 30

K

Kachins, 111
Karens, 111, 146, 149
Kassem, 96

Kennan, George, 243
Kennedy, John, 206
Khan, Ayub, 193
Kohn, Hans, 19, 62
Koirala, P. B., 181
Korea, 117, 182
Krushchev, N., 157, 228
Kublai Khan, 111
Kuomintang: 132, 133; troops in Burma, 150
Kyaw Nyein, U., 140; and A.F.P.F.L. split, 169-70

L

Laos, 117, 247
Laski, Harold, 201
Latin America, 10, 63, 227, 247
Lebanon, 208
Leftist Unity Programme (Burma), 148
Lenin, 49
Lerner, Daniel, 92-3
Lippman, Walter, 243
Livingstone, D., 102
Lohia, Rammanohar, Dr: approach to Asian socialism, 193-6
Lowenthal, Richard, 164

M

Macaulay, 52
Mahalanobis, Prof., 73
Malinowski, Bronislaw, 56
Mandalay, 111
Mao Tse Tung, 159
Mapai, 209
Martin, Kingsley, 172
Marx, Karl, 20, 30, 31, 35, 44, 68
Mass culture: insidious nature of, 22
Maung Maung, Dr, 152
Mehta, Asoka: socialist outlook of, 196-200
Menon, Krishna, 73

INDEX

INDEX